# Tourism in Central and Eastern Europe: Educating for quality

Edited by Greg Richards

ISBN 90-361-9956-5


Printed in The Netherlands.

# Contents

# Preface

This book is one of the outcomes of a conference organised by the European Association for Tourism and Leisure Education (ATLAS) in the context of actions funded by the Tourism Unit of DGXXIII of the European Commission to aid tourism development in Central and Eastern Europe. The conference, entitled *Tourism in Central and Eastern Europe: Educating for Quality*, was organised with the help of the Research Institute for Developing Economies in Warsaw, and was held in Kasimierz Dolny in Poland in September 1995.

The conference was attended by a total of 82 participants, including 41 delegates from Central and Eastern Europe, 36 from EU countries, and two from outside Europe. The even balance between delegates from west and east made a major contribution to the success of the conference, as the major aim of the event was to create dialogue between western and eastern experts.

The conference was the central element of an integrated project, the aims of which were:

1) To review the current state of tourism education and training in Central and Eastern Europe (CEE), drawing on local expertise and EU experts.

2) To examine the current match between education and training provision and labour market needs to identify gaps in provision.

3) To draw up an action plan for CEE to address the issues raised in the review process.

4) To establish a support network in the EU and CEE to facilitate the implementation of the action plans.

The conference itself was the main vehicle for achieving the first three project aims, and ATLAS has been working since the conference was held to build up the support network necessary to carry out the action plan agreed at the conference (a copy of the action plan is reproduced in Chapter 24).

The programme for the conference was drawn up using a similar format to the conference on tourism and leisure education in the European Union, organised by ATLAS in 1994. A Scientific Committee, consisting of six experts from the EU and from Central and Eastern Europe, was appointed in March 1995. The Scientific Committee members were responsible for advising on the structure and content of the programme, for reading and approving abstracts of papers submitted for the conference, and for advising on conference publicity.

The final conference programme included 35 keynote and workshop papers, with 16 presented by delegates from Central and Eastern Europe, and 19 by delegates from Western Europe and elsewhere.

As with all such events, the staging of this conference would not have been possible without the help and support of a wide range of individuals and organisations. The Scientific Committee members, David Airey, Marin Bachvarov, Anton Gosar, Bohdan Jung and Leo Theuns performed sterling work in creating and developing the conference programme. Thijs van Vugt also helped with the initial stages of the project, and continued to give valuable advice after his move to Sheffield Hallam University. The keynote speakers at the conference, Bohdan Jung (Warsaw School of Economics), Adam Pierzchala (DG1A, European Commission), Kryzstof Gerula (ORBIS), David Airey (Nottingham Trent University), Miroslaw Nalazek (Polish Association for the Promotion of Tourism) and Henryk Handszuh (World Tourism Organisation) also helped to provide the basic framework for discussion and the detailed analyses presented in the workshop sessions.

As far as the organisation of the conference was concerned, the staff from the Research Institute for Developing Economies in Warsaw were indispensable. Bohdan Jung not only put together an excellent team to ensure that the conference worked smoothly, but his advice was crucial to the academic and social success of the event. Bohdan's suggestion to move the venue of the conference from Warsaw to the small Polish resort of Kasimierz created a much more intimate event, and gave delegates direct experience of the problems of developing tourism in the rural areas of Central and Eastern Europe. The change of venue did, however, create a number of logistic problems, which were heroically dealt with by the local organising staff, Bożena Mierzejewska, Elżbieta Boniecka and Tomasz Tchórzewski. Thanks must also go to the Director of the Polish Architect's Centre Ryszard Zdonek and his staff for providing such excellent facilities for the conference.

In spite of the subject focus and location of the conference, a great deal of the organisational work, both prior to and following the event, took place at the ATLAS base at Tilburg University in The Netherlands. Having just recovered from organising a conference on tourism and leisure education in the EU, the ATLAS staff, Yvonne van Luxemburg, Leontine Onderwater and Nanda Sanders, showed the same flair and enthusiasm which had made the first event so successful. As the pressure mounted, they were ably assisted by Jeanette van 't Zelfde.

The production of this book would also not have been possible without the support of the ATLAS staff. Leontine Onderwater and Evelyn Mulders worked tirelessly to correct and lay out the text, and Harold van der Werf turned some very rough illustrations into high quality diagrams. As always, however, any remaining errors in this volume are the responsibility of the editor.

Greg Richards
Tilburg
May 1996

# List of contributors


David Airey
Nottingham Business School, Nottingham Trent University, Burton Street, Nottingham NG1 4BV, United Kingdom.

Wieslaw Alejziak
Tourism AWF Krakow, AL. Jana Pawta II 62, Krakow 31-571, Poland.

Marcjanna Augustyn
Akademia Wychowania Fizycznego, Ul. Mikolowska 72a, Katowice 40-065, Poland.

Marin Bachvarov
Faculty of Geology & Geography, Sofia St. Kliment Ohridski University, Mlapost 3 Bl. 317 e 5, Apart. 93, Sofia 1712, Bulgaria.

David Bowen
Oxford Brooks University, Gipsy Lane Campus, Headington Oxford OX3 0BP, United Kingdom.

Bill Bramwell
School of Leisure and Food Management, Sheffield University, Totley Hall Lane, Sheffield S17 4AB, United Kingdom.

Cristiana Cristureanu
Academia de Studii Economice, Plaja Romana Nr.6, R-70167 Bucharest, Romania.

Ana Goytia
Universidad de Deusto, Avda de las Universidades s/n 48007, Bilbao, Spain.

Henryk Handszuh
Quality of Tourism Services, WTO, Capitán Haya 42, 28020 Madrid, Spain.

Ian Henry
Department of Physical Education and Sports Science, Loughborough University, Loughborough LE 11 TU, United Kingdom.

Chris Holloway
Bristol Business School, University of the West of England, Coldharbour Lane Frwehay, Bristol BS16 1QY, United Kingdom.

Frank Howie
Queen Margaret College of Higher Education, Edinburgh EH12 8TS, Scotland.

Bohdan Jung
Research Institute for Developing Economies, Warsaw School of Economics, Ul. Rakowiecka 24, 02-521 Warszawa, Poland.

Alzbeta Királová
Matej bel University, Tajovského 10, Banská Bystrica 975 90, Slovakia.

Eric Laws
Hospitality and Tourism Research Centre, Napier University, 10 Colinton Road, Edinburgh EH1 5DT, Scotland.

Barbara Marciszewska
University School of Physical Education, 80-336 Gdansk, Ul. Wiejske 1, Gdansk, Poland.

Frank McMahon
Dublin Institute of Technology, Cathal Brugha Street, Dublin 1, Ireland.

Bożena Mierzejewska
Research Institute for Developing Economies, Warsaw School of Economics, Ul. Rakowiecka 24, 02-521 Warszawa, Poland.

Margit Mundrucźo
College of Commerce, Catering and Tourism, Alkotmany str. 9-11, Budapest 1054, Hugary.

Franc Pauko
Faculty of Business Administration, University of Maribor, Razlagova 14, 62000 Maribor, Slovenia.

Greg Richards
Department of Leisure Studies, Tilburg University, PO Box 90153, 5000 LE Tilburg, the Netherlands.

Marco Antonio Robledo
Escola Oficial de Turisme, Cra. de Valldemossa km 7.5, Palma de Mallorca 07071, Spain.

John Swarbrooke
School of Leisure and Food Management, City Campus, Pond Street, Sheffield S1 1WB, United Kingdom.

Boris Vukonić
Ekonomski Fakultet, University of Zagreb, Trg. J.F. Kennedyja 6, 41000 Zagreb, Croatia.

Jerzy Wyrzykowski
Geographical Institute, University of Wroclaw, Pl. Uniwersytecki 1, 50-137 Wroclaw, Poland.

Anita Wyznikiewicz-Nawracala
University School of Physical Education, 80-336 Gdansk, Ul. Wiejske 1, Gdansk, Poland.

# Chapter 1

# The development of tourism in Central and Eastern Europe

**Greg Richards**

## INTRODUCTION

The restructuring of Central and Eastern Europe has created both some of the greatest opportunities and also the greatest challenges in global tourism development in recent decades. Unlike the development of tourism in the Third World, the countries of Central and Eastern Europe are not starting with a clean sheet, but must achieve a transformation of an existing and in some respects successful tourism industry. This must also be achieved against a background of fundamental social, political and economic change, the most important aspect of which in the context of tourism is the transition to a market economy. The speed and effectiveness of such changes will be vital to the success of the tourism industry in Central and Eastern Europe in an increasingly competitive global tourism industry.

Not surprisingly, much of the analysis of the changes taking place in Central and Eastern Europe (CEE) has concentrated on the physical aspects of development, such as the upgrading of infrastructure and industry. Rather less attention has been paid to the development of service industries, and particularly the 'soft' elements of the tourism product, such as human resource development and service quality. However, the development of skills and know-how in these areas is likely to be crucial to the ability of CEE to compete in global markets. The exchange of such knowledge between the European Union and CEE has therefore been one of the major policy themes of DGXXIII of the European Commission, which sees the development of tourism in CEE as a strengthening of the position of Europe in the global tourism market.

Central and Eastern European countries already make a major contribution to the European tourism industry, generating some $16 billion in international tourism receipts in 1995 (WTO, 1996). However, the potential for tourism development is much greater. A large proportion of the current visitor arrivals in CEE are day visitors or transit passengers, who make a relatively small economic contribution to the region. Maximising the benefits from current visitor flows, and increasing the volume and quality of tourism requires not just the upgrading of infrastructure

and the tangible aspects of the tourism product, but also improvements in service delivery and marketing. Care must also be taken to ensure that the process of modernisation does not destroy the elements of the natural and cultural landscape that are potentially so attractive to tourists. It must also be recognised that CEE countries have developed considerable expertise in some aspects of tourism development and management. In the scramble to adopt 'Western' free enterprise and market mechanisms, therefore, it is important that the good aspects of the existing tourism system are not simply disposed of on ideological grounds.

In order to achieve an effective restructuring of tourism in Central and Eastern Europe, therefore, it is important to create dialogue between East and West. This is precisely what the European Association for Tourism and Leisure Education (ATLAS) was trying to achieve in staging the conference *Tourism in Central and Eastern Europe: Educating for quality* in Poland in September 1995. The dialogue stimulated by this conference produced a wide range of evaluations of the current state of tourism in CEE and the future prospects for development, most of which are reproduced in this volume. The central themes of the conference, Education, Marketing, Service Quality and Sustainability, reflect some of the major issues confronting CEE in the tourism development process.

The remainder of this chapter presents a background to tourism in the CEE region as a whole, and introduces some of the key themes which are dealt with in the rest of the book.

## The tourism market in Central and Eastern Europe

Tourism is currently an important segment of many Central and Eastern European economies, and is now growing as a result of increasing flows of tourists from the west. The latest figures from the World Tourism Organisation (WTO, 1996) indicate that Central and Eastern European countries attracted over 75 million tourists in 1995, compared with 29 million in 1985. The market share of CEE has grown from 14% of the European market in 1985 to over 22% in 1995. Hungary, Poland and the Czech Republic all featured in the top ten tourist destinations in Europe in 1994.

Hungary, the largest tourist receiving country in the region, attracted over 21 million foreign tourists in 1994, compared with less than 10 million in 1985 (Figure 1.1). International arrivals to Hungary rose by a further 3.1% in 1995, but the rate of growth has now slowed considerably compared with the late 1980s, when double figure growth rates were common. Poland welcomed 17.5 million international tourists in 1994, more than Germany or Austria, for example. In 1995, tourism to Poland grew by 2.3%. The Czech Republic achieved 'take-off' in

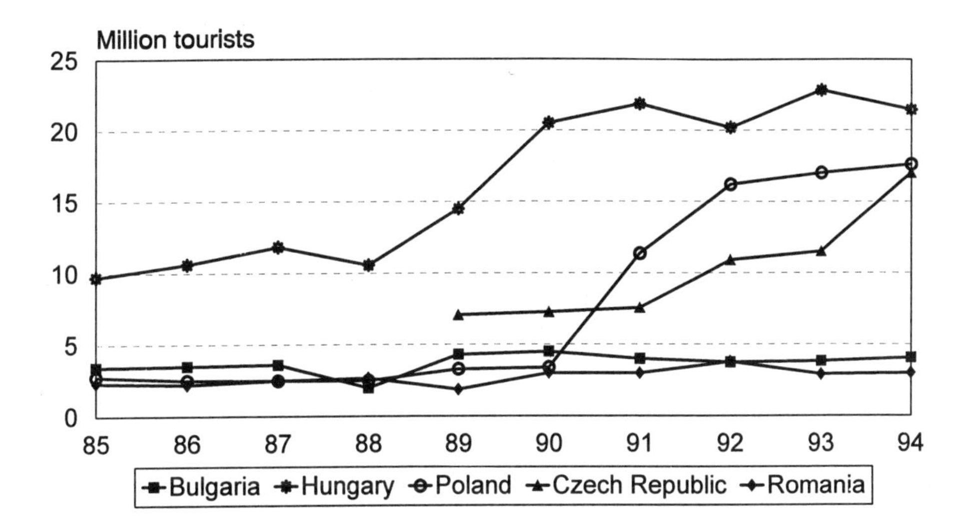


tourism growth rather later than Hungary or Poland, with a growth rate of 48% being achieved in 1994. The 17 million arrivals in 1994 is still slightly below the level of Poland, but the Czech Republic is challenging hard for the number two position in the CEE region.

**Figure 1.1: International tourist arrivals in selected CEE countries, 1985-1994**

In many countries, the official tourism figures represent only the tip of the ice-berg as far as total visitor arrivals are concerned. In most Central European countries there are much larger numbers of day visitors and transit visitors, many of whom come to shop or to trade in countries such as Hungary and Poland. In Poland for example, it is estimated that there were 82 million foreign visitors in 1995, the vast majority of whom come from the EU, particular from neighbou-ring Germany. In the Czech Republic, visitor numbers, estimated at 100 million in 1994, are even higher. Such estimates of visitor numbers should be treated with a certain degree of caution, however. As Theuns (1996) has demonstrated in Poland, estimates of tourist and visitor arrivals are higher than the figures which can be substantiated on the basis of overnight stay or foreign exchange data.

Tourism growth has not been even across the whole CEE region, however. As Figure 1.1 indicates, growth has been particularly strong in those countries which border on Germany, thc major source market in European tourism. For countries further removed from western markets, such as Bulgaria and Romania, growth has been much weaker. Other countries in the region, such as Slovenia and Croatia, have been strongly affected by the war in former Yugoslavia, and will probably grow more rapidly now that hostilities have ceased.

For some of the major destinations in the region, the impact of competition with neighbouring countries is now becoming apparent. In Hungary, for example, falling growth rates have put particular pressure on upmarket hotels, as lower spend tourists from other CEE countries have become one of the major sectors of the market. As the market has matured, other problems, such as rising prices and higher crime rates have also begun to have a negative effect on growth (Hall, 1995; Alejziak, Chapter 23 this volume).

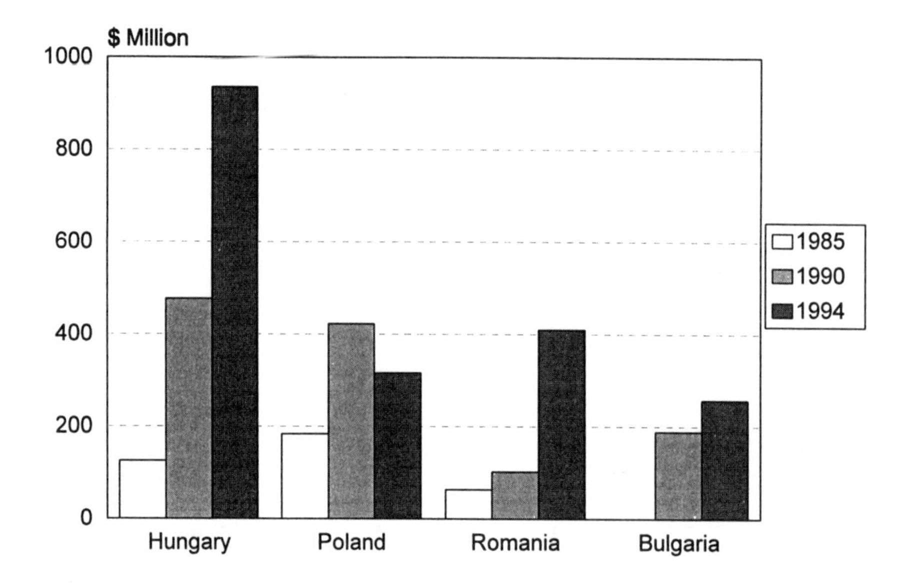


**Figure 1.2: Outbound tourism expenditure for selected CEE countries**

The growth in inbound tourism to the region has been mirrored by a surge in outbound tourism, as CEE residents take advantage of the new freedom to travel. Outbound international tourism expenditure by CEE residents increased from less than $800 million in 1985 to $3.3 billion in 1994, a growth of over 300% (Figure 1.2). Growth in outbound tourism in many CEE countries actually peaked in the period leading up to the fall of communism. Outbound tourism from the former Soviet Union, Hungary and Poland grew by over 100% in the period 1987-1989, but growth rates fell considerably after 1989, as the fall of the old regimes created considerable economic hardship (Hall, 1995). Although the image of CEE tourists as minimum budget travellers is to some extent confirmed by the relatively

low expenditure figures, there is also an emerging market of high spend tourists among the new 'elite' in the region.

## ECONOMIC IMPACT OF TOURISM

Democratisation and the relaxation of travel restrictions in CEE has had a dramatic effect on tourism receipts in most CEE countries. Total receipts for the region grew from just over $1 billion in 1985 to over $11 billion in 1994, an average annual rate of increase of 26% (Figure 1.3). The share of total European tourism receipts accounted for by CEE countries rose over the same period from just over 2% to 6.6%.

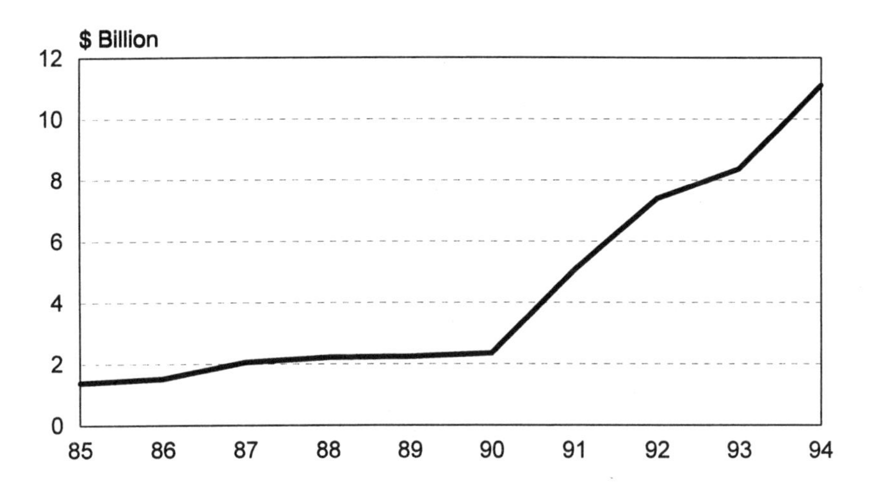


**Figure 1.3: Total international tourism receipts for CEE countries**

Given the fact that CEE accounts for over 20% of all European tourist arrivals, it is clear that the economic return on tourism in the region is still well below that achieved in other areas of Europe. This is at least partly explained by the fact that a large proportion of international arrivals come from other CEE countries. However, as Hall (1995) points out, the distinctions between Western and Eastern tourists has begun to blur in terms of spending power. Tourists from the former Soviet Union visiting Warsaw in 1993, for example, spent $450 per head, compared with an average of $782 spent by North American visitors.

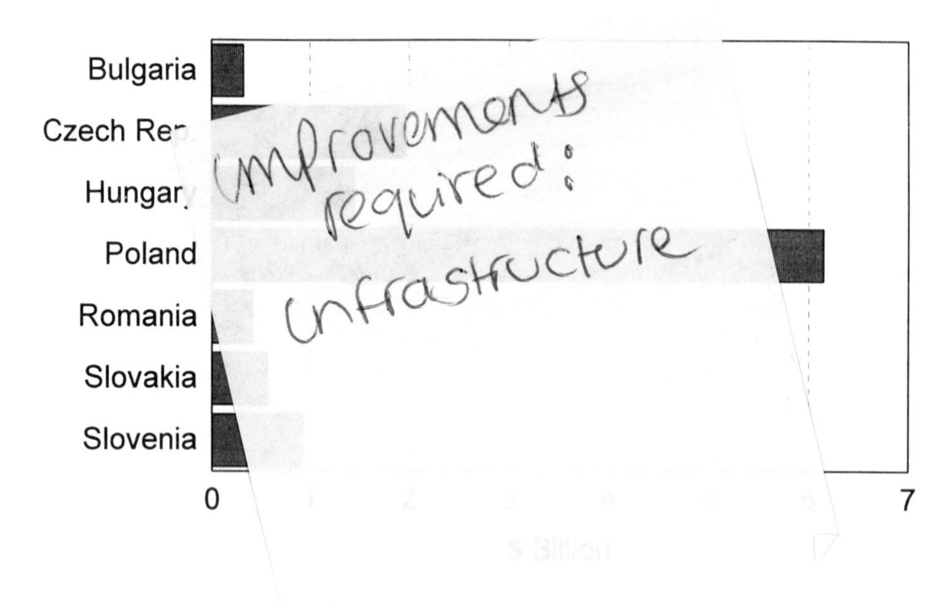


**Figure 1.4: International tourist receipts for selected CEE countries, 1994**

Hungary, Poland and the Czech Republic, which account for 80% of CEE tourist arrivals, also account for over 86% of all tourist receipts (Figure 1.4). Tourism arrivals and expenditure in many other CEE states have been hit by political instability or the conflict in former Yugoslavia.

In the communist period, international tourism was seen as being particularly important as a source of hard currency. That emphasis has softened in the post-communist period, as some CEE currencies have become convertible, and increasing unemployment has made job creation one of the primary goals of economic policy. Estimates presented in the current volume indicate that tourism supports some 250,000 - 300,000 jobs in Hungary, over 100,000 jobs in Bulgaria and about 40,000 jobs in Slovenia. Tourism is therefore an important source of employment in CEE, and is likely to become even more important in the future as the tourism industry develops further.

The tourism market in CEE has therefore developed very rapidly over the past decade. It is clear, however, that there are a number of structural weaknesses of tourism development in the region which will have to be overcome if tourism is to realise its full potential.

## INFRASTRUCTURE AND TOURISM INVESTMENT

There is a need for significant investment in the general infrastructure of CEE to support tourism, including transport links, communications, business services and utilities. Extensive road building programmes are now underway in many CEE countries, including an ambitious plan by the Polish government to develop over 2,500 km of motorways over the next 15 years (Hall, 1995).

In addition, many specific tourism facilities are in need of upgrading and expansion. For example, it is estimated that the Polish hotel industry requires $200 - $300 million of investment in order to reach the standards required by the international tourism industry. The high cost of renovating the tourism infrastructure of CEE, combined with uncertainties over the potential rate of return on such investment has tended to deter potential external investors. Levels of investment have also been fairly uneven in the CEE region, as the Central European countries have attracted the bulk of inward investment, while south-eastern European countries such as Romania and Bulgaria have lagged behind.

In some areas of tourism activity, the pace of change has been very rapid indeed. In particular, major western hotel chains moved very rapidly to secure the commanding heights of the tourism economy, investing in prestige hotel projects in the major capital cities. In Poland, for example, the first foreign-operated hotel, the Marriot in Warsaw, opened in 1989. By 1992, 12 international hotels were operating in Poland, and 14 more were on the drawing board. By the end of 1993, however, there were already signs that oversupply was developing in the four and five star hotel market as a result of the rush of Western investment (Paszucha, 1993).

## RESTRUCTURING THE TOURISM INDUSTRY

The structure of the tourism industries in most CEE countries is different from the models found in the EU. Many former monolithic state enterprises are now in the process of being privatised. The approaches taken to privatisation have varied from one country to the next, and have met with varying degrees of success. In Hungary, for example, the privatisation process initially began with the transfer of state-run enterprises to their former communist managers, often at greatly reduced valuations. This discredited the whole privatisation process, and caused delays in privatising state-owned hotel chains. In the Czech Republic, however, a more 'grass roots' approach was adopted, issuing investment points to individuals which allowed them to purchase stock in former state enterprises. This quickly established a market in shares in these enterprises, which has resulted in a much more successful privatisation process than in Hungary (Lennon, 1995).

The conference presentation by Krzystof Gerula, Vice-President of ORBIS, gave some interesting insights into the effect of privatisation in the travel industry in Poland. ORBIS, which was originally established as a private company in 1920, was nationalised after the second world war to become a virtual monopoly supplier of hotel and travel agency services in Poland. Following market reforms in 1989, ORBIS began the journey back into the private sector. In 1991 ORBIS was transformed into a joint stock company, wholly owned by the state. The company was floated initially by offering 51% of the shares to employees in 1993, followed by complete privatisation in 1994. In the process ORBIS has been transformed into a holding company, which is responsible for the strategic management of the largely independent hotel, transport and travel operations. By increasing managerial responsibility in individual business units, ORBIS hopes to develop the initiative and accountability of individual mangers. To date, the restructuring seems to have been fairly successful, as tour operating turnover has increased from DM 25 million in 1993 to DM 40 million in 1995. Client totals have also risen substantially, from 160,000 in 1994 to 190,000 in 1995. Total ORBIS group turnover in 1995 was DM 95 million. In the longer term, the goals of ORBIS are to further devolve the management of the business, to privatise more of the hotel stock and to improve product quality in order to ensure competitiveness.

As noted above, there is a reluctance from external investors to invest in renovating existing tourism plant. Much Western investment has concentrated on the provision of new, premium quality facilities aimed primarily at business and leisure tourists from abroad. Outside the hotel sector, Western investors have been much slower to invest in tourism (Lennon, 1995). Domestic investment has been concentrated in the creation of small operations, such as budget hotels and travel agencies. In Poland, for example, there are over 3000 travel agencies, about 80% of whom also function as tour operators, but apart from the former state travel company ORBIS, there are no large-scale tour operating companies. This means that the travel industry is not able to compete effectively in international markets, where economies of scale are vital in tour operating.

The lack of investment also means that CEE countries lag behind in terms of information technology. In 1995, for example, there were only 800 CRS terminals in CEE as a whole, compared with 23,000 in Germany alone. This places CEE at a major disadvantage in international markets, because it is not possible to book the product through CRS systems. A combination of investment in information technology and packaging of products through major suppliers is needed to address this problem.

## THE ADMINISTRATION OF TOURISM

The public administration systems for tourism in CEE are in need of change and improvement. Senior managers in state organisations have often been in post since the Communist period, and there is a need to change attitudes. This is reflected in the call in a number of chapters in this volume for re-training of existing administrators and managers, and the recruitment of more graduates from new tourism courses. The improvement of the efficiency and effectiveness of public administration in the tourism area is one of the priorities identified by the European Commission in its tourism aid programmes in CEE.

With privatisation of former state-owned tourism companies, the role of the state is also changing from that of tourism services provider to that of coordination and facilitation of private sector initiatives. Current administrative systems are often complex and to[illegible]. In Poland, for example, there are five separate organisations which have some responsibility for the marketing of Polish tourism. As Miroslaw Nalazek, Director of the Polish Association for the Promotion of Poland pointed out in his presentation, the division of responsibilities often hampers the marketing of Poland abroad. In the domestic market there is also a poor fit between demand and supply, as the marketing of tourism is based on administrative units which usually bear little relation to tourism regions.

## THE ROLE OF THE EUROPEAN UNION

The uneven nature of tourism investment in CEE is to a large extent a reflection of differing levels of economic development and political stability, which are now also important factors in the discussion about the entry of CEE states into the European Union.

In preparation for membership of the EU, many CEE countries are now preparing 'preaccession measures' to bring their legislative frameworks in line with those in the EU. Many countries have also been actively using the EU Phare Programme to assist the development of the tourism industry. In some countries, however, tourism has not been identified as a sector of the economy which should benefit from EU assistance under the Phare Programme.

As Adam Pierzchala from DG1A of the European Commission pointed out in his presentation, the EU is keen to support tourism development in CEE, but this requires more recognition of the importance of tourism on the part of some administrations. The priorities for tourism development as far as the European Commission is concerned are to stimulate product development and regional development in CEE. In order to support this development, CEE governments must recognise the importance of tourism as an economic sector, and to take an active role in stimulating consumer demand. This invariably means upgrading the quality of the tourist offer to meet rising consumer expectations. The EU can support these kinds of developments through the provision of investment capital, advice on policy and marketing and through training programmes. A good example of the support which the EU can give to training programmes is provided by David Airey in Chapter 2 of this volume.

## RURAL TOURISM

Rural tourism is viewed as a key area for tourism development in CEE, because of the relatively rural nature of most of the CEE countries. Developing rural tourism is not without its problems, however. In contrast to the rapid changes in the metropolitan centres, enormous challenges remain in the vast stock of social tourism facilities in domestic tourism centres such as Kazimierz in Poland. It is estimated that Poland alone has about 3,800 social tourism facilities with some 310,000 beds. The modernisation of these facilities cannot be achieved from domestic resources alone, and yet these are areas which are not considered attractive by foreign investors.

The answer perhaps lies in developing a new style of tourism in Central and Eastern Europe. As John Swarbrooke suggests in his analysis of rural tourism in the region (Chapter 13), it is often the lack of Western facilities which is attractive to the incoming tourist. The development of appropriate facilities for international tourism may not therefore require the level of investment which may be suggested by some Western consultants. As Ruukel shows in Chapter 14, the development of `ecotourism' in CEE can be based on local facilities, and the local population can be directly involved in the development of tourism based on natural resources. McMahon (Chapter 15) provides similar evidence of appropriate `agri-tourism' development in rural areas of Poland, Hungary and the Czech Republic.

## TOURISM MARKETING AND SERVICE QUALITY

The greatest need identified by all CEE participants was to improve the quality of the tourism product, tourism marketing and tourism marketing education. The absence of market mechanisms during the communist period obviated the need to develop marketing skills, but these are now essential if CEE countries are to compete effectively for business not only from international tourists but also in the domestic market. In the past, marketing has been very much product based, and has suffered from fragmentation across different administrative areas. There is now growing evidence, however, that marketing is being taken more seriously at all levels in the public sector. In her analysis of regional marketing, for example, Marcjanna Augustyn indicates that a growing number of cooperative marketing schemes are being established in CEE (Chapter 21).

The growing recognition of the importance of tourism marketing at both national and regional levels is provided by participation in regional and global trade exhibitions by CEE countries. Central and Eastern Europe has experienced substantial growth in tourism exhibitions and travel trade market places in recent years. The number of international travel exhibitions held in Central and Eastern Europe grew from 6 events in 1991 to 25 in 1995. Even more significant is the enormous growth in the number of exhibitors at these events, which rose from less than 800 in 1991, to almost 13,000 in 1995 (Richards and Richards, 1996). This growth indicates the extent to which the tourism industry, both East and West, sees Central and Eastern Europe as a major growth market for the future.

It is important, however, that in the rush to attract foreign tourists, marketeers should not lose sight of the importance of the domestic market. Not surprisingly, the potential foreign currency earnings from international tourism have tended to give foreign tourism a higher profile than the domestic market in most CEE states. This can produce a sectoral and spatial imbalance in the development of tourist facilities, and a concentration of investment in key tourist centres frequented by international tourists.

The rapid changes in the tourism flows in CEE have also produced an urgent need to update market information. Up to date and reliable research information is required to help inform the marketing efforts of CEE, and to form the basis for strategic and tactical planning. It was suggested during the conference that a study of consumer attitudes in major origin markets towards tourism in CEE would be a potentially valuable contribution to the development of marketing information across CEE as a whole.

In terms of service quality, the presentation by Henryk Handszuh (Chapter 18) made it clear that much basic work needed to be done in CEE in order to develop a quality tourism product, and to enable them to compete effectively with other world regions. In particular, basic standards for health and safety need to be adopted and enforced in order to provide adequate protection for the consumer.

Once the basic standards are in place, tourism enterprises in CEE still have much to learn in terms of customer orientation. The kind of quality management and assessment systems discussed by Eric Laws (Chapter 20) and Marco Robledo (Chapter 19) have yet to make an impact in service management in CEE. It is clear, however, that in order to compete effectively in the global market, enterprises in CEE will have to pay increasing attention to the issue of quality. As Robledo points out, the increasingly experienced and sophisticated tourist will demand even higher standards of service in future.

### EDUCATION AND TRAINING

There is a pressing need to improve and extend the provision of tourism education and training in CEE, in order to upgrade the quality and effectiveness of tourism services. Although a well-developed system of tourism education existed in many CEE countries during the Communist period, the focus of tourism education was often on spatial planning or economics, and did not have the management focus so common in tourism education elsewhere. As David Airey underlines in his review of tourism education development in CEE (Chapter 2), there are a number of real strengths in the educational system which developed up to 1989. These strengths included an emphasis on geographical and human issues in tourism, and the development of a knowledge base for tourist guides. Major weaknesses of the system, however, included out-of-date curricula, little initiative for students in the learning process, a lack of management and marketing input and poor links with industry. This summary picture is also reflected in many of the national analyses presented in Chapters 3 to 10 of this volume.

The review of individual national education systems in CEE revealed a similar variety of provision to that identified in the EU in the ATLAS conference in Tilburg in 1994. However, some common features were evident. Most notably, there is an emphasis in tourism courses on economics and spatial planning, in contrast to the management emphasis evident in the west. In most countries, the existing curricula are being updated, but there is resistance to change within many of the more traditional institutions of higher education. Links with industry are generally poorly developed, and few academic staff see the relevance of a vocational orientation in their courses, or the need for them to have some experience of industry themselves.

There was considerable discussion during the conference of the educational needs of CEE. In particular, there was a division of opinion about the relative weight which should be given to specialist or generalist forms of education. Although some argued that there was a great need for specialists, for example in the area of tourism marketing, other participants argued for a more general approach to tourism education. The generalist approach was supported by those who felt that a general education provided the flexibility and adaptability necessary to cope with the rapidly changing circumstances in Eastern European tourism, and that specialists may find themselves rapidly outdated.

The presentations by David Airey (Chapter 2) and Chris Holloway (Chapter 12) both underlined the fact that vocational approaches to education need to be developed, and that this required that vocational education be respected, both in western and eastern Europe.

There is a lack of tourism texts for students and practitioners in the languages of CEE, which inhibits the exchange of information and curriculum development. By reviewing the information needs of tourism education and training in CEE, it should be possible to identify suitable texts for translation, or new areas in which texts should be provided. As a basis for such work, it was suggested that a full review of currently available tourism texts should be undertaken.

A major weakness of tourism education in CEE is the relative lack of contact between educators and the tourism industry. In the past, contact with the industry was not considered important for the development of courses, and this is still not perceived as a priority by many educators. In addition, the tourism industry itself does often not see the need to recruit tourism graduates, which tends to limit the motivation of people from industry in getting involved in tourism courses.

There is a need to build up staff and student exchanges and other forms of academic exchange to improve the quality of tourism education in CEE. This applies not only to exchanges with EU institutions, but also to the re-establishment of exchange systems between CEE countries themselves, which were often well developed in the past. Some educational institutions in CEE have developed courses in English, which can provide a basis for extending exchange programmes in the region.

In order to support such developments, there is a need to review in detail the provision of tourism education and training in CEE, in order to establish specific development needs, identify potential partner institutions in the EU and within CEE themselves and to establish the standards and levels of course provision.

## Summary

Central and Eastern European countries are facing major challenges in tourism development, tourism marketing, human resource development and education. The analyses presented in this volume show that considerable progress has been made in some areas since the democratisation of CEE, but there remains a huge challenge in converting an outdated product to the needs of western markets, and in educating and re-educating people for jobs in tourism. The chapters which follow will hopefully provide a sound basis for assessing the current situation of tourism education in Central and Eastern Europe, and give some pointers as to potential ways forward.

## References

Hall, D.R. (1995). 'Tourism change in Central and Eastern Europe.' In: Montanari, A. and Williams, A.M. (eds.). *European Tourism: Regions, Spaces and Restructuring*. Wiley, Chichester, pp. 221-244.

Lennon, J. J. (1995). 'Hotel privatisation in Eastern Europe: progress and process.' In Leslie, D. (ed.). *Tourism and Leisure: Culture, Heritage and Participation*. LSA Publication No 51, Leisure Studies Association, Eastbourne, pp. 45-58.

Paszucha, M. (1993). Investment opportunities in Poland's tourist industry. Paper presented at the conference, Privatisation in the Tourism Industry, London, April 1993.

Richards, G. (1995). *European Tourism and Leisure Education: Trends and Prospects*. Tilburg University Press, Tilburg.

Richards, W.S. and Richards, G. (1996). *International Travel Trade Market Places*. Tourism Research and Marketing, London.

Theuns, H.L. (1996). 'Tourism statistics in Poland.' *Cahiers du Tourisme*, C, no. 197.

World Tourism Organisation (1995). *Tourism Market Trends: Europe 1995*. WTO, Madrid.

World Tourism Organisation (1996). *International Tourism Overview: Highlights 1995*. WTO, Madrid.

# Chapter 2

# Tourism education and manpower development in Central and Eastern Europe

**David Airey**

## INTRODUCTION

Three thoughts prompted the title for this chapter on *Tourism Education and Manpower Development in Central and Eastern Europe*. The first was that these three topics lie at the heart of the successful development of tourism in this part of the world. The second was that all three are in a process of fairly rapid change and in some cases reappraisal, not only here, but in other countries as well. The third was that many readers will be experts in one or perhaps two of the topics, but there are few who would claim expertise in all three.

With these three thoughts, this chapter sets out some of the basic issues about the three topics and to develops some of the linkages between them. In doing this, the aim is to stimulate further debate and assist in the process of education for quality both here and in other parts of the world.

The chapter draws on the author's experience of two worlds. The first is the world of tourism education in The United Kingdom (UK) as a teacher and inspector for the best part of twenty years. The second is the world of manpower development for tourism in Poland for two years, until the end of 1994, as the technical adviser for the Commission of the European Communities (CEC) PHARE programme for the Development of Tourism. Neither world, of course, gives the authority to speak on behalf of the whole of Western Europe or of Central and Eastern Europe (CEE). But it is hoped that the experiences help in understanding some of the basic issues.

In line with the three topics included in the title, the chapter is in three main parts. The first part is devoted to tourism education itself. The aim is to briefly set out the nature of tourism education and some of the current issues which it is facing. This draws particularly on the experience of Western Europe, but countries of Central and Eastern Europe are rapidly reaching a point where they are facing the same issues. The chapter then moves on to manpower development and in particular to consider the ways in which the providers of education can assist in the process of manpower development in tourism. The final part focuses specifically on the experience of Central and Eastern Europe, and drawing upon the work of the CEC PHARE Tourism Programme, ident-

ifies some of the important characteristics and gaps in tourism education in Poland. The chapter ends with a brief comment on work for the future.

## TOURISM EDUCATION

Taking the first topic of tourism education, it is obviously impossible in a chapter like this to provide a comprehensive view of all its aspects and characteristics. Instead, five particular features have been selected to help set out its nature and some of the current issues which it faces.

The first of these, and perhaps the most remarkable, is its rapid rate of growth. Taking the UK as an example, the first two postgraduate degree courses in tourism were introduced in 1972, with a combined enrolment of about 20 students and the first two bachelor degree courses started in 1986, with a combined intake of about 110 students (Airey 1995). The most recent evidence is that there are now over 50 degree courses enroling over 2500 new students each year. And this is just at degree level. There are tens of thousands of other students studying tourism at lower levels and tourism is now included in the curriculum of many schools. The rate of growth is far in excess of the growth of tourism itself and this raises important questions about the second feature, which is the over-provision of young people educated in tourism. At present there is no hard evidence of what happens to those who study tourism at lower levels. Some may succeed in gaining employment in tourism but it is likely that there are many more who do not, and go into other sectors of employment or continue into higher education or become unemployed. The best information we have about this relates to the graduate level. At this level in the UK only about 20% gain employment in tourism after their course (Airey *et al.*, 1993). But it also needs to be noted that a further 50% gain employment elsewhere in the service sector. In other words, the study of tourism appears to be successful in providing an education which contains sufficient transferable skills to enable graduates to compete for employment in a range of other sectors such as the retail trades, finance and banking, even though it does not necessarily lead to jobs in tourism. There are clearly some important messages here for those who are in the business of developing tourism studies about the importance of developing transferable knowledge as well as specialist skills.

The third feature of tourism education relates to its coverage. As an activity, tourism embraces a wide range of different sectors: accommodation, the travel trade, transport, tourist attractions, tourist boards, etc. It also provides employment at a number of different levels: management, technician/supervisory and craft/operative. These can be set out as a grid as given in Figure 2.1. One authority (Medlik 1993) has made the point that a comprehensive system of education and training for tourism needs to provide coverage of all the sectors as well as all the levels. In many countries, this is not the case. Some sectors have been inadequately covered and some levels are poorly addressed. For example, managerial education for tourism is poorly developed in some countries, while in others it sometimes seems that management education is growing too fast in relation to the other levels or in relation to the jobs available. Perhaps the grid given in Figure 2.1 can act as a reminder of the importance of achieving balance in tourism education.

| Sectors / Levels | 1 | 2 | 3 | 4 | 5 | 6 | 7 |
|---|---|---|---|---|---|---|---|
| Management | | | | | | | |
| Technician/ Supervisory | | | | | | | |
| Craft/ Operative | | | | | | | |

1 Government and tourism organisations
2 Attractions, entertainment, recreation
3 Passenger transport
4 Hospitality
5 Tour operators and travel organisers
6 Retail travel agencies
7 Guides, information and interpretation

**Figure 2.1: Sectors and levels of tourism**
*Source:* Medlik (1993)

There is another kind of balance which is also important in tourism education and that is between the sharply vocational content of tourism courses and the more theoretical aspects of the study of tourism. Of course, for non-vocational courses this is not an issue. But most tourism courses are vocational, at least in as far as they attract students by relating their work to possible employment. With this in mind there is an important need for those designing and delivering the courses to maintain a balance between vocational and theoretical content. In practice what this means is that the courses are not solely concerned with training in specific competencies for immediate employment. There is also strong pressure from employers for this. But on the other hand, the theoretical aspects should not be exaggerated. The important point is that vocational education needs to be exactly what it says, both vocational and educational, to assist in the development of what Medlik (1993) has referred to as "educated, versatile and highly adaptable people who can think". In many cases this balance is achieved by setting tourism in the context of other areas of study, notably business studies, but also other areas such as environmental studies.

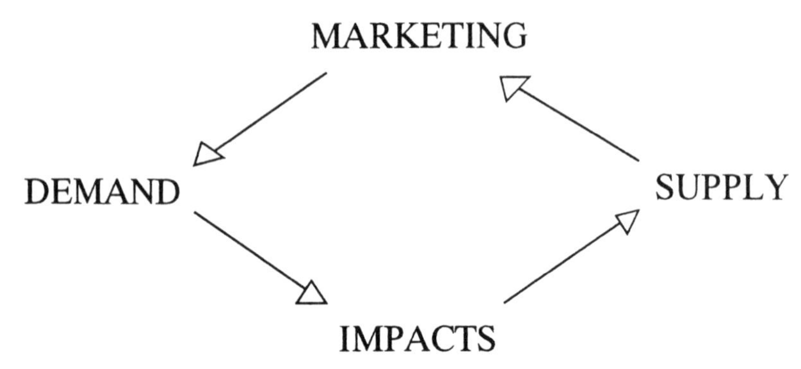


**Figure 2.2: The study of tourism**

The fifth and final feature of this brief look at tourism education relates to the content of tourism courses. There are a number of ways of looking at this. Figure 2.2 provides a starting point in which the study of tourism can be described as embracing the study of demand by people travelling and staying away from home; the study of the supply of resources used during travelling and staying away from home (this includes the tourism industry and tourist destinations); the study of the economic, environmental, social and other impacts of demand on supply and *vice versa*; and the study of the marketing links between demand and supply. A more sophisticated elaboration of this has been produced by Leiper (1981) as shown in Figure 2.3.

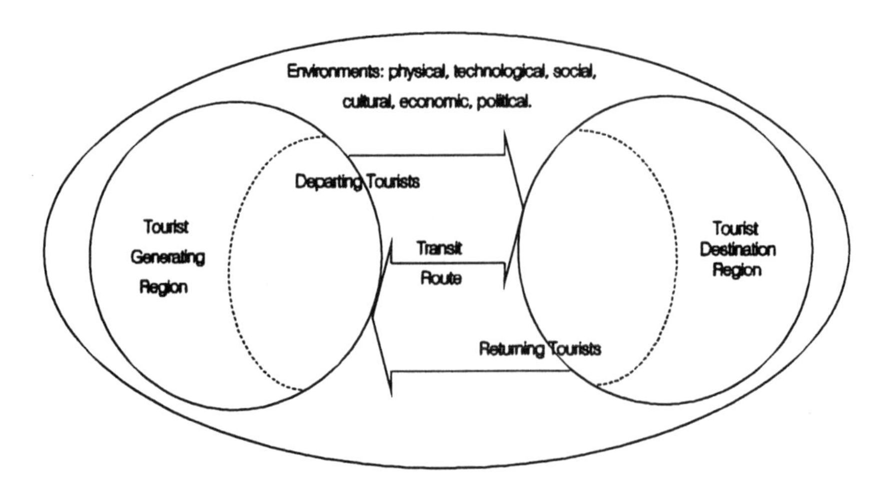


**Figure 2.3: The basic tourism system**

But while these and other models provide a starting point for the study of tourism, in reality, as tourism has grown and developed, a danger has arisen that as a new area of study tourism has come to mean what academics want it to mean. This has led to confusion and sometimes disappointment on the part of students and potential employees and it may also limit the opportunities for tourism to continue its development as a robust and coherent area of study. With this in mind work is currently underway in the UK (National Liaison Group, 1995) on the development of a minimum common core of tourism studies, at higher levels, which gives an indication of the main elements of tourism studies. These are set out in Figure 2.4.

The meaning and nature of tourism and its relationship with leisure and recreation

The structure of the tourism industry

The dimensions of tourism

The significance and impact of tourism

Marketing - tourism applications

Planning and development - tourism applications

Policy issues, management, finance, organisation

**Figure 2.4: Minimum common core for tourism**
*Source*: Council for National Academic Awards (1993)

## MANPOWER DEVELOPMENT

The second part of this chapter is concerned with manpower development which, in many ways is now seen as the key to successful operation and maintaining competitive advantage.

Over the past decade or so the focus of attention for the successful development of tourism seems to have gone through a number of shifts. Initially the focus was on physical development. In this context physical masterplans formed the key element in the development process. Attention then shifted to marketing and promotional activities, during which time marketing plans and strategies featured prominently in the development activities. The most recent move is for manpower development to receive greater prominence both at the level of the individual enterprise as well as at the level of the destination. In many ways the reasons for this are obvious. With labour costs representing one third or more of total costs, the effective use of labour is crucial to the cost side of operational success. In addition, as a service industry, effective staffing vitally affects customer satisfaction and can be the key to maintaining the distinctiveness and quality of the product and hence crucially affect the revenue side as well.

Against this background, tourist destinations and companies in all parts of the world are embracing and developing schemes to improve the quality and effectiveness of their workforce. At the national level, for example, general schemes of government assistance are being introduced to tourism to improve manpower. In the UK the Investors's in People (IIP) initiative provides government support for organisations which devote a part of their resources to identifying and providing opportunities for staff development which will improve competitive performance. In the same vein, at the level of the destination, a training scheme developed in Canada with the name "Welcome Host" is being taken up by tourist boards and similar organisations to improve the quality of the manpower and training in their area. This is a one day programme, mainly devoted to customer care, which is taken by a diverse range of workers involved in tourism from taxi drivers to those operating farmhouse accommodation.

Turning to Central and Eastern Europe, the tourism development programmes in this part of the world nearly all devote attention to manpower issues. In Poland, for example, one third of the first tourism programme was devoted to management and manpower development. Under this heading a range of activities were developed to train the trainers, to train the professionals working in tourism and to strengthen the resources available to tourism education. This is just the start of the long term process of improving the competitiveness of tourism in this part of the world.

The important question for those concerned with tourism education, is how can the education providers best contribute to this process of improving manpower quality. One of the conclusions which was reached in considering the contribution of the educational system to manpower development in Poland was that, while there was no ideal system of education and training and nor was there one which could easily or simply be transferred across international boundaries, there were pointers to good practice. The four pointers which were used to plan the work of providing development assistance in Poland are set out in Figure 2.5.

| | |
|---|---|
| 1. | Provision is up-to-date and reflects best standards and practice |
| 2. | Effective links between education and industry |
| 3. | Adequate coverage by sector, level and employment group |
| 4. | Breadth, understanding and challenge |

**Figure 2.5: Pointers to successful vocational education in tourism**

The first of these pointers is the fairly obvious one that the provision should be up-to-date and reflect best standards and practice both in education and training as well as in industrial terms. The second is in many ways related to this. There should be sufficient and effective links between education and training, on the one hand, and industry, on the other, so that they can benefit from each others' experience. The third goes back to a point about coverage made earlier, that there should be adequate provision for all levels and sub-sectors of tourism. In addition, the coverage should also include the needs of different employment groups, not only young people at the start of their careers but also employees, the self-employed and the unemployed. And the final pointer is that the provision is not simply concerned with training for a specific task but also provides sufficient breadth, understanding and challenge from which the individuals can develop further skills and knowledge as well as their own thinking and initiative.

Obviously these pointers are not comprehensive. But they do provide a starting point for thinking about the provision made by schools and colleges. Against this framework a list of gaps and weaknesses in the education provision in Poland was formed.

## CENTRAL AND EASTERN EUROPE

The final main part of this chapter deals with the experience of Central and Eastern Europe in general and Poland in particular. However, before turning attention to educational issues it is worth briefly reflecting on the contextual background. For this purpose three features have been selected to help set the context.

The first, and perhaps the most important point is that these countries should not be considered as developing countries in the traditional sense of the word. In common with many developing countries they have a high proportion, up to 30%, of employment in agriculture (Hall, 1991). This compares with 3% in the

UK. But, unlike traditional developing economies, they have long-established manufacturing sectors. Also, unlike many developing countries their academic standards and much of their educational provision compares well with those of Western countries and their cultural and artistic traditions are in many ways similar to those of the West. The real difference from the developed countries of the West stem not so much from the level of development *per se* but from the fact that they have developed in a different social and economic setting.

Secondly, the countries have experienced significant economic dislocation following the changes of 1989. In many ways they are going through, in a few years, the same changes, for example, in the decline of manufacturing industry, which in the West has been taking place over decades. At the same time, also just like the West, they are experiencing a growth in the service sector, of which tourism is a part, and this is creating changing requirements for manpower and associated education and training.

The final feature is that tourism was not invented for these countries in 1989. They all have a long tradition of travelling and staying away from home and they all have unique tourist attractions and supplies of tourist facilities. For example, in 1985, Hungary was recording 10 million international tourist arrivals, and Romania five million (Economist Intelligence Unit, 1994). Poland received eight million visitors per year in 1980 and in the same year 40% of the Polish population took a holiday of at least five days (Institute of Tourism, 1993). The important point of difference is that tourism, particularly domestic tourism, was seen primarily as a social rather than an economic activity, with the implication that attitudes to competitiveness, customer care and investment developed in a very different setting.

Against this background it is not surprising that tourism education and training up to 1989 developed on rather different lines in Central and Eastern Europe than in the West. In some aspects it developed real strengths. These include geographical and human issues related to tourism and the knowledge base for tourist guides. But set against the pointers to vocational good practice, given in Figure 2.5, it also contained a number of significant weaknesses.

As indicated above, these pointers were used to consider the provision of tourism education in Poland and against these, following an extensive programme of visits and discussions with representatives of industry, education and others in different parts of Poland a number of important weaknesses and gaps in the provision compared with Western Europe were identified.

In relation to the first pointer, provision is not always up-to-date and does not always reflect best standards and practice either in education and training or in industrial terms. Particular gaps include those areas of the curriculum concerned with successful business operation, particularly finance, economics,

marketing, management and customer care. For the individual tourist from the West, the latter is possibly the strongest reminder that the countries of this part of the world have had a different recent history. There are also important gaps in resources, particularly textbooks and computers.

Turning to the second pointer, links between industry and education are poorly developed. For example, employers are rarely involved in courses or curriculum design, few teachers have recent experience of the tourism industry and industrial secondments for teachers are virtually unknown, case studies based on industry rarely form part of the teaching and while most courses include industrial placements for students, these are rarely well integrated into the courses.

As far as the adequacy of the coverage is concerned there are some important gaps, particularly for those already in employment and for the unemployed. In countries experiencing high structural unemployment and major economic change this is a crucial area for development.

From the point of view of teaching methods and curriculum design few of the courses, particularly at the lower level, provide the kind of breadth, understanding and challenge that are common in the West. The extent to which students are encouraged to take responsibility or initiative is also very different from the practices which are now common in many countries in the West.

It needs to be emphasised that this is a summary picture. There are notable exceptions, not only in Poland but, in many others parts of the countries of Central and Eastern Europe. There are also plenty of examples where gaps and weaknesses have already been recognised and are being addressed successfully by the individual institutions and national authorities, in some cases with bilateral and multilateral support programmes such as the CEC PHARE programme. Nevertheless, the agenda for change remains a formidable one, but it is one which must take place if these countries are to compete with the countries of the West in attracting tourist expenditure.

In response to these gaps and weaknesses, the programme which was developed in Poland contained four broad elements as set out in Figure 2.6. A "train the trainer" programme of courses and study visits was organised, concentrating on marketing, customer care, finance and curriculum and course development. In addition to courses in Poland these included a study visit to the Netherlands, following which a small support group was established within Poland designed to continue the process of exchanging ideas. The "train the professional" programme, concentrated mainly on marketing issues for key personnel working in the tourism industry. This programme also included a series of customer care courses for those employed at the gateways to Poland: the border guards, the customs officers, the airport and airline personnel. The programme to strengthen the resources mainly concentrated on the translation of textbooks and manuals and in addition support was given to the development of an open learning centre which is being set up in Krakow. This is to provide written, electronic and other resources for those engaged in education and training throughout Poland. The final element concerned developing the environment within which tourism education and training is taking place. This concentrated on two issues: industry and education links and developing tourism as a subject for study in schools. For these a series of seminars and conferences in Poland was organised (Airey 1994).

| Train the Trainer |
|---|
| Train the Professional |
| Strengthen the Resources |
| Develop the Environment |

**Figure 2.6: Development of vocational tourism education in Poland**

This particular programme has now come to an end. During its operation, which ran over three years, only a few thousand individuals came into contact with one or more of its components. Given the size of Poland, its population of 38 million, and given the scale of its needs, with the unemployment rate over 20% in some areas, this is a small contribution. But given the enthusiasm, commitment and speed of learning of those who took part in the process and who are now in a position to spread their knowledge and experience the potential for change is very strong. We shall be surprised how quickly countries in this part of the world begin to provide real competition for those in the West, and not just in tourism.

## CONCLUSION

The themes of this chapter have been *tourism education, manpower development* and *Central and Eastern Europe*. As indicated at the beginning, all three lie at the heart of the issues covered in this book and all three are in such a process of rapid change and development that it is often difficult to identify the key issues and priorities for the future.

Nevertheless, there are some fixed points which can provide a basis for developments and discussion. First, tourism as a subject for study is now well established, with a growing community of scholars and teachers, journals, textbooks, conferences and professional associations. It is better established in Western than in Central and Eastern Europe but that is rapidly changing. Second, the development of manpower is recognised as one of the key components of tourism competitiveness in an increasingly competitive world and this provides an important challenge and opportunity to those involved in tourism education. Third, Central and Eastern Europe is once again fully linked to the West.

Against these fixed points those working in tourism education are presented with two challenges and opportunities. Firstly, how to contribute to the quality of manpower and thus competitive industry and secondly, how to spread good practice between East and West. This book provides a continuation to the discussion on both these topics.

## REFERENCES

Airey, D., Ladkin, A. and Middleton, V.T.C. (1993). *The Profile of Tourism Studies Degree Courses in the UK 1993*. National Liaison Group for the Tourism Society, London.

Airey, D. (1994). 'Education for Tourism in Poland: the PHARE Programme'. *Journal of Tourism Management*, Vol 15 No 6., pp.467-471.

Airey, D. (1995). *Tourism Degrees Past, Present and Future*. Inaugural Lecture, Nottingham Business School.

Economist Intelligence Unit. *International Tourism Reports*, Nos. 3 (1992) p.69, 2 (1993) p.29 and 3(1994) p.12.

Hall, D.R. (1991). *Tourism and Economic Development in Eastern Europe and the Soviet Union*. Belhaven, London.

Institute of Tourism (1993). *Polish Tourism in Figures*. Warsaw.

Leiper, N. (1981). 'Towards a Cohesive Curriculum for Tourism Education: Problems and Prospects'. *Annals of Tourism Research, 3,* 13-34.

Medlik, S. (1993). *The Study of Tourism*. Institute of Tourism, Warsaw.

National Liaison Group (1995). *The Core Body of Knowledge for Higher Education in Tourism*. NLG, London.

# Chapter 3

# The current state of tourism and tourism education in Bulgaria

**Marin Bachvarov**

The decline of communism as a political and economic system and the loss of ex-socialist states and especially the USSR as economic partners, created an extremely difficult situation for the Bulgarian economy as a whole and for its tourism industry in particular. Since the end of the 1980s the country has been in a total crisis. An unprecedented dimension of the crisis is the transition from centralised planning to a market economy. One of the popular beliefs in this period, typical for many ex-socialist countries, is that tourism should be a priority sector during the transition, along with sectors such as commerce, agriculture, consumer goods industry and communications. These priority sectors are defined by the volume of their present or expected contribution to the national economy and especially to its foreign currency earnings. On a per capita basis, Bulgaria is one of the most indebted countries in the world (over $ 8 billion owed to different foreign creditors).

## 1. SITUATIONAL ANALYSIS

The assumption that the 'priority sectors' would lead the economy did not prove to be correct for Bulgaria after the 1989 political changes. Among the sectors mentioned above only commerce provided a real boost. The expected tourism development did not occur - just the opposite, the share of Bulgaria in world tourism revenues fell from 0.30% in 1985 to 0.16% in 1990. The number of foreign tourists in the country in 1992 fell by half compared with 1988, the number of the tourist nights by two-thirds and the revenues by three-quarters.

Foreign currency earnings were estimated to be $500 million in 1993, while neighbours Turkey and Greece earned $3 billion each. A slow recovery was noticed in the second half of 1993, which continued throughout 1994. The contribution of the tourism sector to GNP was recently estimated at 3.5%, which also reflects its share in total employment.

This situation indicates that tourism is not a priority sector in post-communist Bulgaria, although the politicians are claiming so. In fact, there is a serious drawback in Bulgaria's market position and in tourism investment, while the quality of tourism services has not improved substantially.

All this is against the background of a dramatic change of the foreign tourist flows to the country by regions of origin. The East-European tourists who represented 80% of overnight stays in 1990, disappeared abruptly afterwards. Visitors from adjacent countries increased, but as a rule their stays are short or on transit, so the economic effect is meagre. Only the West-European market is relatively stable, Germany and United Kingdom being the major tourist partners of Bulgaria.

**Table 3.1: International arrivals in Bulgaria in 1994 in thousands**

| Visitors origin | All Tourists | Holiday and Recreation | Visitor Origin | All Tourists | Holiday and Recreation |
|---|---|---|---|---|---|
| Austria | 11 | 3 | Jordan | 3 | - |
| Belgium | 7 | 4 | The Netherlands | 15 | 9 |
| Canada | 3 | 1 | Norway | 12 | 11 |
| Chech Republic and Slovakia | 47 | 8 | Poland | 39 | 8 |
| CIS | 1829 | 711 | Romania | 1874 | 139 |
| Denmark | 11 | 6 | Spain | 3 | 2 |
| Finland | 5 | 3 | Sweden | 11 | 8 |
| France | 20 | 12 | Switzerland | 6 | 3 |
| Germany | 157 | 131 | Turkey | 2006 | 87 |
| Greece | 357 | 141 | UK | 60 | 48 |
| Hungary | 40 | 3 | USA | 24 | 9 |
| Iran | 5 | 1 | Yugoslavia | 3153 | 1166 |
| Iraq | 3 | 1 | Other | 329 | 92 |
| Israel | 7 | 4 | | | |
| Italy | 30 | 12 | Total | 10068 | 2623 |

According to the frontier crossing statistics in 1994 (Table 3.1), Bulgaria was visited by 10 million foreigners, which is 21.3% more than in the previous year. There is some recovery of the tourists from the former Soviet Union countries and a further increase in visitors from the Balkan states. At the same time the number of arrivals from Western and Central Europe decreased. The major contributors are in descending order: Yugoslavia (former), Turkey, Romania, the former Soviet Union states, Greece, Germany and the United Kingdom. They account for over 95% of the visits paid to Bulgaria.

The holiday and recreation trips are of particular interest, and these reached 2.6 million in 1994. Here the increase compared to 1993 is smaller but a still considerable 12.9%. Particularly strong is the growth of arrivals from the former Soviet Union states (6 times, 1993 levels) and Turkey (3 times).

Still, considering the volume of real tourist flows and the income contribution, the one-third decrease in the West-European market (including the Germany and UK) is a serious reduction.

## 2. Basic features and constraints of Bulgarian tourism

A major feature of foreign tourism in Bulgaria is the very low percentage of non-organised individual trips to the country. A great majority of the tourists come for group package holidays on the Black Sea coast, or in the winter resorts. Another peculiarity is that except the business trips attracted by the capital Sofia and a few other urban centres, foreign tourism is almost entirely bound to hotel concentrations, called 'tourist complexes'. The biggest complexes on the Black Sea coast are at Slunchev Briag, Zlatni Piasatsi, Albena, St Konstantin, Duni, Eleni and in the mountains at Borovets and Pamporovo.

The strong geographical concentration of the foreign tourism is clear. The coastal zone attracts 81.5% of the total overnights. The Sofia region in second place is far behind with 11.2% of the nights and third is the area of the second biggest town, Plovdiv, with only 4% - in spite of its international fair, cultural attractions and development of mountain skiing facilities in the nearby Rhodope mountains. The remaining territories on the Danube plain and in Upper Thracia - about half the surface area of the country - absorbed only 3.3% of the foreigners' overnights.

The concentration of heavy tourist infrastructure in tourist complexes, created a number of technological and urbanistic advantages, but led also to saturation and some management problems. Most of the hotels were constructed in 1960s and 1970s (generally 2-star seasonal hotels), so they need considerable renovation and adaptation to the new market environment. If the conditions were satisfactory for the local and Soviet block clients in the past, the Bulgarian tourist complexes now need investment and management efforts to make them competitive in the West-European market.

Traditionally, foreign visitors to Bulgaria are unevenly distributed by season - 69% coming in the second half of the year (Figure 3.1). After the record month of August with 13.7% visits, July, and interestingly enough, December rank second, both with 11.8% of the visits. Of course, the seasonal concentration of holidays and recreation and foreigners' overnights is much higher in the summer months, with 78.9% of all arrivals from June to September in 1993 (NSI, 1993-1994).

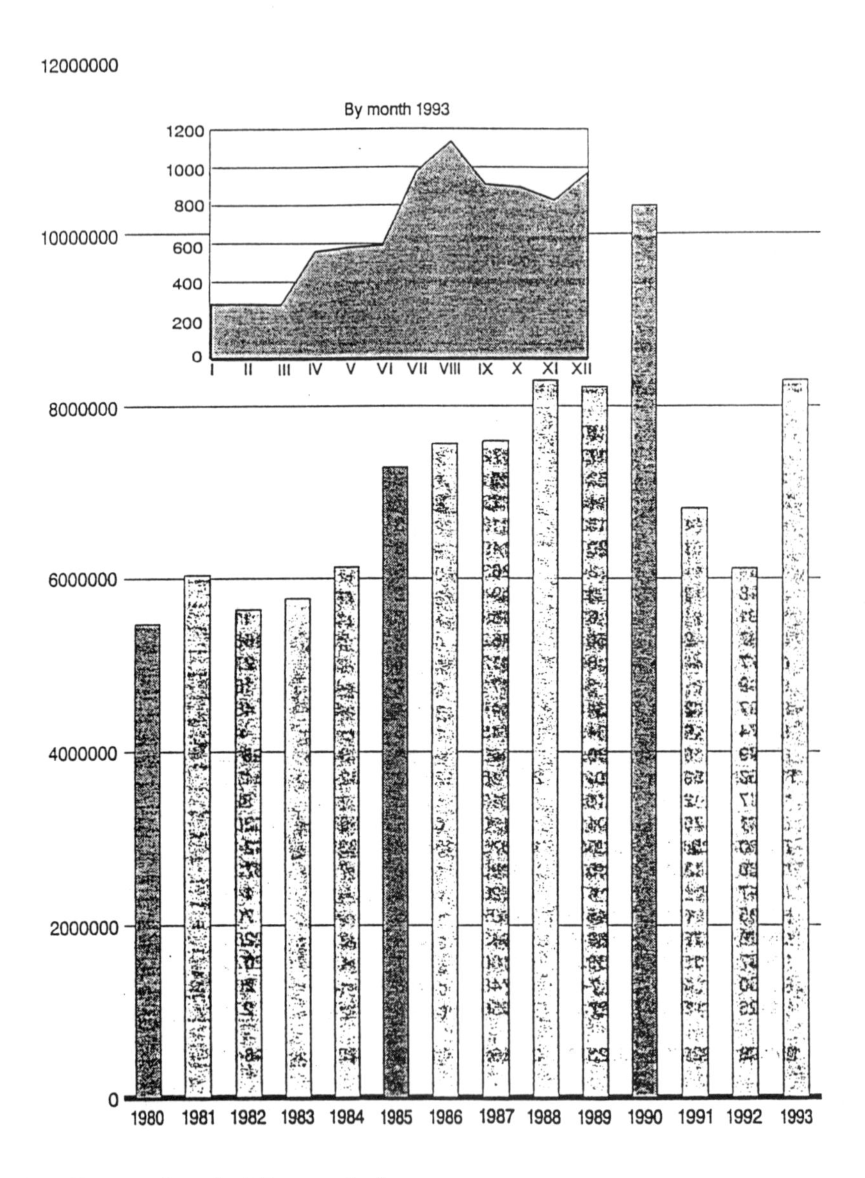


**Figure 3.1: International visitor arrivals**

The overall nights spent by foreigners declined from 7.5 million in 1993 to 6.4 million in 1994. The average length of stay fell below 3 days.

Except for some business and transit trips from Middle-Eastern countries, Bulgaria is not a holiday destination for the markets outside Europe. As could be expected, the flows from Germany and the UK are economically more important, while the visits originating from the surrounding states are short and mostly non-touristic. A recent inquiry disclosed that only 2% of the foreign tourists in the Black Sea region belong to the affluent segment of the market.

It is also interesting, that for the first time of its history, the country became a generator of significant outgoing visits. With 4.4 million departures in 1994 Bulgaria now ranks 55th among the World tourism spenders, with $189 million tourism expenditures (WTO, 1993). Bulgarians are mostly visiting adjacent countries such as Turkey, Greece, Romania and Macedonia. The main reason for this neighbourhood pattern, typical for outflows and to a certain extent also for the inflows to the country, is the dramatic increase in transportation fares and especially air-fares. This factor, which affects all of Eastern Europe, causes a shrinking of the geographical perimeter of tourist trips.

The institutional structure and ownership situation in the Bulgarian tourist industry is typical for the transition to a market economy. Most of the catering sector is either private or leased to private managers. On the other hand, nearly all 591 hotels are state owned, the representative of the State being the Committee for Tourism. Their privatisation advances slowly. Only recently two luxury hotels were sold and a number of others entered the privatisation process. The commercial sector had 139,000 beds in 1994, 118,000 of them in hotels (NSI, 1993/94). There is a reduction of more than 10% of the accommodation capacity in comparison with the previous year, but practically, this is due only to the reduction of the mountain hostels and room letting. Less than 7% of the beds are in hotels of 4 and 5-star or de luxe categories. A new phenomenon is the emergence of private hotels in the big towns and resorts or in their vicinity. This has not been statistically monitored yet, but there is no doubt that private hotel capacity exceeds the reduction of officially monitored accommodation.

Until 1990, the state company Balkantourist had a monopoly in all essential aspects of international tourism. Later Balkantourist was split into some 130 smaller state holdings, determined on geographical basis. Balkantourist limited its activities to wholesale tour operating and marketing. Many of the installations and activities were leased. Probably the greatest change in the tourism sector affected tour operating and marketing, which became much more decentralised as a multitude of small private travel agencies emerged (4,500 in 1994), some of them connected with important tour operators in the country and abroad. Another major wholesale tour operator is Balkanholidays - initially a subsidiary of Balkantourist, now a mixed private firm based in several European countries and the USA, acting as a competitor of Balkantourist. The newest important development is the purchase of 51% of the shares of Balkantourist by the most powerful Bulgarian private group Multigroup, which is also active in banking, industry and other sectors. This is regarded as an important step toward the privatisation of tourism in Bulgaria in favour of the national capitalists, who are linked with supranational

hotel chains and financial groups. Up to now foreign companies were present in the Bulgarian tourist industry mostly as joint ventures with the state, in management contracts (for instance in the Sofia Sheraton hotel) and in the consultancy and assessment of the facilities envisaged for privatisation. There are signs also that some foreign companies are interested in buying hotels mostly in the urban centres.

The role of the Committee for Tourism has been reduced to the normal functions of the government body administering tourism in the country. The Committee also takes part in the privatisation process, but only as a partner of the State Agency for Privatisation, to which is delegated the decisive competence.

Bulgaria emerged in the international tourism market in the early 1960s as a typical sun, sea and sand destination. This characteristic has not changed significantly up to the present day. More than 75% of foreign bed nights and 63% of the available hotel beds are bound to the Black Sea coast - a band of nearly 400 km of sandy and rocky sea shores with several hotel concentrations in the vicinity of the ports of Varna and Bourgas.

Considering the recreational and cultural attractions of the country, there is no doubt about its great potential as an international tourism destination.

Business visits tend to concentrate only in the bigger towns with hotels of a high standard. During the last two years the number of business tourists has markedly decreased as a result of the stagnation of the economic reforms and the progress in privatisation. The curative visits to the mineral springs resorts, rural tourism, game hunting and congress tourism are numerically incompatible with sea-side tourism. Those who spend a holiday on the sea coast, seldom undertake sight-seeing tours inside the country. Only a couple of winter resorts in Rila and the Rhodope mountains, managed to create some sort of alternative to the preponderant recreation flows towards the Black Sea coast in summer, which is a mature recreational region of international magnitude.

So, theoretically, tourism has a bright future in Bulgaria. In reality though, tourism development is hampered not only by the severe economic crisis, typical for all post-communist societies, but also by outdated legislation, lack of fresh investment and slow privatisation. The bulk of the hotels and the major tourist companies are still state-owned. No national strategy for development of the tourism sector has been drawn up yet.

## 3. EDUCATIONAL STRUCTURE AND NEW RELEVANT DEVELOPMENTS

The number of those permanently employed in tourism and recreation is about 60-70,000 (the total population of the country is 8.5 million). Part-time or seasonal employment in tourism account for at least another 100,000 jobs mostly during the summer. Altogether, tourism accounts for 5% of the overall employment in the country.

There are contradictory assessments of whether the share of the high and higher schools graduates is increasing or decreasing. The magazine *Cash* from 19 July 1995 announced that 5% of the tourism employees are university and 10% vocational college graduates, 15% have completed vocational secondary schools and as many as 70% are grammar school graduates. The article insists that the educational structure is improving. However, Hadjinikolov (1984) disclosed that in the early 1980s, the higher schools and hospitality colleges graduates were providing respectively 9% and 37% of the 45,000 workers then employed in tourism, a level much higher than their current proportion. Probably the discrepancy is a result of adding to the 1980s data the employees with non-tourism professions (jobs in health services, technical maintenance etc.), which are no less important for any tourism destination than the tourism professions proper.

A negative feature of employment in Bulgarian tourism is that the personnel are generally getting older. In the light of this, in spite of the educational merits of 4-5 year studies, the necessity of more rapid preparation of tourism employees, appears to be a priority for the industry (Rakadjiyska 1990). At the same time, the higher education establishments (dependent on the Ministry of Education, and not on the State Committee for Tourism), do not seem to favour shorter courses.

Presently eight higher education schools in Bulgaria are offering degrees and diplomas in tourism and tourism-related fields. There are 535 places available for recruitment of students for the 1995/96 academic year (Table 3.2). Some of the places are supported by the Ministry of Education, the rest (with lower scores on the entry exams) are paid for by the students.

The first generation schools, established in the 1960's, include the vocational colleges in Varna and Bourgas and the Tourism departments in Varna Economic Institute and Sofia University. It is not surprising that tourism education was then concentrated in the Black sea coastal region, and more specifically in Varna, since Bulgaria was and still is a country of sea-side summer tourism monoculture. In Bourgas a centre for training and re-training of the tourist cadres was also established, sponsored by the International Labour Organisation (ILO) to also serve the neighbouring countries. It became a national center for short-terms (1 week to 6 months) upgrading and recycling of the employees in the state tourism firms. The firms were compelled to supply participants for the courses and pay the centre, according to a plan drawn by the State Committee of Tourism.

**Table 3.2: Tourism higher education in Bulgaria**

| Higher School | Place | Name of course | Founded | 95/96 intake | Fee 95/96 1000 Lev |
|---|---|---|---|---|---|
| Higher Economic Institute | Sofia | International Tourism | 1990 | 200 students (both forms) | 34<br>17 (extr.) |
| University | Sofia | Tourism | 1968 | 55 (regular only) | 18 |
| New Bulgarian University | Sofia | Tourism | 1993 | ? (continuing education) | 14 |
| Institute of National Economy | Varna | International Tourism | 1965 | 200 (both forms) | 28<br>8 (extr.)<br>20 (eve.) |
| Pedagogical Institute | Blagoevgrad | Geography of Tourism | 1991 | 55 (regular only) | 24 (reg.)<br>12 (extr.) |
| University | Veliko Turnovo | Geography and Economics of Tourism | 1994 | 40 (correspon-dence only | 16 |
| Vocational College | Bourgas | Hospitality and Touroperations | 1969 | 110 | 28 (reg.)<br>8 (extr.)<br>20 (eve.) |
| Vocational College | Varna | Hospitality and Touroperations | 1963 | 100 | 28 (reg.)<br>8 (extr.)<br>20 (eve.) |

reg.= regular students; extr.= extramural; eve.= evening students.

As an average, those permanently employed were anticipated to take part in the courses at least once every 4 years. The Bourgas centre was very active in 1970s and 1980s, but since the 1989 changes the firms are no longer obliged to ensure training and re-training, and the activity of the centre has decreased dramatically.

As for tourism education and research, historically, quantitatively (regarding both staff and graduates) and qualitatively, the first academic institution in Bulgaria is the Varna Institute of National Economy.

The vocational secondary schools were founded in Sofia and in the nearby spa resort Bankya, in the second Bulgarian town Plovdiv, in Veliko Turnovo and three more such schools are in the Black sea region (in Pomorie, Varna and Dobrich). They train personnel mostly for catering in hotels and restaurants.

The second generation of tourism education is a new development. As can be seen from Table 3.2, several academic institutions opened tourism related courses between 1990-1994. In the Sofia Economic University a Department of International Tourism was created in 1990, though several tourism oriented modules have been taught to students in the Faculty of Commerce and Transportation since 1970, where research was carried out and teaching materials were developed. Similarly tourism-oriented modules exist in the curricula in Blagoevgrad Pedagogical Institute not only in the Faculty of Economics, but also in the Faculty of Ecological Engineering.

The New Bulgarian University in Sofia is a Soros sponsored private university registered abroad and opened in 1992. Its structure, curricula and diplomas are designed on American and European standards. It is fully paid, the teaching is usually during the weekends or in the evenings, as most of the students are working or learning in other schools. Tourism development and modules on tourism subjects are taught also in the Department of Heritage Management (cultural tourism course) as well in the radio course. Due to its recent development, the New Bulgarian University is offering only certificate and diploma (first and second level), but the bachelor degree is anticipated as well.

The second generation tourism education is also characterised by decentralisation of schools' branches in many different locations. For instance, the Blagoevgrad Pedagogical Institute is offering modules in tourism in its branches in Smolyan and Turgovishte. This is typical also for the Sofia Economic University, and is planned for the University of Veliko Turnovo subsidiary in Pleven. The general feeling is that the diffusion of the Tourism higher schools courses is not helping the quality of the education.

At the high school and post-graduate level, the establishment of the Dutch Hotel School in the Albena sea resort should be noted (2-year intensive course) run by the Maastricht Hospitality Institute. Another interesting case is the Danish-Bulgarian college in Botevgrad near Sofia. Its 2-year courses are in Trade, Marketing and Tourism. In general though, the private schools are not yet numerous in Bulgaria.

Typical for the country is the functioning of about 20 linguistic secondary schools (English, German, French, Russian, Spanish and Italian). The majority offer on a voluntary basis additional preparation in Tourist Guidance and Interpreting.

Several private firms are offering short-time courses for guides, cooks, small hotel managers, etc. The quality of this education is generally inferior.

It should be mentioned also, that the big hotels, 5 and 4-star hotels, such as the Sofia Sheraton, the Sofia Intercontinental and the Grand Hotel Varna, have their own strict programmes of training and re-training.

## 4. Strengths and weaknesses of Bulgarian higher education in tourism

The positive features are rather different for the schools of the first and the second generation. The common characteristics seem to be as follows:
- almost four decades of tourism development created a favourable climate for its acceptance by society and the recognition of the needs of professionalism and respective education and training;
- the high intellectual capacity of those joining tourism courses, which is due to the attractiveness of the tourism professions on one hand, and the good image of the departments offering respective courses on the other;
- a demanding secondary education level as far as the content of the subjects is concerned. Education is high in the hierarchy of priorities of the average Bulgarian family. During the post-socialism crisis the number of students has doubled. An important source of enrolment is the linguistic school graduates;
- the existence of a national network of tourism education and training establishments with two main cores - Varna and Bourgas on the Black Sea coast, and the capital city of Sofia. In the first generation departments there is a tradition and achievements in both research and education, including some high level monographs/textbooks;
- the academic staff is motivated to improve its performance. Many of the lecturers are specialists invited from the industry. This gives a pragmatic dimension to the generally theoretical education;
- the tourism departments have set examples of internationalisation in curricula design, techniques of teaching etc., in their schools, which has boosted their internal image. Several TEMPUS projects, including two very successful projects coordinated by the Dublin Technological Institute and the University of Palma, as well as two British Know-How Fund projects, have been established or are in the process of realisation.

The deficiencies and shortcomings of Bulgarian tourism higher education reflect the present situation of the country, the weaknesses of this industry in Bulgaria and of the education system in particular:
- the lack of a new education law legalising the European structure of course levels. No national accreditation of schools exists. All students in the universities and higher institutes currently graduate at a level close to the Masters degree, which is not recognised as such in developed countries. A new education law introducing three levels (certificate, bachelors and masters) has recently been debated in Parliament, so it will hopefully be operative in the academic year 96/97;
- conservatism, inertia and opposition to practical forms of education, characterises the milieu inside some higher educational institutions;
- the low level of computer training of both students and lecturers, insufficient hardware and the absence of specific national software;
- teaching, although based on modern curricula and syllabi, is old-fashioned

stressing mainly the memorising and reproduction of theoretical knowledge. Some modules reflect the old situation and not the transition to a market economy. The vocational colleges have been more successful in connecting the training with the contemporary industry requirements;
- practically, student mobility between schools and even between faculties is very low. Accreditation of academic scores and modules is a difficult and long process. Paradoxically, accreditation of the results and diplomas obtained by a group of students in the EU countries (mainly within TEMPUS), proved to be smoother;
- the weakest link in the teaching process is industrial placements. Placements are ill-organised, ill-paid and too short. This is an area where all East-European educational institutions need know-how and help. Especially grave is the situation with the placements of extramurals as the recent rapid development of extramural education students are joining secondary school graduates many without any experience in the industry;
- the underdevelopment of short-term and vocational forms of education and training, while the university level is over-represented by too many centres (Figure 3.2) of varying teaching quality. Considering that worldwide the great majority of the tourist cadres are trained in vocational schools, the emphasis should be on this type of schooling;
- the facilities and equipment of the educational establishments are inadequate. Special attention should be paid to the libraries, labs, computers and other communication facilities;
- the permanent staff in the tourism teaching units is too small numerically in comparison with the number of the students. A positive feature is, that all schools invite specialists from the industry but they do not take part in activities other than teaching (such as research, planning, auditing, or overall assessment of departmental performance);
- with the notable exception of the Varna institute linked with the Varna and Bourgas vocational colleges, the educational establishments are acting without any co-ordination. The State Committee for Tourism is hypnotised by its privatisation programme and does not pay any attention to education and training. It has even omitted to mention education in the recently prepared tourism law;
- the severe budget cuts have affected the whole system of education. In this situation the funding provided by several international projects is crucial, although the emphasis is often not where it should be - on equipment and software provision and student placement mobility. Western partners are not always aware, that the development is hampered not by the intellectual capacity of the staff, but by organisational, legal or technical problems;
- there is a structural inadequacy within the Bulgarian schools of different type and level. Travel services are well represented in the curricula and placements, while catering and especially hotel management remain underrepresented. Little or no provision is made in the area of leisure, sports and crafts management.

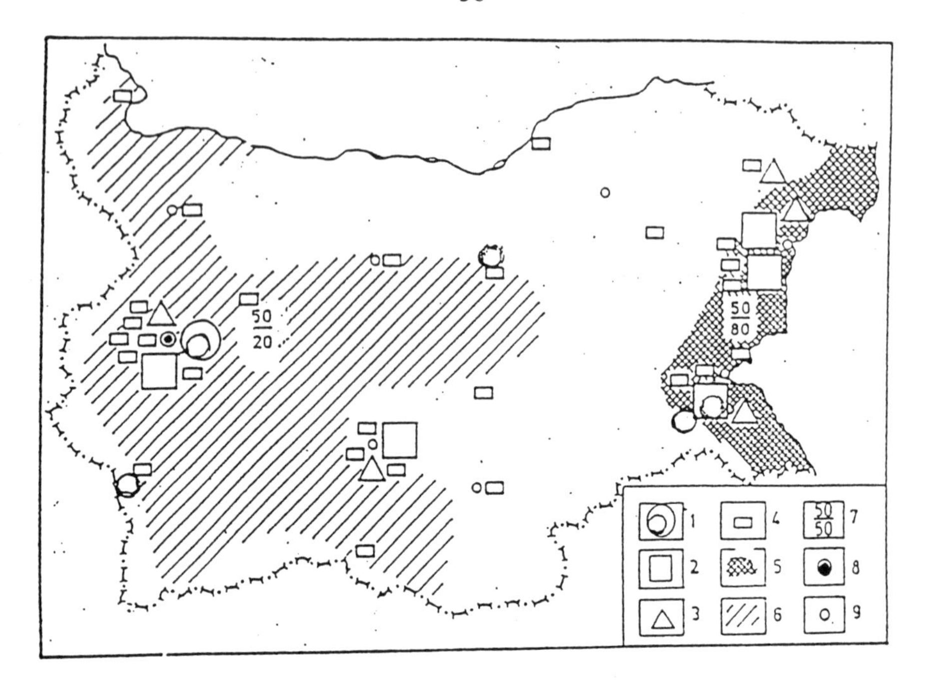


Legend:
1. Universities offering teaching in tourism (Sofia, Blagoevgrad, Bourgas, Velko Turnovo);
2. Other higher institutes (Varna economic institute, Varna vocational institute, Bourgas vocational institute, Plovdiv food processing institute);
3. Institute for retraining of tourism cadres (in Bourgas, Plovdiv, Sofia and Albena);
4. Professional and secondary schools offering qualification in restauration, hotel and touring services (in all districts centres and some other bigger towns);
5. Black sea tourist area;;
6. Tourist areas in the interior;
7. Percentage of the permanent (above) and the seasonal (below) tourist employment;
8. The capital Sofia;
9. District centres.

**Figure 3.2: The tourism educational network in Bulgaria, situation end of 1994**

Bulgaria has no alternative to the development and re-structuring of the tourism industry to adapt to the market economy. Therefore, it is obvious that serious efforts are necessary in tourism education. These efforts need the active support of the State Committee for Tourism and the elaboration of a concept of the Bulgarian Tourism with emphasis on the education, training and re-training. The existing loosely related educational units should be linked in a network, to capitalise on their considerable past experience and on the new prospects of europeanisation and education for quality.

## REFERENCES

Hadjinikolov, H. (1984). *The Services in International Tourism and the Quality of Labour*. Tourism and Recreation Bulletin 9, State Committee for Tourism. Sofia.

Rakadjiyska, S. (1990). *Tourism Training and Education in Bulgaria*. Annals of Tourism Research, vol.17, pp.150-153.

NSI, (1993-1994). *Tourism, annual and trimestrial bulletins*. National Statistical Institute Sofia.

WTO, (1993). *Yearbook of Tourism Statistics*. Vol.1, ed.45. WTO, Madrid.

# Chapter 4

# Tourism education in Croatia

**Boris Vukonić**

## INTRODUCTION

Education of personnel for the needs of tourism in Croatia has a long tradition, which is to be expected if we consider the fact that the first signs of tourism in Croatia were registered 150 years ago. In the course of its development tourism education has been through very many changes, as many external factors have influenced the form, type and volume of tourism education. For example, through the last 150 years Croatia has been a part of various state formations, and this is only one of many factors that have influenced the form and content of tourism education. The present tourism educational system is still strongly influenced by the recent past. Therefore, the very first task of the young Republic of Croatia in this field is the reconsideration of educational programmes in their totality and their adjustment to the philosophy and logic of the free market. The significance of such education has become even more obvious now, in the course of the war against Croatia, which resulted in shortages of personnel in tourism for different reasons. On the other hand, according to its development plans, Croatia has a great need for trained and high quality tourism personnel.

## THE DEVELOPMENT OF TOURISM EDUCATION

As in other European countries, education for the tourism industry in Croatia started in the form of training for caterers, namely waiters. From today's perspective, we remember only the foundation dates of the schools at the beginning of the century, whereas we tend to forget about the time consuming process of convincing people of the need for tourism education which as a rule preceded every action in this field. This was the case in Croatia, too. The single process of defining a model for the first catering school, the so called "Scientific Scheme of the School Specialised in Training Innkeepers and Coffee-House Keepers of the Free and Royal City of Zagreb", took a few years. Another three years passed until this School was founded in 1917 by a special Viceroy's decree.

It must be mentioned that this School has been active ever since (with a small interruption from 1943 to 1949). Today it exists under somewhat changed name and aim: to educate caterers as well as personnel for other sectors of tourism. To this first catering school in Croatia was later added the School for Hotel Management. They have been moving from one location to another, and today this is the biggest educational centre for catering and tourism personnel training in Croatia with almost 3,000 students.

As tourism in Croatia developed, especially in the regions along the Adriatic coast (there has been a permanent growth noted since the end of WWI), the need for qualified catering and hotel personnel increased, leading to the opening of vocational schools in almost all the bigger towns on the Adriatic. After the 1960s, the great tourist boom in the region caused the development of a wide network of more than 40 schools specialised in catering in Croatia. Along with the schools goes the grave problem of trained personnel. Logically enough, such a number of schools demanded a great amount of money which could not always be provided. Thanks to the well-known present circumstances in Croatia, this is the case today again. That is why many of the schools are relatively lacking in technical facilities. Only a few of them are directly connected to hotels where students can put their knowledge into practice, and the majority of the schools have a very small number of students.

In the period preceding the best tourism years in Croatia, in the academic year 1983/84, there were 5,705 students registered in schools specialised in teaching catering and hotel management in the whole of Croatia. There were four scientific and teaching institutions providing courses of study aiming to produce economists specialised in tourism and hotel management. In the same academic year the number of regular students was 897 and there were 272 part-time students.

There was a need for highly educated catering and hotel management personnel in Croatia, so the logical step was to found several high schools, and later, degree-granting educational institutions specialised in catering and tourism. The best known such schools were in Opatija (since 1960), Zagreb and Dubrovnik. Due to the various changes in the educational system in Croatia, these schools have either changed their status or have become Faculties (this is how the Faculty of Hotel Management in Opatija came into being), and sometimes they merged with other educational institutions (which was the case with the High School for Hotel Management and the Faculty for Foreign Trade in Zagreb).

Several universities provide courses for tourism personnel: Zagreb University, Split University (in Dubrovnik and Split) and Rijeka University (in Rijeka and Pula). The very first independent two year course on tourism was founded in 1970 in Dubrovnik. The great majority of such courses still take place within Faculties of Economics, which is also the case with the only Faculty of Hotel Management in Croatia (founded in 1973 in Opatija), where the accent has been placed upon economical aspects of the subject studied. In the beginning, in most Faculties or high schools the tourism topics were taught in the form of an optional subject usually called 'Tourism' or 'Tourism Economy'. At the Zagreb Faculty of Economics this subject has existed since 1956, which can be considered to be the beginning of degree granting educational programmes in tourism in Croatia.

Nevertheless, the very first complete study of tourism in Croatia was organised at the Faculty for Tourism and Foreign Trade in Dubrovnik. Later on, the same course of study was established in Zagreb (in 1977 at the Faculty for Foreign Trade and at the Faculty of Economics) and in Pula (at the Faculty for Economics and Tourism). It is quite interesting that even before the regular four-year course of study was introduced in Croatia in 1962, there existed a post-graduate study in the field of Tourism Economy at the Zagreb Faculty of Economics. In fact, this post-graduate study and similar courses developed at the same Faculty later on, have become a major source of tourism experts who have often continued to pass their knowledge to students in high schools and at Universities.

There have been many attempts in the past to standardise the content of the tourism courses or, at least, to unify some basic subjects so that the same diploma from different schools would 'weigh' the same. So far no one has completely succeeded, although the process of standardisation has been more efficient in the educational system in secondary schools. Still, the pressure to standardise is nowadays becoming more and more intense in university education as well.

If we wanted to draw conclusions about the circumstances in the past and the problems concerning education for the tourism industry, it would be possible to identify four basic points:

- Firstly, in the last 90 years of intense development of tourism in Croatia, tourism personnel have been educated at four basic levels: primary, secondary and high schools with specialised teaching programmes for the needs of tourism, as well as universities. Although neither continuous nor systematic, extra educational programmes have been developed in the form of seminars and specialised courses for all kinds of personnel.

- Secondly, the level of education and competence of the personnel, along with other material prerequisite conditions, determine the level of tourist service offered. This, again, influences the structure of the consumers of the (Croatian) tourism industry and affects its economic impact. It is, therefore, logical that much more attention has been paid to education of personnel for the needs of tourism, since nowadays the tourism industry is taken much more seriously in Croatia.

- Thirdly, the development of the tourist offer in the past lacked adequate personnel education as well as the corresponding quality and variety of courses of study, teachers and lecturers.

- Fourthly, tourism education covered only catering and hotel management profiles and personnel working in travel agencies. Nevertheless, there is a much wider range of qualified staff needed in tourism: in transport, marketing, financial institutions, handicraft industry, etc. Educational programmes lacked adequate courses of study on such fundamental topics.

## EDUCATION OF PERSONNEL FOR THE CURRENT NEEDS OF CROATIAN TOURISM

Tourism education can make a major contribution to improving the quality of Croatian tourism in its totality. Well advanced tourism, catering and hotel managing personnel are surely very important determinants of the actual realisation of the development strategy of Croatian tourism, which is a priority segment of the national economy.

Although the educational system has been reformed at all levels, it is still being carried out within a poor network of schools and institutions, in very stingily equipped classrooms. Most teaching staff were educated in the non-market conditions of the former state and, even more importantly, they taught students according to courses of study relying upon a completely different political and socio-economical system (that of former Yugoslavia).

After the new state of Croatia came into being, some radical changes had to take place in education. The differences between the former and the new system of education and educational programmes were enormous: from the socialist approach towards the world and economy one had to switch to the free-market system. In terms of theoretical and political approaches this meant a switch from the principle of socialist self-management towards life and earning to the capitalist, entrepreneurial and free-market approach. This is a great change in the educational system and it is virtually impossible to achieve in a short period of time, in spite of the significant actions already being taken in courses of study at all levels of education in Croatia.

There are three Ministries of the Republic of Croatia (Ministry of Education, Ministry of Tourism and Ministry of Science) working together on reforming all educational profiles for the needs of tourism. Two boards have been founded (one for secondary school education, and the other for university education) which have set the basic aims of the many reform processes that are yet to come:

a. to develop courses of study which will correspond to the changes in the Croatian economy and the role of tourism as one of its fundamental sectors;

b. to adjust these courses of study to changes in global tourism practice;

c. to widen the number of educational profiles within the regular teaching programme;

d. to limit the network of educational institutions in order to concentrate all the relevant financial and other means so that higher quality equipment (in classrooms, laboratories, libraries and workshops) and highly educated teaching staff can be provided;

e. to coordinate secondary school teaching programmes with high school courses of study, so that the so-called graduated hotel staff and 'tourism technicians' can continue their education in tourism, hotel management, economy or geography at university;

f. to determine the number of pupils and students enroling in state educational institutions according to the actual needs of tourism industry;

g. to ensure professional advancement especially of young teaching staff, assistant professors and professors by sending them to high quality universities and schools abroad;

h. to ensure a sufficient number of high quality textbooks for all the most important subjects lectured in secondary and high schools and universities;

i. to continue the unification of educational programmes of the same level at various specialised schools and universities.

These are the very basic tasks. There are many details involved in every task identified so far and it is not possible to mention all of them. Nevertheless, there are many changes and improvements which are being discussed and which are already taking place in practice. I strongly believe that right now, Croatia is taking the right path towards solving its educational problems at all levels since such education has to develop top quality and skilled personnel for the needs of Croatian tourism in the future.

# Chapter 5

# Tourism and tourism education in Hungary

**Margit Mundruczó**

## INTRODUCTION

Hungary is one of the most popular tourist destinations in Europe. This is due to its geographical location, its relatively developed tourist industry and services, its rich cultural and historical heritage and the well-known Hungarian hospitality. In addition to the heritage attentions concentrated in Budapest, Hungary also has an abundant supply of thermal water and Lake Balaton, Central Europe's largest lake.

## THE ROLE OF TOURISM IN HUNGARY

Tourism is becoming an important sector in the Hungarian national economy. In the last decade tourism was the only industry which was not seriously influenced by the economic recession. More and more people are employed in the tourism sector while other sectors of the economy (e.g. industry and agriculture) have seen structural changes and employment difficulties. A representative survey made in 1994 shows that foreign tourists and one-day visitors together spent approximately $ 3 billion in Hungary. The net balance of officially registered foreign exchange income and expenditure contributed $ 0.54 billion to the balance of payments.

Tourism provides jobs for about 250,000-300,000 people. It is also able to provide permanent jobs in economically distressed, underdeveloped areas. In Hungary tourism has a strongly stimulating impact on private enterprises. Due to the strong multiplier effect (over 2) tourism has both a direct and an indirect impact on 25-30% of total demand in the Hungarian economy. Direct and indirect full and part-time income from tourism therefore benefits every fourth family.

## THE TOURISM INDUSTRY IN HUNGARY

### Accommodation

In the peak tourist season of 1994 there were over 800,000 beds offered to tourists. Unlike other tourist destinations, three quarters of Hungary's accommodation consists of private rooms. Hotel capacity is about 85,000 beds, about 25,000 more than five years ago. This increase is due to the construction of new hotels and the refurbishment and expansion of existing ones. Privatisation has continued in the hotel industry. Following Hungarian small investors, foreign institutions and companies have been involved in the Hungarian hotel industry (e.g. ACCOR, Marriott).

Tourism continues to have a supporting, stabilising effect on catering sales, with foreign and domestic tourists contributing an estimated 55-60% of the total. Nearly three-quarters of the 44,500 commercial catering establishments are run by private entrepreneurs. The number of privately owned facilities increased more than three times since 1989. As part of the privatisation process, several well-organised new catering chains have been formed in recent years. In 1994 nine international fast-food chains operated more than 60 units across the country (two thirds in Budapest).

**Infrastructure**

Recently, significant advances in the development and modernisation of transportation have assisted Hungarian tourism. In air transport the number of companies providing services increased to 150. MALÉV has been privatised and has continued with its fleet realignment acquiring new, efficient jet aircraft and expanding its flights.

Important elements in the development of the road network were the building and upgrading of motorways, bridges and border crossings. The Budapest-Hegyeshalom (Vienna) railway commenced improvements in 1993. Telecommunications have developed rapidly. The telephone exchanges opened in 1993 provided 700,000 new lines for clients.

**Travel agencies**

Currently, more than 800 registered agencies are operating at 1,300 locations in Hungary. The majority of travel agencies organise and retail tourism products, international as well as domestic. Most travel agencies are totally Hungarian owned, others are joint ventures, and only 20 are fully foreign owned.

**Public sector tourism**

A market economy based on private ownership makes it necessary for the State to undertake a new role in the area of tourism. As a result, tourism responsibilities have changed. The Hungarian Tourist Board is an organisation within the Ministry of Industry and Commerce and its missions are to stimulate, catalyse, co-ordinate planning, to create conditions for development, and to publicise and promote. Recently the Tourist Board prepared a National Tourism Development Strategy.

## DEMAND FOR HUNGARY

### 1994 Data summary

In 1994, Hungary had 39.8 million foreign visitors, which is 1.9 % less than in 1993. Of the visitors 21.4 million were tourists. It should be noted that the majority of 'tourists' coming from Eastern Europe arrive without real tourism purposes (refugees, shopping, working) and stay in the country for relatively short periods without making any tourist expenditure. The total length of stay of foreign tourists was over 140 million nights. As was mentioned above, $ 1.4 billion was officially registered by banks as hard currency revenue. The total hard currency income was estimated $ 3-3.5 billion. Hungarian citizens crossed the nation's borders 14.3 million times and spent 33.7% more in hard currency than in 1993.

## TOURISM EDUCATION IN HUNGARY

In the Hungarian higher education system there are three institutions which provide tourism programmes for students. These institutions are as follows:

- College of Commerce, Catering and Tourism
  (undergraduate and post-graduate programmes in Tourism & Hotel Management)
- Budapest University of Economic Sciences
  (tourism subjects and a postgraduate programme in tourism)
- Kodolányi College (Székesfehérvár)
  (undergraduate tourism programme only)

Beside these institutions a few other institutions teach tourism subjects for one semester.

## COLLEGE OF COMMERCE, CATERING AND TOURISM

The origin of the College may be traced back to 1857 when the Budapest Academy of Commerce, the first commercial higher educational institution in Europe, was founded. In 1885 this institution moved to the present site in Alkotmány street. During its history it has seen many changes. In 1962 the Ministry of Commerce established a School for Commerce and Catering, which was reorganised in 1968 as a College of Commerce and Catering. In 1993 the College was renamed The College of Commerce, Catering and Tourism (CCCT).

**Courses and students**

The College is the largest higher educational institution in Hungary in the field of catering, hotel and tourism. The college houses faculties of Commerce, Catering, Tourism and Teacher Training, which offer courses at post-secondary, undergraduate and postgraduate levels.

The post-secondary programmes include:
- tour-guiding and tour management;
- catering management;
- commercial management;
- small business;
- manager assistant;
- advertising management and
- fashion management.

The College offers undergraduate programmes in:
- commercial management;
- catering and hotel management;
- tourism management - hotel management (run jointly within the tourism management and hotel management course portfolio taught in English);
- tourism management - hotel management (run jointly within the tourism management and hotel management course portfolio taught in German);
- teacher training for vocational schools in the areas mentioned above.

Postgraduate programmes are available in:
- tourism and hotel management;
- household economics teaching;
- business management;
- catering management;
- marketing management.

The language of teaching is Hungarian except for the new English language Tourism Management and Hotel Management (THM) undergraduate programmes which commenced in September 1994.

Table 5.1 presents the actual and forecast number of students in the College over a four-year period.

**Table 5.1: Students at the College of Commerce, Catering and Tourism**

| | 1992/93 | 1993/94 | 1994/95 | 1995/96 |
|---|---|---|---|---|
| *Undergraduate* | | | | |
| Students in total | 1451 | 1702 | 2625 | 2820 |
| Full-time students | 820 | 929 | 1410 | 1520 |
| THM students English | | | 41 | 80 |
| Evening and correspondent students | 631 | 773 | 1215 | 1300 |
| *Postgraduate* | | | | |
| Students in total | 180 | 180 | 340 | 400 |
| *Post-secondary* | | | | |
| Students in total | 540 | 970 | 1000 | 1100 |

## TOURISM AND HOTEL MANAGEMENT PROGRAMME TAUGHT IN ENGLISH

A major development spearheaded by a programme of co-operation between CCCT and the Manchester Metropolitan University (MMU) and funded by the British Government through the British Council, has resulted in the development of a new programme in Tourism and Hotel Management, which will be taught in English. The course was designed to provide a vocational education for students and results in a learning experience and qualification which are both internationally recognised and accredited. It will seek to satisfy the growing international demands for future managers in Tourism and Hotel operations who will be required to understand, analyse and plan operational and management policies in a variety of international environments.

### Course aim

The aim of the course is to provide an educational programme which seeks to prepare students for a changing society and to develop those skills and competence necessary for management careers internationally in hotel and tourist organisations.

### Outcome

The Tourism and Hotel Management course taught in English is a four-year programme of full time study, with 36 weeks of industrial experience in the third year. The students finishing the course satisfactory will receive an undergraduate Diploma in Tourism Management or Hotel Management. The diploma will be accredited by the Hungarian Ministry of Education and by European Foundation for the Accreditation of Hotel School Programmes (Option Hotel & Catering) or the United Kingdom Institute of Travel and Tourism (Option Travel & Tourism).

**Structure of the programme**

The course is operated in English and extends over a period of four years. Each academic year consists of two semesters of 14 weeks. These normally commence in September and February.

*Year I*

The first year is common to both courses. It is designed to provide a fundamental understanding of both the practical and operational elements of hotel and tourist organisations, and of those business aspects necessary for their organisation and support. Economics, mathematics, statistics, accounting, computing, hospitality and tourism studies, communication and languages provide the core programme.

*Year II*

The common core elements of Year I are developed further and applied in Year II through studies in management, law, human resource management, marketing, accounting and languages. Additionally, the programme provides for students who wish to specialise in either Hotel and Catering or in Travel and Tourism. These options are supported by industry specific subjects, for example, for Hotel and Catering students the course provides modules in food and beverage, hotel management, hotel accounting and gastronomy. For Travel and Tourism students, there are modules in the geography of tourism, tour organisation and sales, management, ticketing and tourism projects.

*Year III*

In order to reinforce the first two years of study, and to provide an industrial orientation to the course, the third year will consist of a period of industrial placement, usually abroad. Those specialising in Hotel and Catering will work within hotels, those with Travel and Tourism interests will work in travel agencies, tourist information centres and convention bureaux. This year of industrial placement will not only enable students to validate acquired theories, skills and competencies from the first two years of the course but will also provide the necessary industrial orientation required to underpin more advanced management studies in Year IV.

*Year IV*

The final year of the course contains a core of advanced managerial theory and practice - operations management, finance, strategic and human resource management. In addition, students will have the opportunity of developing further their special interest. In Hotel and Catering there are modules in food and beverage management, hotel management, marketing and finance. In Travel and Tourism specialisation will be developed through studies on tour operation and retail management, marketing and strategic management.

| | Year 1 | | Year 2 | | Year 3 | Year 4 | |
|---|---|---|---|---|---|---|---|
| SUBJECT | sem 1 | sem 2 | sem 1 | sem 2 | | sem 1 | sem 2 |
| *Common Core Subject* | | | | | INDUSTRIAL PLACEMENT | | |
| Introduction to Food & Beverage | 4 | 3 | | | | | |
| Mathematics | 2 | | | | | | |
| Economics | 4 | 2 | | | | | |
| Information Technology | 3 | 3 | | | | | |
| Communications | 2 | 4 | | | | | |
| English Study Skills | 4 | 6 | 2 | 2 | | | |
| Foreign Language | 6 | 3 | 6 | 6 | | 6 | 6 |
| Introduction to Tourism | | 3 | | | | | |
| Statistics | | 4 | | | | | |
| Accounting | | 2 | 4 | | | | |
| Behavioural Studies & Management | | | 2 | | | | |
| Cultural Studies | | | 2 | | | | |
| Law | | | 2 | | | | |
| Human Resource Management | | | | 2 | | 2 | |
| Marketing | | | | 4 | | | |
| Operations Management | | | | | | 2 | |
| Financial Management | | | | | | 2 | |
| Strategic Management | | | | | | 2 | |
| Informations System Management | | | | | | | 2 |
| Feasibility Studies/ Business Games | | | | | | | 2 |
| Dissertation | | | | | | 1 | 1 |
| **SUBTOTAL** | **25** | **30** | **18** | **14** | | **15** | **11** |
| ***Option in Hotel & Catering*** | | | | | | | |
| Food & Beverage | | | 6 | 6 | | 2 | |
| Hotel Operation | | | 4 | 4 | | | |
| Hotel Accounting | | | | 4 | | 2 | |
| Hotel Management | | | | | | 2 | 2 |
| Hotel Marketing | | | | | | | 2 |
| **SUBTOTAL** | | | **10** | **14** | | **6** | **4** |
| **TOTAL** | **25** | **30** | **28** | **28** | | **21** | **15** |
| ***Option in Tourism & Travel*** | | | | | | | |
| Geografy of Tourism | | | 4 | | | | |
| Tour Operations/ Travel Retailing | | | 4 | 6 | | | |
| Public Sector Tourism | | | 2 | | | | |
| Economics of Tourism | | | | 2 | | | |
| Ticketing | | | | 2 | | | |
| 'Live' Group Project | | | | 4 | | | |
| Tourism Marketing | | | | | | 2 | |
| Travel Retailing Management | | | | | | | 2 |
| Tour Management | | | | | | 2 | |
| Convention/ Meeting Management | | | | | | 2 | |
| Tourism Strategic Management | | | | | | | 2 |
| **SUBTOTAL** | | | **10** | **14** | | **6** | **4** |
| **TOTAL** | **25** | **30** | **28** | **28** | | **21** | **15** |

*In weekly units: one unit = 45 minutes*

**Table 5.2: The curriculum. Tourism and Hotel Management Undergraduate Programme taught in English by modules and teaching hours**

The methodological approach to the final year studies will centre upon independent learning strategies - projects, case studies, seminars etc. These are designed to encourage course participants to develop their analytical and evaluative skills and competencies. This approach will be enhanced further by the requirement for all students to complete and submit a dissertation to indicate their ability to undertake independent learning. The curriculum is shown in Table 5.2.

## EXTERNAL RELATIONS

As a professional higher educational institution, the College has good contacts with the industry, industrial professional bodies, Government institutions and with other economic higher educational institutions.

The College is working closely with the industry in the following areas:
- course design and development;
- course delivery;
- course quality control;
- industrial placement;
- careers;
- student sponsorship;
- short courses offered to managers from industry.

The College is a member of:
- Hungarian Chamber of Commerce;
- Association of Hungarian Hotels;
- Association of Hungarian Travel Agencies;
- Association of Hungarian Chefs and Confectioners.

Some College staff are also members of relevant professional organisations.

From 1962 until 1993 the College was supervised and subsidised by the Ministry of Commerce and Industry. The fact that the College was the only higher educational institute belonging to the Ministry gave the College a unique opportunity to work in close co-operation with the different departments of the Ministry (e.g. Hungarian Tourist Board, Department of Human Resources).

## STAFF DEVELOPMENT

The College's current research and staff development policy has evolved from the development strategy of CCCT agreed in June 1994 by the College Council.

The main objectives of this development strategy have been identified as follows:

- to develop the research and consultancy programmes which meet the demands of the industry;
- to establish small research teams that combine academic staff, industrialists and students;
- to establish a case study centre;
- to develop a special kitchen research lab;
- to assist staff in improving their pedagogical performance and their professional knowledge;
- to assist staff in developing their foreign language skills;
- to seek necessary resources for staff development in Hungary and abroad.

Over the last few years the College has had a special staff development programme relating to the new course taught in English. Every full-time teacher who is (and will be) involved in the THM course portfolio has participated in staff development programme(s) and an English language training course.

Staff development programmes included the following elements:

- curriculum developments seminars in Hungary and abroad held by foreign professors;
- visiting lecturers coming into the College provide an important vehicle for staff development;
- senior Faculty Awards programme in the UK from 3 to 12 weeks;
- the Senior Faculty Awards programme includes visits to industry as well as to educational establishments;
- visiting foreign universities and studying their teaching methods;
- meetings with industrialists in Hungary and abroad;
- attending conferences in Hungary and abroad;
- participating in short courses;
- research/consultancy work which helps to keep the staff up to date;
- English Language Training.

**Difficulties and problems**

The College and staff appear at times to be overextending themselves by having agreed to embark on too many courses and projects at the same time. Since the Hungarian Government has reduced the financial support given to educational institutions the College has to increase its revenue coming from different post-secondary and postgraduate programme tuition fees. There is a problem that heavy workloads either within the College and/or to do with external projects may act as a constraint on their implementation.

# Chapter 6

# Tourism education in Poland: An Overview

**Bohdan Jung and Bożena Mierzejewska**

## 1. THE STRUCTURE OF TOURISM EDUCATION IN POLAND

Specialised tourism education in Poland is delivered, as in most countries, at secondary and higher (post-baccalaureate) level, as well as, on a lesser scale, though specialised extension courses offered by companies to their employees or purchased from third parties. In the post-war tradition there existed a narrow linkage between, on the one hand, the professional and vocational secondary schools and, on the other, between firms in the public sector, which acted as natural sponsors of this type of education (equipping schools with the necessary equipment to carry out practical training), places of internship or industrial placement, as well as logical future employers of young trainees and graduates. With the advent of economic reforms in late 1989 this whole system of linkages, based around planned symbiosis of public education and state ownership of firms, was blown apart. One of the important consequences of this breakdown was a much more varied and uncertain pattern of entry into the labour market for young people (Roberts and Jung, 1995).

The path from tourism education to work, which was in force until 1995, provided for a number of independent entry levels, starting with two years of secondary (vocational) education and ending with a full doctoral cycle (total of 13 years in secondary and higher education).

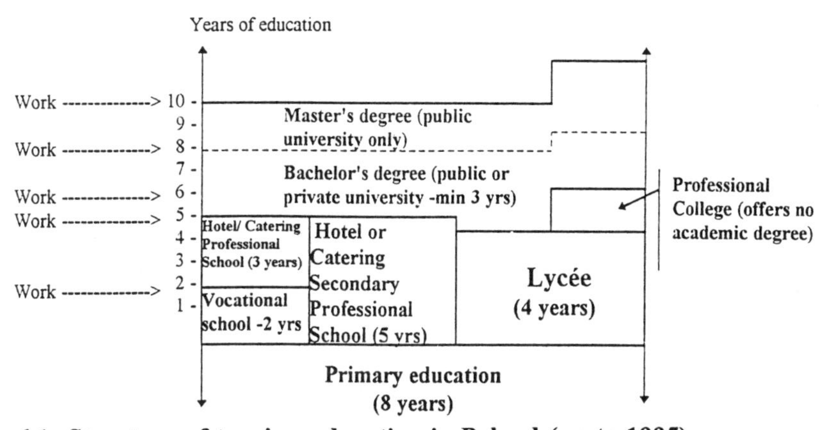


**Figure 6.1: Structure of tourism education in Poland (up to 1995)**

Vocational schools (post-secondary education) provide courses leading to professions connected to the tourism industry and catering services/gastronomy. They are for students of at least 15 years of age who have graduated from primary schools. In tourism, this type of school typically trains cooks and waiters. From the point of view of the employer, students that obtain diplomas in these schools are considered as having a professional qualification. Under Polish conditions, vocational schools generally do not enjoy a good standing either with the students or with the employers. However, those which prepare for a catering qualification are quite popular with young applicants and usually have many candidates wishing to study there.

While no data even on the approximate number of students in these schools could be obtained from the Ministry of Education, the number of schools offering vocational training in gastronomy and catering suggests (taking into consideration a two-year cycle of training, 30 students per class and two classes studying in parallel) that this number is close to 20,000, of which slightly over 10% in private schools, all of which were established after 1989. Vocational schools offering skills in gastronomy and catering account for 6% of all vocational schools in Poland (GUS, 1995).

**Table 6.1: Number of vocational schools offering courses in gastronomy and catering**

| Type of school | Public | Private |
|---|---|---|
| Vocational school | 149 | 17 |

From the career point of view, vocational schools are close to being a dead end. There are special 3-year professional schools (*technikum*) in hotel and catering that allow graduates of vocational schools to complete their secondary education with a baccalaureate (rather than a skill) and continue on to university or college education, but the actual numbers wishing to improve their educational status through this trajectory are very small.

A full cycle of secondary education in tourism is offered by professional schools (usually *technikum* or, on more rare occasions, by professional *lyceum* or lycée). Those which prepare for a career in tourism usually offer qualifications in gastronomy and catering and hoteliery. Full secondary education, which is accompanied with industrial placement or training takes 4-5 years. Successful graduates of the *technikum* obtain a baccalaureate or *matura* (essential prerequisite of university or college education) and diplomas which qualify them to work in hotels, tourist offices and restaurants.

**Table 6.2: Number of professional secondary schools offering courses in hoteliery and gastronomy**

| Type of school | Public | Private |
|---|---|---|
| Professional schools in hoteliery | 49 | 5 |
| Professional schools in gastronomy | 194 | 6 |

Again, no official data on enrolment in these schools could be obtained from competent authorities. If similar assumptions were made as those for vocational schools (but allowing for a 5-year cycle of education), the approximate total enrolment in these schools could be evaluated at some 76,000 pupils, with less than 4% in private schools, all of which were established after 1989. By our very cursory estimates, in 1995 there were about 96,000 pupils enrolled in vocational and professional secondary schools which offered a qualification or skill in tourism and gastronomy/catering. This was slightly over 10% of total enrolment in this type of school. Professional schools in tourism and gastronomy and catering constitute about 5% of the total number of professional schools in Poland (GUS, 1995).

Next step up on the ladder of tourism education in Poland are the colleges (*szkoty pomaturalne* - or post-baccalaureate schools), which offer 2-year courses for graduates of secondary schools who have obtained their baccalaureate. Their intake is usually those who failed to pass their competitive entrance exams to public universities and (a recent development!) have no financial means to pay tuition in private universities or 'evening studies' in public universities, where no entrance exam is necessary, but where fees are paid for each semester of study. Graduates of these colleges obtain no academic degree, but earn a certificate for skilled and qualified technicians, which in theory gives them access to middle level management. There are two specialisations in colleges that prepare for work in tourism: hotel management and management of tourist services.

**Table 6.3: Number of colleges offering courses in hotel management and tourist services management**

| Type of school | Public | Private |
|---|---|---|
| Colleges (*szkoty pomaturalne*) | 29 | 2 |

Many of the public colleges were created after 1989 in response to the potential demand for this education, which followed a rapid increase in the number of private hotels, motels, restaurants, cafes and bars in Poland after market reforms. They were swift in modifying their teaching programme to offer skills needed on the job market, but their weakness lies in the fact that they continue to be perceived as a surrogate of higher education and many of their students drop out as soon as they succeed in entering a university. The number of colleges offering courses in tourism and hoteliery accounted for 3% of all schools of this type in Poland (GUS, 1995).

At the highest level there are 7 universities that offer masters degrees in tourism. Two of them are so-called Academies of Physical Education (AWF), and the others are economic universities (*Akademia Ekonomiczna*). Over a 5-year study course, they offer majors in tourism, which is viewed from a very general and broad perspective. Only one university offers a major in what is strictly defined as hotel management. One of the latest developments in higher education is the launching of four private universities that offer majors in hotel management at a bachelors level (3 years' course). This development was in response to higher demand for qualified hotel managers in Poland as several new chains of hotels have opened in the last few years[1]. As for higher education in gastronomy, there are 6 universities which offer a major in this field. None of them cater specifically for professionals, who aim at a career in hotels and tourism. The bulk of students pursuing a full cycle of higher (academic) education, which leads them to a Master's degree, are graduates of general lycées and have no practical experience in the tourism industry.

Both in the case of colleges and universities, variations in the size of classes and student groups do not allow even for rough estimates of enrolment in tourism, hotel or gastronomy majors. In 1993 all Academies of Physical Education had a combined enrolment of 3,236 students, and one private Higher School of Tourism and Hoteliery had 381 students (GUS, 1994).

The proposed direction of change in the system of tourism education is towards simplification. As can be seen in Figure 6.2, under the planned system of tourism education there is no place for 2-year colleges with no academic degree and for 3-year professional secondary schools for those who received a vocational education.

---

[1]These operators encountered some problems with qualified staff (especially management), so in many cases they had to hire foreign managers, who in turn had no knowledge of the local market.

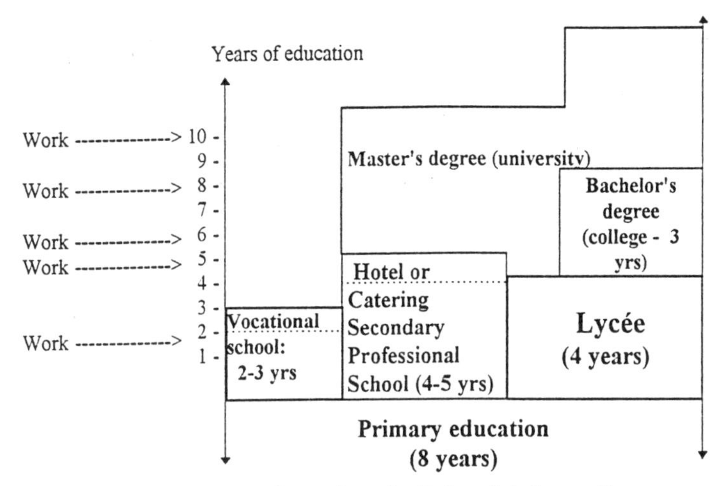


**Figure 6.2: Structure of tourism in Poland (planned)**

In what is a sanctioning of the status quo, in the proposed system the vocational trajectory looks even more like a dead end. Preparation of skilled technicians is increasingly delegated to professional schools, whereas the strengthened role of 3-year colleges, which offer a bachelors degree in areas related to the hospitality industries, is a reflection of the expanding role of private colleges/universities, but which practically rule out the possibility of pursuing a Masters degree[2].

## 2. ORGANISATION OF TOURISM EDUCATION AND ITS GEOGRAPHIC DISTRIBUTION

Tourism education in Poland is split along three lines. In terms of the number of schools and enrolment the bulk of it takes place in public schools, colleges and universities, even though expansion of private schools is certainly the single most important and dynamic development since the post-war years. The distinction between public and private education should at this point be made more clear. Public schools belong to and are financed by central or (recently on a much broader scale) local government. Their dependence on the Ministry of Education (MEN) for approval of their curriculum is total. Financing for operation of these schools also comes from the state budget. No tuition is

[2]With one exception, the 35 private universities/colleges that operate in Poland in all fields of study (most are in management and business administration) do not meet the Ministry of Education's requirements on the composition of academic staff (especially the number of full professors and academics with a post-doctoral degree) necessary to have rights to confer masters degrees.

charged by these schools, but it has become frequent practice among parents to contribute financially and give assistance in kind to the schools in order for the latter to organise extra or more varied activities (such as school trips or modernisation of computer labs). Private schools must be licensed by the Ministry of Education. This licensing is largely dependent on the conformity of their curriculum with guidelines established by MEN, as well as on use of an adequate number of qualified teachers or professors, whose education meets national standards. Private schools collect tuition, but they may also apply (and indeed many of them do) to the Ministry of Education for subsidies to cover their partial or even full operating cost.

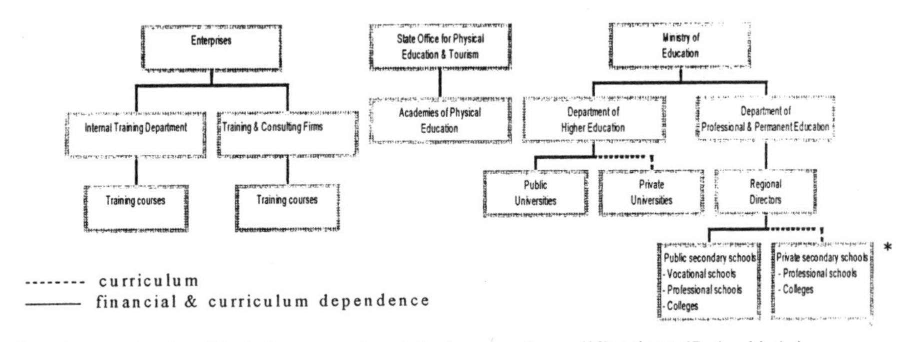


* -private schools with rights to confer state degrees & qualifications (B.A., M.A.) can obtain subsidies

**Figure 6.3: Organisation of tourism education in Poland (1995)**

The most important split takes place at the level of higher education (especially majors leading to a Masters in Tourism), where tourism education is divided, on the one hand, between Academies of Physical Education (AWF), which both in terms of curriculum and financing are dependent on the State Office for Physical Education and Tourism, a junior ministry within the structure of the Polish government and, on the other hand, economic universities. Other institutions are in the various stages of the process of entering the educational market for tourism (geographic faculties at universities hitherto specialised in humanities, more academies of physical education and economic and management faculties at general universities). It is also characteristic of tourist education in Poland that training courses which are organised for and at the behest of the industry are either done by companies' internal training centres (as in the case of ORBIS and most large hotels) or by specialised training/consultancy firms. Training is therefore almost entirely separate from the education system.

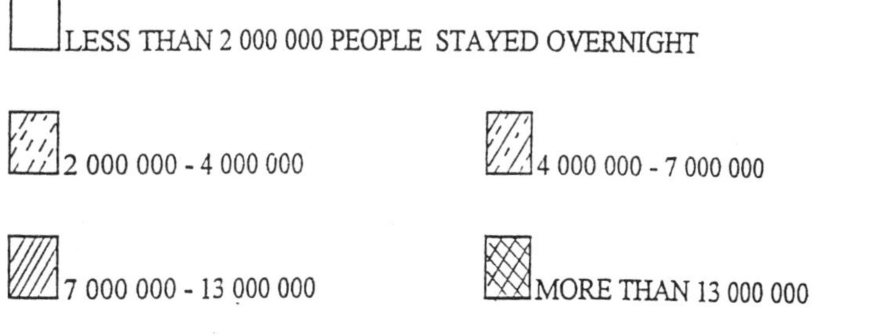


• PUBLIC SCHOOL ✱ PRIVATE SCHOOL

**Figure 6.4: Intensity of internal travel (Jan-Sept 1992) and tourist schools in Poland in 1992**

While on the organisational level three independent ways of organising tourism education and training, as shown in Figure 6.3, could be suggestive of an erratic pattern of distribution of schools, a comparison between the spatial distribution of tourism education and the demand for tourism services (as exemplified by the number of tourists per *voievoidship* or region) shows a good correlation between the number of schools and visitors in a given region (see Figure 6.4).

## 3. REFORM AND PROSPECTS

Tourism education in Poland is undergoing reforms under pressure from both internal and external factors. Internal factors can be mainly attributed to the structure of demand for labour and the restructuring of the tourism industry. In the years 1980-1993 the number of beds in Polish hotels grew from 49,900 to 74,300, motel beds increased from 1400 to 3300, and beds in pensions from 6,100 to 12,000 (GUS 1994). This was accompanied by a tremendous growth in the number of private tourist agencies and travel agents, small restaurants, bars etc. On the other hand, employment in social tourism (such as holiday centres belonging to state-owned enterprises) was clearly in decline. External pressure came from demand and requirements of foreign visitors, as well gentle persuasion from Western consultants helping the Polish government to reshape the country's tourism industry (the so-called TOURIN project co-financed by the European Union's PHARE programme and the Polish government programme).

One of the priorities of the TOURIN project is the restructuring of Polish tourism education. Much effort has gone into the programming of secondary and higher tourism education. Up to 1992 all secondary education in tourism was administered (both financially and in terms of curriculum) by the Ministry of Education while some of higher (academic) education was supervised by the State Committee for Physical Culture and Tourism. Since 1993 a joint programming body was created by this junior ministry. This programming body features experts from the Ministry of Education, as well as PHARE consultants involved in the TOURIN project (see Figure 6.5).

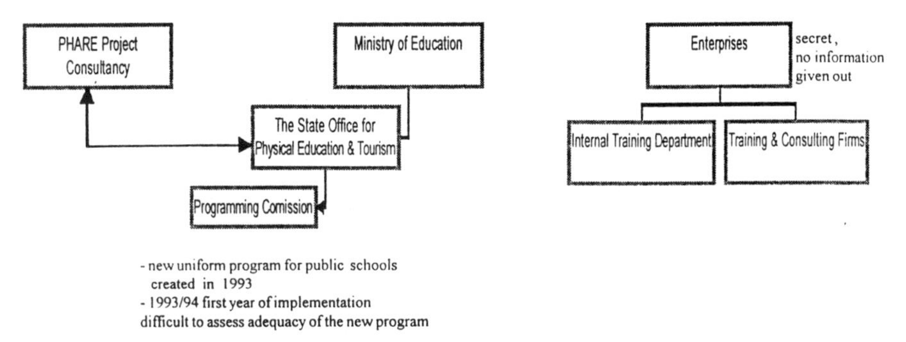


**Figure 6.5: Programming of tourism education after 1992**

There is still no linkage between the system of tourist education and training/updating for industry. As for the uniform curriculum in tourism, catering and gastronomy and hotel education, which was applied to secondary professional and vocational education in the school year 1993/94, it is too early to assess its adequacy, which will only become apparent when the first graduates make their entry on the job market. From the perspective of 1995 the prospects of tourism education in Poland look better than a few years ago since the awareness of the need for change is backed by individual and institutional action, such as implementation of reform programmes which are part and parcel of a larger restructuring package for the whole industry.

Uniform curriculum is only a part of the larger effort to reform tourism education. Other elements of these reforms include programming of curriculum through regular co-ordination and consultations between the State Office for Physical Culture and Tourism, the Ministry of Education, secondary schools, universities, representatives of the industry, local government and foreign consultants. Efforts are made to set up updated libraries of Western textbooks, translate into Polish some key literature, as well as to create data banks on schools offering courses in tourism and hotel management. With the assistance of the TOURIN Phare project, a process of the training of trainers is now well under way (see also Airey, Chapter 2 this volume). International co-operation is developing, with seminars and conferences on curriculum development and restructuring of education taking place both in Poland and abroad.

While both content and form of tourism education in Poland are changing, much remains to be done. The future of the Academies of Physical Education, which eagerly open themselves to tourism education, or which modify the existing curriculum, is largely uncertain. These academies view tourism from an extremely broad perspective, as exemplified by Figure 6.6.

**Table 6.4: Curriculum in tourism higher education in an Academy of Physical Education**

| Subject | Hours |
|---|---|
| BASIC COURSE (2 YEARS, 4 SEMESTERS) | |
| Introduction to law | 42 |
| Economics | 56 |
| Psychology | 42 |
| Pedagogy | 42 |
| Introduction to tourism, recreation and hotels | 28 |
| Geography of tourism | 80 |
| History of culture and arts | 80 |
| Statistics | 56 |
| Man and environment | 82 |
| Landscape geography | 82 |
| Sociology | 45 |
| Introduction to informatics | 45 |
| Introduction to marketing | 28 |
| Introduction to food and catering service | 42 |
| Electives (BASIC COURSE) | 28 |
| Foreign language 1 | 523 |
| Foreign language 2 | 241 |
| Physical education | 381 |
| SPECIALISED GRADUATE COURSE IN ORGANISATION OF TOURIST SERVICES | |
| Elements of spatial planning and tourist management | 42 |
| Organisation and management | 42 |
| Informatics in tourism | 42 |
| Economics of tourism | 56 |
| Economics of tourist firms | 42 |
| Seminar (diploma) | 84 |
| Sociology of tourism | 42 |
| Marketing in tourism | 42 |
| Biometeorology of tourism | 42 |
| Specialising seminar | 42 |
| Electives (3 subjects chosen from 5 blocks) | 224 |
| Practical training | 200 |
| Qualified tourism | 80 |
| Foreign language 1, foreign language 2 (as above) | (as above) |
| Physical education (as above) | (as above) |

Higher tourism education in Poland still largely suffers from a clear lack of focus. In tradition, it was activity-oriented (preparation for 'animators' of social and qualified tourism), spatially-oriented (preparation of spatial planners specialised in tourism and recreation, destined to work in planning commissions and local government) or functionally-oriented (administrators of state-owned hotels and travel agencies). There is still little tradition and indeed not enough professors able to offer courses with a managerial focus.

The second source of worry is the continuing split between higher education in tourism carried out in universities subordinated to the Ministry of Education and the State Committee for Physical Education and Tourism, as well as the continuing marriage of tourism and physical education in the latter. In the light of other priorities in reforming the country's administration, there is no political interest in ending this unfortunate linkage, which was created when tourism was mainly seen through the prism of social activities. Tourism education continues also to be largely detached from the industry and focused on young people, rather than upgrading and updating of the skills of those already working in tourism or gastronomy.

The current reform of education in tourism, as prepared by the State Committee for Physical Education and Tourism and depicted in Figures 6.1 and 6.2, also runs counter to the general reform of education prepared by the Ministry of Education. Under the experience of the last five years, when young people with vocational and specialised professional training were experiencing the highest levels of unemployment and were also hardest to re-train, MEN decided to boost general education (especially of gymnasium or lycée type), which gives greater flexibility to future graduates and prepares them for a more varied set of careers.

The quality of private schools and universities, the most dynamic segment of the market for tourism education in Poland, is yet to be ascertained on the job market. The composition of the body of teachers in some of these schools suggests that some fresh blood is desperately needed, as those with a very poor record in public schools and universities are presented as the intellectual backbone of these new institutions. Compared to graduates of public schools and universities, those from private ones are also in a more fragile position. When not able to pay for private education, these graduates find themselves in a tight spot since credits earned in their private courses are not recognised outside of their schools. The image of a tourism professional is also jeopardised by the low ethics of the industry, which was recently hit by a number of scandals, caused by fraud practised by greedy and dishonest operators.

On the whole, the process of reforming tourism education in Poland is, despite the above shortcomings, well on its way and it is to be expected that the best graduates will have interesting job prospects linked to the development of both Polish and foreign-owned tourist infrastructure, as well as in the tourism and travel agencies catering for increasingly travel-oriented Poles. The situation in which new Western hotels recruiting their staff in Poland had one precondition for their prospective staff - namely that they should never have worked in Polish tourism or gastronomy - is over, but both private and public schools, colleges and universities must yet prove their worth on the increasingly demanding and competitive job market.

## References

Blotny, J. (1993). *Rozmieszczenie zagranicznej turystyki przyjazdowej do Polski w 1992 roku.* Warsaw, Instytut Turystyki.

Borne-Falencik, H. (1993). *Informator o szkolach srednich przygotowujacych kadry dla turystyki w roku szkolnym 1992/93.* Warsaw, Instytut Turystyki.

Erdman, L. (1994). 'Integrated concept of study for leisure science personnel'. In: H. Ruskin, A. Sivan, (eds.). *Leisure Education: Towards the 21st century.* Utah, Provo, Brigham Young University.

Gotowt-Jezierska, A. (1992). 'Dzialalnosc Urzedu Kultury Fizycznej i Turystyki w sprawie reformowania szkolnictwa turystycznego w Polsce'. *Problemy Turystyki,* No.2, pp. 39-44.

Górecki, T. (1992). 'Ksztalcic by suyli ludziom'. *Problemy Turystyki,* No.2, pp. 33-38.

GUS, (1994). *Rocznik Statystyczny,* Warszawa, GUS.

GUS, (1995). *Rocznik Statystyczny,* Warszawa, GUS.

Kaspar, C. (1995). 'Coopération Est-Ouest au développement du tourisme'. *Revue de Tourisme/Tourist Review,* AIEST 1/95.

Richards, G. (ed.) (1995). *European Tourism and Leisure Education: Trends and Prospects.* Tilburg, Tilburg University Press.

Roberts, K. and Jung, B. (1995). *The first post-communist generation.* London, Avery Publishers.

Zawadzki, M. (1993). *Natezenie krajowego ruchu turystycznego.* Warsaw, Instytut Turystyki.

# Chapter 7

## The regional system of tourism education in Lower Silesia, Poland

**Jerzy Wyrzykowski**

Lower Silesia is a historical-geographical region which embraces five provinces in South-West Poland: Jelenia Góra, Legnica, Opole, Walbrzych and Wroclaw (see Figure 7.1). It can also be treated as tourist region, with Wroclaw, a large sightseeing center, as the major tourism centre.

The main tourism areas of Lower Silesia are the Sudety Mountains, the Opawa Mountains, the Sleza Mountains, Trzebnica Hills and the Turawa Lakes. The main tourism resorts are the sightseeing centers Wroclaw (a large sightseeing center), Jelenia Góra, Klodzko, Legnica, Lwówek Slaski, Brzeg, Nysa, Opole, Paczków and Swidnica, and Karpacz, Szklarska Poreba, Duszniki Zdrój, Kudowa Zdrój and Polanica Zdrój as more important holiday and health resorts. The dominant types of tourism are mountain tourism and urban tourism. In 1993 about 8 million visitors came to Lower Silesia, the majority from Germany. Only a small number of visitors spent more than one day in Poland. The potential tourist capacity of Lower Silesia is estimated as about 250-300,000 visitors. The accommodation capacity of the region consists of 885 establishments and 57,500 beds (1993).

In the universal system of school education, in primary and secondary schools, tourism education is provided mainly by tourist and country lovers groups and by social organisations, which are active in schools, such as the PTTK (Polish Tourist and Country Lovers Society), PTSM (Polish Youth Hostel Association), ZHP (Polish Scouts Union) and other youth organisations.

In the last few years a set of author tourist courses has been launched. The basic programme of education is being adapted by teachers-authors to their needs. New subjects are being introduced, covering, for example the history of art, the history of architecture, the methodology of tourism, the geography of tourism, foreign languages, tourist excursions around the region and the country, the organisation of winter holidays, summer wandering camps, and sometimes also foreign excursions. The general aim of the creators of these courses is the provision of general education while taking an active and conscious part in tourism, with special attention for learning about one's own region.

During their stay at the schools, especially in tourist classes (courses), pupils have the possibility to gain tourist marks of distinction and PTTK and PTSM competences, as leaders of walking tourism, managers of tourism, protectors of monuments (architecture, nature), guardians of nature protection, and also tourist guides and leaders of foreign excursions. These tourist courses are organised in several schools in Wroclaw, Jelenia Góra, Legnica, Lubin, Milicz, Sobótka and Swidnica.

Professional secondary education in tourism is mainly related to the Economic and Catering Schools which offer 5 year hotel technician courses and 4-5 year courses in 'tourist services'. Hotel technical schools are located in Jelenia Gora, Walbrzych and Wroclaw, and courses in 'tourist services' only in Wroclaw. Professional secondary education in tourism is located in bigger towns and tourism centres.

For the last few years work has been done, under the auspices of The State Sport and Tourism Administration in Warsaw, to reconstruct the programmes of these schools, in order to adjust them to the needs of the free market. It is recognised that special emphasis should be placed on economic subjects, better knowledge of foreign languages and good professional practice. This process is not finished yet and greater participation of tourism industry managers, the potential employers of the students, is necessary. Another problem is to ensure a supply of high quality teachers for these programmes.

Other professional courses in tourism are provided by the post-grammar schools. These schools run two kinds of courses 'Hotel management' and 'Tourist services'. These schools are located in Jelenia Góra, Klodzko, Nysa, Walbrzych, Wroclaw. A special post-grammar school is the State Postmature Studies of Culture Animators and Librarians with a course in Animation Tourism.

The restructuring of the national economy in Poland is causing an intensive search for carreer changes, and the bright prospects for the future development of the tourism industry have caused a high level of applications for tourism courses. The programmes and educational levels of these schools are highly differentiated, and their existance will probably be justified by the possibility of work in the tourism industry for graduates.

Tourist agencies and social organisations also organise additional education for tourist guides and leaders of foreign excursions. There are not enough jobs for the hundreds of guides trained each year. There is also no official obligation to have a guide license. A new chance for increasing demand for these services should be provided by the organisation in Wroclaw of the World Eucharistic Congress (1997).

There is no Higher Tourism School in Lower Silesia. Wroclaw Higher Schools offer only 2-3 year courses in tourism within studies of physical education, geographical studies or economical studies. The course in Recreation and Tourism at the Academy of Physical Education in Wroclaw prepares specialists in animation, organisation and servicing of recreation and tourism. The course in Regional and Tourism Geography at the University of Wroclaw provides training in the environmental basis of tourism development for the needs of travel agencies, tourist enterprises, regional and local administrations and institutions of regional and spatial planning.

The Department of Regional and Tourism Geography in Wroclaw participated in a TEMPUS project (1992-1995) related to development of higher tourism education in Central and Eastern Europe. In the framework of this project, teachers from Wroclaw took part in seminars abroad, students participated in one-year courses at West European universities and special professional courses were organised by West European partners in Wroclaw. As result of this cooperation, additional economic subjects, a computer laboratory and professional practice were introduced on the courses. A modern computer laboratory has been set up with TEMPUS funds, prepared also for distance learning, with the use of international computer and satellite television nets.

The course in the economics of tourism and hotel management at the Academy of Economics in Jelenia Góra prepares specialists in economics for the tourism industry.

Postgraduate Studies in Tourism at Wroclaw University and Postgraduate Studies in Recreation at the Wroclaw Academy of Physical Education also prepare adults to change their profession and to apply their knowledge in the tourism industry. The main weaknesses of the system of tourism education in Lower Silesia are: the unfinished process of the restructuring of educational programmes, the lack of a higher tourism school, insufficient co-operation between different elements of system and its lack of recognition by the tourism industry. There is a need to organise a Higher Hotel and Tourism School and to provide studies at master of science level in different higher schools. This, however, requires general changes in the system of higher education in Poland.

**Figure 7.1: Lower Silesian provinces**

## APPENDIX: LOWER SILESIA REGIONAL SYSTEM OF TOURISM EDUCATION

### Elementary schools

- Tourist and country lovers groups
- Author programs with emphase on tourism problems
- Activity of social organisations disposed toward development of tourism (PTTK, PTSM, ZHP)

**Secondary education**

1. Grammar schools
- Author tourist courses (I LO Jelenia Góra, I LO Legnica, I LO Lubin, LO Sobótka, LO Swidnica, II LO Wroclaw, V LO Wroclaw, XII LO Wroclaw, XV LO Wrocaw)
- Tourist and country lovers groups
- Activity of social organisations disposed toward development of tourism (PTTK, PTSM, ZHP)

2. Groups of economic and catering schools
- Hotel technical schools (5 years) (ZSEiT Jelenia Góra, ZSEiG Walbrzych, ZSG Wroclaw)
- Course: Tourist services ( 4-5 years) (ZSE nr 2 Wroclaw)
- Tourist and country lovers groups
- Activity of social organisations disposed toward development of tourism (PTTK, PTSM, ZHP)

3. Post-secondary professional schools (2 years)
- Course: Tourist services (ZSEiT Jelenia Góra, ZSE Klodzko, ZSE Nysa, ZSEiG Walbrzych, ABOR Wroclaw, PTSM Wroclaw, Spóldzielnia ‘Oswiata’ Wroclaw)
- Course: Hotel management (ZSEiT) Jelenia Góra, ZSEiG Walbrzych, Spóldzielnia ‘Oswiata’ Wroclaw)
- Course: Animator of tourism
- Post-secondary School of Culture Managers and Librarian in Wroclaw (2 years)

**Higher schools**

- Academy of Physical Education in Wroclaw
  course: Physical education
  speciality: Recreation and tourism ( 2 years)

- University of Wroclaw
  course: Geography
  speciality: Regional and Tourism Geography (2 years)

- Academy of Economics in Wroclaw Faculty of Regional and Tourism Economy in Jelenia Góra
  course: Economics
  speciality: Economics of tourism and hotel management (3 years) (proposed new name: Management and marketing in tourist services)

**Postgraduate studies (1 year)**

- Academy of Physical Education in Wroclaw:
  Postgraduate Studies in Recreation

- University of Wroclaw:
  Postgraduate Studies in Tourism

# Chapter 8

# The current state of tourism and tourism education in Romania

**Cristiana Cristureanu**

## 1. TOURISM MARKET-CURRENT POSITION

Romania has a variety of tourism assets and attractions which have been developed and promoted for international and domestic tourists. Prior to the mid 1960s tourism development was focused on health spas, and also a limited number of traditional resorts in the Carpathian mountains and on the Black Sea coast. From the mid 1960s to the early 1980s, tourism became a development priority and there was rapid development, particularly on the Black Sea coast and in mountain resorts. Because of the policy of isolation in the 1980s, tourism development ceased to be a priority and the tourism product declined. This chapter looks particularly at the development of tourism and tourism education during the 1990s, which have seen a revival of tourism demand accompanying the transition to a market economy.

### 1.1. Tourism attractions

Tourism attractions in Romania can be categorised into those which are the major reason for attracting tourists and those which enhance the experience of tourists during their stay. Romania also has other natural, historic and cultural assets which for international markets, currently serve the role of enhancing tourists' experience, for example through inclusion on excursion programmes.

With almost one third of the country comprising mountains, Romania has a major potential asset for winter and summer tourism. For international tourism the most important areas are currently in the Prahova Valley and the Brasov area. The Black Sea coast has the advantage of sandy beaches and a length of approximately 70 km of coastline developed in the late 1960s and 1970s with purpose built resorts. The coast also includes natural health treatment resources which are exploited. The River Danube runs from the Black Forest in Germany to the Black Sea. Over one third (1,100 km) of its course is in Romania, culminating in the Danube Delta. The Danube Delta is designated by UNESCO as a World Heritage site and a Biosphere Reserve. Approximately a quarter of Romania's land area is covered by forest and there is also a wide range of flora and fauna. Because hunting was largely prohibited during the past regime, there are large numbers of animals including the brown bear, wolf, deer, lynx and fox. Romania has rich resources of mineral water, therapeutic mud and emanations of carbon dioxide which, together with local climatic characteristics, have formed the basis for the development of over 160 spas. Other natural attractions include areas and routes of scenic beauty and caves.

Attractions dating from Neolithic times reflect Romania's history. Of particular interest for tourism are: the monasteries, the painted churches, the wooden churches, the fortified churches and towns, Greek, Dacian and Roman sites, and the legend and associated sites of Count Dracula. Bucharest and a number of other major towns and cities also have historic and cultural attractions (see Figure 8.1).

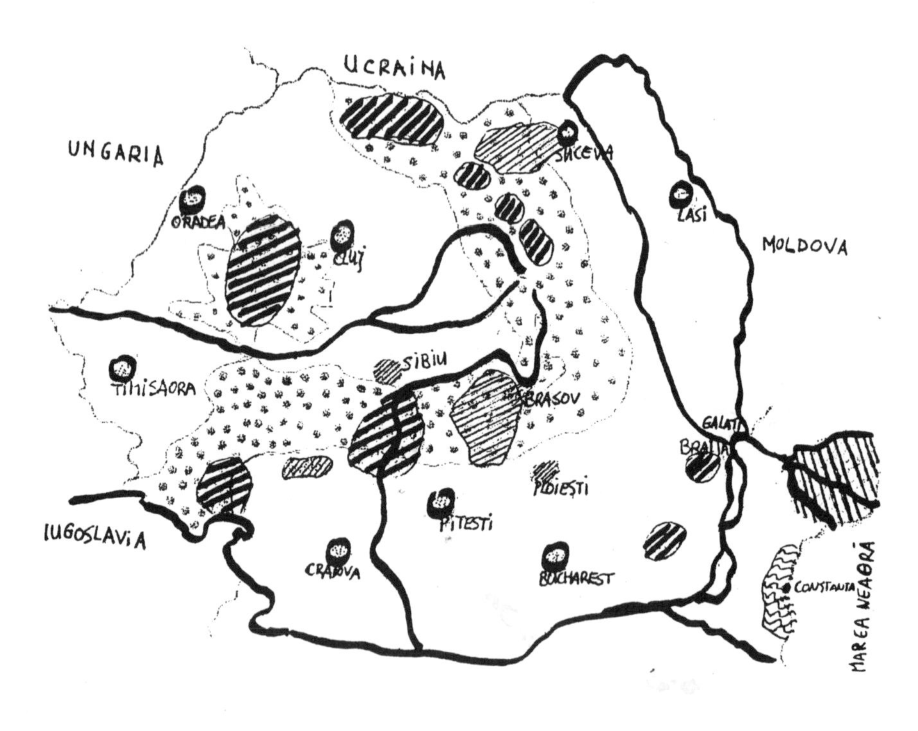


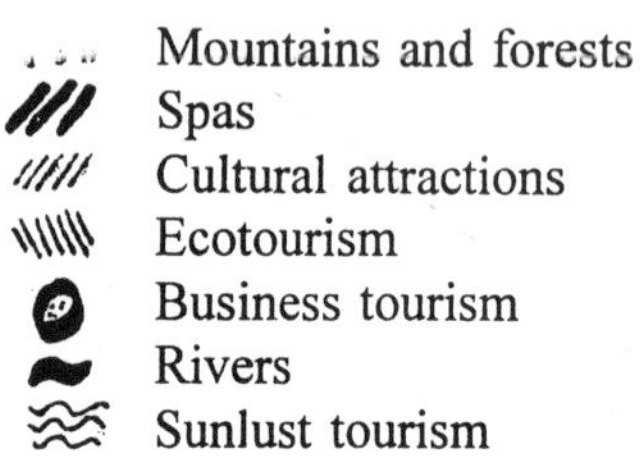


**Figure 8.1: Tourist attractions**

Other attractions include, for holiday tourism, the handicrafts and performing arts, festivals and vineyards. What is certain is that the interest of foreign tourists in these 'assets' is fluctuating and the fluctuations are significant. The collapse of the communist regime, a declared enemy of tourism obsessed only by the economic gains which could be obtained from it, did not coincide with an 'invasion' of foreign tourists.

### 1.2. Tourism products

Romania's major tourism products are, in order of importance, as follows:

- *Beach tourism* which accounts for approximately 40% of the country's tourist accommodation capacity and 25% of demand. The resorts are very seasonal in their operation.

- *Health spa tourism* located in over 160 spas throughout Romania, of which less than 20 are considered to have potential for international tourism. They offer a wide range of treatments.

- *Winter sports tourism.* There are a large number of winter ski resorts which also cater to summer tourism. They fall into three general categories: international resorts, secondary resorts and local resorts.

- *Circuit tourism* which includes major historic, cultural and scenic attractions.

- *Business tourism* mainly in Bucharest where there are many conference facilities, but also in some other big cities.

- *Ecotourism.* The most important areas for ecotourism are the Danube Delta, including ornithology, viewing safari, hunting and fishing; the Carpathian Mountains, including hiking, trekking and caving; and many of Romania's extensive forest areas, which include good quality hunting.

- *Agricultural tourism.*

- *Transit tourism.*

Virtually all foreign arrivals by air (5% of total arrivals) pass through Romania's three international airports: at Bucharest, Timisoara and Oradea. During the summer there are also some flights to Constanta and other domestic airports which serve Scandinavian and German demand. Road accounts for the vast majority of foreign arrivals to Romania (75%). There are 20 international entry points by road. Most of them are generally very congested. The second largest number of arrivals is by rail (18%) with 10 entry points. Tourists can also enter Romania by the Black Sea port of Constanta (2%).

### 1.3. Tourist accommodation

Tourist accommodation registered by the Ministry of Tourism is given a star rating (from one to five stars) and classified under one of nine types: hotel, suite hotel, motel, villa, bungalow, cabana, camping, holiday village or pension. The total registered supply in 1994 comprised 227,114 beds in 105,740 rooms, 80% of which are in hotels. The methodological norms meet the demands imposed by future integration into the European Union.

### 1.4. Food and beverage facilities

Restaurants are classified as deluxe or Category I to IV. There are some 38 types of restaurants, plus a further 9 types on rail, ship and air transport. Restaurants within hotel complexes are separately graded, but in accordance with the hotel's accommodation.

### 1.5. Tourism workforce

Statistics relating to the workforce are poor and often inaccurate (Burns, 1995). However, there were estimated to be 240,800 tourism employees in the whole industry in 1993. By sector, the tourism work force is employed as follows: hotels and restaurants, 148,000 (61%); transport, 38,500 (16%); tourist companies, 25,000 (10%); leisure facilities, 29,300 (12%). In the accommodation sector, an indicator for comparing of human resource inputs is the staff to room ratio. The range of staff per room by type of hotel location is shown in Table 8.1.

**Table 8.1: Staff per room by hotel location**

| | |
|---|---|
| Spa Hotels | 0.4 to 0.9 |
| Black Sea Coast | 0.2 to 0.4 |
| Bucharest | |
| 1 and 2 stars | 0.3 to 0.5 |
| 3 and 4 stars | 1.1 to 2.1 |
| Mountains | 0.6 to 1.2 |

An employment multiplier for the industry has been calculated locally by the National Institute of Tourism Research as 1.52. Given that the base year direct workforce was 240,800, the total direct and indirect workforce supported by tourism in Romania is 367,000. Of the total tourism workforce, 36% is skilled and 64% is unskilled. By category of employment 6% is managerial, 8% is supervisory, 22% craft (skilled) and 64% operative (unskilled).

### 1.6. Demand

Domestic demand far exceeds foreign tourist demand. In 1992 22.9 million domestic tourist nights were recorded in registered tourist accommodation compared with 3.2 million foreign tourist nights. The distribution of demand by location is shown in Table 8.2.

**Table 8.2: Distribution of tourist nights by location**

| | % tourist nights | | |
|---|---|---|---|
| Location | Foreign | Romanian | Total |
| Spa | 9.1 | 24.6 | 22.7 |
| Coast | 23.5 | 25.6 | 25.4 |
| Mountain | 10.9 | 9.9 | 10.0 |
| Other | 56.5 | 39.9 | 41.9 |

The demand pattern does not fully reflect the dominance of the accommodation supply on the Black Sea coast because of the short season there. Other locations include Bucharest, which accounted for over 30% of foreign tourist nights but only 6% of domestic demand.

Table 8.3 details the main trends in arrivals from 1988 to 1994. The most important demand generating region is Europe, which accounted for over 96% of total arrivals in 1993, and has consistently accounted for over 95% of frontier arrivals.

**Table 8.3: Trends in arrivals to Romania (000s)**

| | 1988 | 1989 | 1990 | 1991 | 1992 | 1993 | 1994 |
|---|---|---|---|---|---|---|---|
| Africa | n/a | n/a | 15.0 | 9.3 | 6.4 | n/a | n/a |
| Americas | 32.8 | 34.1 | 52.9 | 50.9 | 50.3 | n/a | n/a |
| East Asia/Pacific | 84.5 | 86.9 | 29.8 | 33.9 | 31.3 | n/a | n/a |
| Europe | 5,376.0 | 4,710.5 | 6,326.8 | 5,089.0 | 6,070.4 | 5,554 | 5,662 |
| Middle East | n/a | n/a | 32.7 | 34.7 | 39.4 | n/a | n/a |
| South Asia | n/a | n/a | 22.8 | 26.6 | 20.1 | n/a | n/a |
| Other | 20.7 | 20.7 | 55.3 | 115.8 | 62.1 | n/a | n/a |
| Total | 5,514.0 | 4,852.2 | 6,535.3 | 5,360.2 | 6,280.0 | 5,785.6 | 5,898.1 |

*Source:* WTO

The countries of Central and Eastern Europe account for over 70% of arrivals but less than half of recorded tourist nights. The main purpose of visit of foreign arrivals is leisure tourism (62%), the rest being business (3%) and transit (35%). Romania accounts for 2.3% of total European arrivals and only 0.069% of the revenues.

Tourist activity has a simple structure with low tariffs and no additional offer. An integrated and complex offer is supplied by an extremely reduced number of Romanian tourist companies. The opinion of specialists in this field is that Romanian tourism is further subject to almost all the restrictions and bears the burden of all the deficiencies of a command centralised economy and collectivism. Attempts at raising quality standards are hampered by the modest financial means available in a transitory country which has other priorities and is marked by profound imbalances. This situation will probably delay by a few years the rehabilitation of tourism as an economic branch.

## 2. TOURISM EDUCATION

### 2.1. Structures for training

Training for tourism in Romania is conducted by four bodies:

- The department of Economics at the National University.

- Lycees with tourism profiles (Ministry of Education).

- The National Institute for Tourism Training and Management (INFMT) which is controlled by the Ministry of Tourism.

- The Ministry of Labour and Social Protection, which operates a number of skilling programmes for tourism at regional level.

Likewise, the Ministry of Education conceives, substantiates, sanctions and applies the overall strategy of education programmes as a whole, and sets education goals by learning cycles and specialities. The recent Protocol between the Ministry of Education and Ministry of Tourism, which reflects national policy on vocational education, confirms that the Ministry of Education is the competent authority for delivering pre-entry training, with technical advice provided by the Ministry of Tourism in a national strategy for tourism training.

The focus of training is dominated by the formal sector, particularly hotel and catering training, with little participation of small and medium-sized enterprises. Training for hotel and tourist activities is provided through high school education, vocational training, complementary or apprentice education, speciality postgraduate education and higher learning (university, post-university and doctoral studies).

*2.1.1. High school education*

There are various types of high schools, including the economics and administration high schools with tourism classes, which educate almost 1% of the total number of pupils enrolled in high schools. Surveying the existing curriculum for economic high schools (employee in tourism) one finds subjects like: organisation and management of tourism activities, operative filing and accountancy in tourism, technology of hotel services, supply and development of tourism activities and practical activities.

*2.1.2. Vocational training*

Vocational training is provided by vocational schools. Their 3 or 4 year courses include vocational training, practical training and general instruction on the basis of curricula set by the Ministry of Education. The courses end with a graduation exam which allows those who pass it to get a diploma in order to practice the trade they were trained for. The curricula and the syllabi for the vocational schools are better conceived and more balanced, but are meant for those working in catering units. In some schools, students are encouraged to start up small entrepreneurial businesses as part of the learning process. The major problems in the vocational schools are: the capability of the trainers, the educational materials, low levels and poor state of equipment, and a lack of up to date textbooks.

*2.1.3. Postgraduate schools*

Postgraduate schools train high-school graduates who want qualify as tourist services technicians, hotel technicians or catering technicians. The curriculum (Appendices: A, B, C) has already been restructured and is to be further improved. The distribution of specialty postgraduate schools by sector is shown in Table 8.4.

**Table 8.4: Postgraduate tourism education**

| Speciality | Number of schools | Number of pupils | Number of courses |
|---|---|---|---|
| Tourist service technician | 12 | 650 | 23 |
| Catering technician | 6 | 218 | 7 |
| Hotel technician | 3 | 83 | 4 |
| TOTAL | 21 | 951 | 34 |

Alongside public education provision there are also other forms of vocational training organised by the Ministry of Tourism, namely by the National Institute for Tourism Training and Management (INMFT). The Institute aims at "...qualitatively improving the entire vocational and training activity in keeping with the exigencies of the market economy characteristics and international tourism development...".

The INMFT has seven basic targets:
- development of courses at medium to high level which are both on a par with European standards, and suitable for accreditation by the Ministry of Education;
- organisation of basic trade training with a pilot scheme to be introduced in the near future;
- adoption of new forms of foreign language teaching methods;
- rapid development of management programmes with a focus on operational aspects of market economy requirements;
- development of diploma curricula framed by modern teaching and learning methods;
- finalisation of all teaching aids;
- development and finalisation of a hotel and tourism training research scheme.

INFMT has organised several courses, which are presented in Appendix D.

*2.1.4. Higher education*
Higher education is conceived as a continuation, in an open system, of the training provided by high-school education and contains:
- university education which includes: short-term university education (university courses of 2-3 years) and long-term university education (4-6 years);
- post-university education which includes speciality post-university courses, Masters Degree Studies and Doctoral Studies.

Tourism is offered as part of the BA Economics within the Faculty of Commerce and the Faculty of International Business and Economics at the Academy of Economic Studies in Bucharest. The two different faculties have different curricula. The Faculty of Commerce has two divisions: Commerce and Tourism. The tourism division includes in its curricula subjects such as tourism marketing, tourism management, geography of tourism, tourism statistics and accountancy in tourism. About 90 students graduate from the course each year. A few have found employment in the Ministry of Tourism, but many remain unemployed. However, in common with many university courses internationally, the tourism course is regarded as too theoretical. The Faculty needs to create a better relationship with the industry, so that the young graduates are recruited more widely by the tourism industry.

The Faculty of International Business provides specialised training in the field of international economic relations with goods and services. Among the international services, International Tourism and International Transportation are the most important components. The content and balance of the curricula were discussed with the teaching staff of the faculty and with specialists in research fields, experts from public institutions and business people. The participation of the teaching staff in training programmes abroad played an important role in the modernisation process of the Faculty. A research group has been set up in the field of International Transactions which include international tourism business as well.

The teaching process is organised according a new pattern that involves three educational cycles. The first cycle comprises the first and second years of study, the second cycle comprises the third and fourth years of study, including two tourism specialisations: International Tourism Business and International Tourism Economics and Policies. The third cycle contains a one-year module leading to a masters degree in the field of inter-European relations which includes tourism as well.

The curricula of the second cycle in International Tourism Business contains courses on World Tourism Geography, International Tourism Economics, International Tourism Marketing, Tourism Business Management, Tourism Market Research, Business Negotiations, Tourism Statistics, Financial Analysis in Tourism, International Transactions, Foreign Investment Analysis, Applied Research, International Logistics, International Trade with Services, International Trade Law, International Payments and Finance, Case Studies and Economic Projects and Foreign Languages. The curricula of the second cycle in International Tourism Economics and Policies is completed with: Tourism Planning, International Specialisation in Tourism, Comparative Studies of Tourism Policies, Tourism International Organisations, International Public Law, Diplomatic Customs, Comparative Studies of Environmental Policies and World Cultural Environment (Case Studies).

There are 1,962 students enrolled for full-time, part-time and extra-mural courses. About 250 students graduate each year. Many of them are hired by domestic and foreign companies operating in international tourism business and foreign trade business.

After 1990 a number of private universities were established, some of which offer tourism as part of a wider subject, such as the Ecologic University.

### 2.2. Quality of training

The strategy of national tourism training has a number of strengths and weaknesses. Among the *strengths* are:

- the strategy recognises that the system is in need of reform;
- the strategy is linked to the emerging standardisation of EU vocational qualifications;
- the creation of links with other European training schools, including the study of non-traditional forms to train managerial staff;
- a strong unity at the university level though a research group in the field of world tourism markets which includes professors, specialists, experts and business people.

Countering these strengths are a number of weaknesses that unless redressed will impede progress towards a sufficiently trained and educated workforce. The major *weaknesses* are:
- the Ministry of Tourism decides the requirements of the sector rather than involving the tourism industry and responding to training needs identified and prioritised by the industry itself;
- the strategy includes a list of several trades and specialities for which the tourism training system assures diplomas. This does not take into account the fundamental changes in the tourism workforce that have taken place in the rest of Europe over the past decade. These changes are characterised by flexibility and multi-skilled working.

The strategy redresses two of the major constraints on tourism education for the past two decades:
- lack of overseas exposure;
- the professional development of staff.

The strategy is doing little to redress the fundamental problem: that of building a service relationship between the commercial sector and the training structure which equips the industry for self-development. In the strategic plan, the industry is clearly placed in a subordinate position and is dependent upon government to supply all its training needs. There are also a number of cases where industry has failed to recognise the need for training.

Technical and interpersonal service skills in the tourism sector in Romania are generally poor. In most cases, the procedures still being used are cumbersome, geared towards maximising employment and inwardly focused. They therefore meet the needs of the enterprise rather than satisfy customer needs. The operational culture remains defined by division of labour with the concomitant inflexibility. However, there are sharply contrasting levels of competence and service within the tourism workforce, arising from at least two factors:
- different styles of service given within differing styles of tourism accommodation;
- the extent to which access is available to education and training courses.

The common perception of Romania's tourism workforce is of overmanning and under-employment.

## 2.3. Future requirements

Market forces will make fundamental changes to the characteristics of Romania's workforce. However the transition to the free market economy distorts the relationship between demand and employment. It is estimated that the tourism sector may, in the short term, have to shed staff as productivity increases. The estimated total workforce of 240,000 has been taken as the base for the projection of future human resource requirements in tourism for Romania. The future needs by sector are expected to be: hotels 61.5%, transport 16%, tourist companies 10.4%, other facilities and attractions 12.1%. Employment categories will be as follows: managerial 6%, supervisory 8%, craft 22%, operative 64% (see Table 8.5).

**Table 8.5: Forecast human resources requirement in tourism**

| | Employment categories 1998 | | | |
|---|---|---|---|---|
| Sector | Managerial 6% | Supervisory 8% | Craft 22% | Operative 64% |
| Hotels | 7,562 | 10,083 | 27,729 | 80,666 |
| Transport | 1,968 | 2,623 | 7,214 | 20,986 |
| Tourism companies | 1,279 | 1,705 | 4,689 | 13,641 |
| Other/leisure | 1,488 | 1,984 | 5,455 | 15,871 |
| Direct employment | 12,297 | 6,395 | 45,087 | 131,164 |

Total direct employment............204,943 = 65,8%

Total indirect employment.........106,570 = 34,2%

Total tourism employment.........311,513

| | Employment categories 2003 | | | |
|---|---|---|---|---|
| Hotels | 9,253 | 12,338 | 33,929 | 98,702 |
| Transport | 2,407 | 3,210 | 8,827 | 25,679 |
| Tourism companies | 1,565 | 2,086 | 5,738 | 16,691 |
| Other/leisure | 1,821 | 2,427 | 6,675 | 19,419 |
| Direct employment | 15,046 | 20,061 | 55,169 | 160,491 |

Total direct employment..............250,767

Indirect employment....................130,399

Total Tourism employment..........381,166

Based on forecast tourism demand, direct tourism output, and increases in direct output per employee, the human resource requirements by category and sector for 1998 and 2003 are shown in Table 8.5.

**Table 8.6: Training requirements for tourism, 1995**

| Training Target Inputs | Lycees | INFMT | University | In-house | Other |
|---|---|---|---|---|---|
| Hotels Sector | 70,3% | 74,9% | 56,6% | 52,7% | 50% |
| Managers | | 750 | 150 | 3,500 | 500 |
| Supervisors | 200 | 750 | 150 | 5,000 | 750 |
| Craft | 2,000 | 1,500 | - | 7,000 | 1,300 |
| Operative | 2,000 | 2,000 | - | 7,000 | 1,000 |
| Total | 4,200 | 5,000 | 300 | 22,500 | 3,550 |
| Transport Sector | 10,9% | 7,5% | 14,2% | 18,1% | 19,7% |
| Managers | | 50 | 25 | 750 | 200 |
| Supervisors | 50 | 50 | 50 | 1,000 | 200 |
| Craft | 300 | 200 | - | 2,000 | 500 |
| Operative | 300 | 200 | - | 4,000 | 500 |
| Total | 650 | 500 | 75 | 7,750 | 1,400 |
| Tourist Companies | 8,4% | 9,7% | 15,1% | 11,6% | 16,9% |
| Managers | | 50 | 30 | 200 | 100 |
| Supervisors | 50 | 100 | 50 | 750 | 300 |
| Craft | 150 | 200 | - | 1,000 | 300 |
| Operative | 300 | 300 | - | 3,000 | 500 |
| Total | 500 | 650 | 80 | 4,950 | 1,200 |
| Leisure/Other | 10,4% | 7,9% | 14,1% | 17,6% | 13,4% |
| Managers | | 50 | 25 | 750 | 100 |
| Supervisors | 75 | 75 | 50 | 750 | 150 |
| Craft | 300 | 200 | - | 2,000 | 300 |
| Operative | 250 | 200 | - | 4,000 | 400 |
| Total | 625 | 525 | 75 | 7,500 | 950 |
| TOTAL | 5,975 | 6,675 | 530 | 42,700 | 7,100 |

Recent research indicates that almost all staff will require training in customer skills. They will also require an understanding of the operational opportunities and constraints of working in the market economy. This is a major task which is best addressed as part of a national awareness campaign for all sections of society.

Training requirements by category and sector, based on the tourist market targets, productivity increases and future staff turnover are shown in Table 8.6.

## 2.4. Managerial development

The lack of market orientation is critical to management training. Most, if not all, managers were developed and gained their experience in a centrally planned economy. In most situations the delivery of training solutions is carried out by managers.

Management and planning for tourism in Romania is carried out by the Ministry of Tourism. In terms of staff development, there is no system of regular performance appraisal that enables staff to set work performance goals in consultation and agreement with their managers. The formal system of promotion is not suitable. It is estimated that at least one-third of the staff at the Ministry require specialist skills in various aspects of tourism. These skills include tourism marketing, appraisal of tourism attractions, tourism planning, tourism development appraisal (including planning at a local level), environmental audit and impact assessment, social and cultural impact and hotel classification and inspection. So, the main requirement is to change the role of the Ministry in the transition to a market economy and to equip the managers to lead the transition to a customer and service oriented market economy by themselves undergoing a process of re-orientation.

Current organisational structures and practices restrict the introduction of management practices as they are known in Western Europe. Training should be targeted at the individual establishments and also at the commercial sector companies. Training and development needs for managers include:
- acceptable operational techniques, which will require a dramatic cultural change with managers encouraged to be creative, decisive and willing to take the initiative;
- managers will have to carry a considerable burden in training the rest of the workforce, so many managers will require training in training techniques;
- service strategy developments and techniques and the management of quality;
- corporate strategy in a competitive environment;
- developing a hospitality marketing orientation;
- selecting and recruiting staff.

For travel agencies and tour operators, where there is growing private sector involvement, training for all levels of staff will be needed in the following specific areas:
- packaging, costing and organising inbound and outbound tour groups (includ-

ing legal implications);
- introducing and dealing with holiday insurance;
- developing inbound and outbound business travel;
- selling skills, product knowledge and client database;
- financial planning of the travel business.

Travel agents and tour operators are highly sensitive to competition and market forces. International companies which deal with ground handling companies soon establish expected standards which, if not reached, lead to cancellation of agreements. Underpinning training needs for this sector will be the awareness of and the need for international standards and expectations. This sector of the tourism industry is likely to be dominated by the introduction of new information technology.

Another area of change will be in the reorientation of the sector with strategic alliances being made between newly privatised hotel groups, the financial services sector, car rentals and hotel booking agencies.

It is proposed that the supervisors should be the main implementers of the practical on the job training programmes. They must also be trained in service delivery concepts, focusing on meeting customer needs, flexibility and team building. Their training should focus on:
- communication techniques;
- motivation and informal reward systems;
- stock control systems and cost controls;
- controlling hotel and catering systems.

Given the training implications arising from the moves towards operating in the market economy, competent management which knows how to function under conditions of competition is essential to the success of Romania's tourism. The main issues in order to achieve the training goals are:
- encourage the universities to develop post graduate courses in strategic management with a focus on creating an ability to match product development and marketing;
- develop mobile management development training teams to work with managers in their own properties;
- extend the co-operation between Romanian universities and Western and/or Eastern universities and/or Western Tourism Companies in order to improve the book stock, the teaching methods and to give apprentice opportunities for teachers and students;
- better co-operation between the Ministry of Tourism and the Ministry of Education;
- the renewal of the staff in the Ministry of Tourism by recruiting recent graduates from the universities.

The organisational structure of tourism units and companies needs modification to meet needs of the new operating environment. This includes more integrated operations, and emphasis on staff development and motivation (with a priority on the development of personnel managers), marketing and profitability.

## REFERENCES

Burns, P. (1995). Hotel management training in Eastern Europe: Challenges for Romania. *Progress in Tourism and Hospitality Research,* 1, 53-62.

## APPENDICES

### Appendix A: Curriculum for speciality postgraduate school

Field: Tourism
Speciality: Tourism technician

| No. | Subjects | Number of classes/year per week | | TOTAL NUMBER OF CLASSES |
|---|---|---|---|---|
| | | I | II | |
| A. | GENERAL TECHNICAL-ECONOMIC TRAINING | 186(6) | 186(6) | 372 |
| 1. | Modern language + business correspondence | 62(2) | 93(3) | 155 |
| 2. | Modern language 2 | 62(2) | 62(2) | 124 |
| 3. | Law and legislation | - | 31(1) | 31 |
| 4. | Business correspondence | 31(1) | - | 31 |
| 5. | Psychosociology | 31(1) | - | 31 |
| B. | SPECIALITY TRAINING | 341(11) | 341(11) | 682 |
| 1. | Technology of tourism activities | 124(4) | 155(5) | 279 |
| 2. | Hotel technology | 62(2) | - | 62 |
| 3. | Technology of activities in catering units | 62(2) | - | 62 |
| 4. | Tourism manegement | - | 62(2) | 62 |
| 5. | Tourism marketing | - | 62(2) | 62 |
| 6. | Tourism administration | 62(2) | 31(1) | 93 |
| 7. | Applied informatics | 31(1) | 31(1) | 62 |
| C. | PHYSICAL EDUCATION | 31(1) | 31(1) | 62 |
| D. | FORM-MASTER CLASSES | 31(1) | 31(1) | 62 |
| E. | PRACTICAL ACTIVITIES: | | | |
| | - school | 372(12) | 372(12) | 744 |
| | - production | 4/160 | 4/160 | 320 |
| | TOTAL NUMBER OF CLASSES: | 1.121 | 1.121 | 2.242 |

## Appendix B: Curriculum for speciality postgraduate school

Field: Tourism
Speciality: Tourism technician

| No. | Subjects | Number of classes/year per week | | TOTAL NUMBER OF CLASSES |
|---|---|---|---|---|
| | | I | II | |
| A. | GENERAL TECHNICAL-ECONOMIC TRAINING | 186(6) | 186(6) | 372 |
| 1. | Modern language 1 + business correspondence | 62(2) | 93(3) | 155 |
| 2. | Modern language 2 | 62(2) | 62(2) | 155 |
| 3. | Law and legislation | - | 31(1) | 31 |
| 4. | Business correspondence | 31(1) | - | 31 |
| 5. | Psychosociology | 31(1) | - | 31 |
| B. | SPECIALITY TRAINING | 341(11) | 341(11) | 682 |
| 1. | Technology of tourism activities | 124(4) | 155(5) | 279 |
| 2. | Hotel technology | 62(2) | - | 62 |
| 3. | Technology of activities in catering units | 62(2) | - | 62 |
| 4. | Tourism manegement | - | 62(2) | 62 |
| 5. | Tourism marketing | - | 62(2) | 62 |
| 6. | Tourism administration | 62(1) | 31(1) | 93 |
| 7. | Applied informatics | 31(1) | 31(1) | 62 |
| C. | PHYSICAL EDUCATION | 31(1) | 31(1) | 62 |
| D. | FORM-MASTER CLASSES | 31(1) | 31(1) | 61 |
| E. | PRACTICAL ACTIVITIES: | | | |
| | - school | 372(12) | 372(12) | 744 |
| | - production | 4/160 | 4/160 | 320 |
| | TOTAL NUMBER OF CLASSES: | 1.121 | 1.121 | 2.242 |

## Appendix C: Curriculum for speciality postgraduate school

Field: Tourism
Speciality: Catering technician

| No. | Subjects | Number of classes/year per week | | TOTAL NUMBER OF CLASSES |
|---|---|---|---|---|
| | | 1st year | 2nd year | |
| A. | GENERAL TECHNICAL-ECONOMIC TRAINING | 155(5) | 186(6) | 341 |
| 1. | Modern language + business correspondence | 62(2) | 62(2) | 124 |
| 2. | Modern language 2 | 62(2) | 62(2) | 124 |
| 3. | Law and legislation | - | 31(1) | 31 |
| 4. | Business correspondence | 31(1) | - | 31 |
| 5. | Psychosociology | - | 31(1) | 31 |
| B. | SPECIALITY TRAINING | 372(12) | 341(11) | 713 |
| 1. | Technology of activities incatering units | 155(5) | 155(5) | 310 |
| 2. | Hotel technology | 62(2) | - | 62 |
| 3. | Technology of tourism activities | 62(2) | - | 62 |
| 4. | Catering unit manegement | - | 62(2) | 62 |
| 5. | Tourism marketing | - | 62(2) | 62 |
| 6. | Catering unit administration | 62(2) | 31(1) | 93 |
| 7. | Applied informatics | 31(1) | 31(1) | 62 |
| C. | PHYSICAL EDUCATION | 31(1) | 31(1) | 62 |
| D. | FORM-MASTER CLASSES | 31(1) | 31(1) | 62 |
| E. | PRACTICAL ACTIVITIES: | | | |
| | - school | 372(12) | 372(12) | 744 |
| | - production | 4/160 | 4/160 | 320 |
| | TOTAL NUMBER OF CLASSES: | 1.121 | 1.121 | 2.242 |

## Appendix D: Training courses and programmes

Organised by INFMT, at the end of which graduation certificates are granted.

| | | |
|---|---|---|
| MANAGERIAL TRAINING COURSES (20 weeks) | work in the job | INTENSIVE FOREIGN LANGUAGE COURSES (8-36 weeks) |
| - travel agency manager<br>- hotel manager<br>- catering unit manager | | - English/French: hotel,restaurant, common language, correspondence<br>- German: hotel,restaurant, common language |
| | work in the job | |
| SPECIALISATION PROGRAMMES (8 weeks) | | FIRST LEVEL MANAGERIAL TRAINING PROGRAMMES (5-10 days) |
| - front desk manager<br>- hotel house keeper<br>- bartender<br>- maitre d'hotel<br>- sommelier | | - management of tourist trade companies<br>- financial and administration control organisation and exercising<br>- computer operation<br>- VAT in hotel and tourism industry<br>- the new accountancy system |
| | work in the job | |
| QUALIFICATION COURSES (12-48 weeks) | | PROFESSIONAL INPROVEMENT PROGRAMMES (5 days) |
| - travel agent<br>- national guide<br>- receptionist<br>- chambermaid<br>- cook<br>- waiter<br>- bartender | | - ticketing in tourism<br>- public relations in tourism<br>- pastry<br>- dietetical menus<br>- bar drinks preperations<br>- enforcement of the new accountancy system |
| UNSKILLED STAFF EMPLOYED IN TOURISM AND HOTEL INDUSTRY | | SKILLED STAFF EMPLOYED IN TOURISM AND HOTEL INDUSTRY |

# Chapter 9

# Tourism education in Slovakia in a European context

**Alzbeta Királová**

## INTRODUCTION

The development of tourism as a dynamic branch of the national economy is a great asset for the majority of developed states. In many cases, even in countries that are not considered tourist destinations in themselves, tourism participates to a high degree in the creation of national income, has an influence on employment, and contributes to the balance of trade as a service export.

The attention paid to the development of tourism in Slovakia in the last 40 years has never been sufficient, considering its potential for economic benefit. Opening the borders for the development of tourism is not enough. Low investment, low employment of often unqualified and unwilling employees, outdated suprastructure, insufficient infrastructure, inadequate prices, poor information systems, outdated technology and equipment, together with the lack of state promotion are all reasons for the slow development of tourism in Slovakia.

In this connection it is necessary not just to create the institutional conditions for the development of tourism in Slovakia, but to formulate the legislative conditions for state support for tourism. A programme of economic support for tourism in Slovakia must include structural changes in the economy, support for employment, increases in the incomes of municipalities and regions and increases in the foreign exchange self-sufficiency of tourism. This programme must not only create a marketing concept of tourism in Slovakia and in its districts, but must also create the conditions for the development of an advanced educational system in tourism, which is applicable at the level of the individual entrepreneur and compatible with tourism education in a European context.

## ORGANISATION OF TOURISM EDUCATION IN SLOVAKIA

Slovak students can, after finishing the basic school, continue their studies at several types of scientific or vocationally oriented high schools. Some of these prepare students for the tourism and hospitality industry. One of the vocationally oriented schools is the so called *Stredne odborne uciliste* (SOU), a special type of high school where the study ends without (three years) or with a comprehensive exam (four years). This type of school prepares students for professions such as cook or waiter. Another opportunity for students is so called *Hotelova akademia* - Hotel Academy, where students can study for three or five years. After the first three years students have to take exams at which time they reach the same level as students of SOU's. Students who pass their exams can continue their studies for another two years and can choose one of three specialisations - Hotel Management, Hotel Keeping or Gastronomy. In their 5th school year they take a comprehensive exam. Ten Hotel Academies exist at present in Slovakia.

Students who take their comprehensive exam at grammar school (high schools preparing students for university) and decide not to continue their study at the university can attend a three-year course of study at one of three Hotel Academies specialising in Hotel Keeping (Brezno) or Tourism (Piestany and Kezmarok). The 'Tourism' specialisation prepares students for work as tourist guides for travel agencies.

Students who take their comprehensive exam at grammar schools can continue their studies at University. At the Faculty of Economics, Matel Bel University they can choose from four specialisations at bachelors level and four specialisations at masters level.

The Faculty of Economics at the Matej Bel University in Banská Bystrica has more than 30 years tradition of tourism education in Slovakia. Apart from this university, students can also attend some tourism courses at the University of Economics in Bratislava and in Kosice, where an Institute of Tourism and Hotel Management was established in 1995, although it has no accreditation at present.

## TOURISM EDUCATION AT THE FACULTY OF ECONOMICS, MATEJ BEL UNIVERSITY

The Faculty of Economics of Matej Bel University was established on July 1, 1992 from the former Faculty of Economics of Services and Tourism. The curriculum of the Faculty is subject to accreditation by a commission of the Slovak government. The Faculty offers, as mentioned above, four specialisations of study: Tourism and Hospitality, Marketing and Management, Public Economics and Administration and Banking and Finance.

The study at the Faculty can be either full-time or part-time. Part-time students attend consultations and evening courses. The length of study is five years at two educational levels. The first three years provide general common and oriented tourism and hospitality courses with optional subjects in each study year, and one semester practical placement in the tourism and hospitality industry.

The aim of the first grade of study is to prepare a flexible, highly motivated and independent professional, interested in people, who is able to communicate in two foreign languages and to manage economic processes at the middle management level.

To be admitted to the second level of study (specialised) in the 4th and 5th year the student needs:
- to have successfully finished the first grade of study;
- to pass the state final examination in special subjects and economics;
- to have a state exam in one foreign language.

In the second level of the Tourism and Hospitality specialisation the optional subjects comprise 21% of the course in the 4th and 50% in the 5th year of study. Students can choose from courses such as Tourism Management, Hotel and Hospitality Management, Travel Agency and Convention Management, Spa Management and Tourism Enterprise Management. In the 4th and 5th year of study the specialised subjects account for 79% of the hours while 21% are allotted to foreign languages and economics. A practical placement is carried out in the 10th term.

The second level of study finishes with the state final exam which consists of the defence of written `diploma work' and scientific discussion, according to the subject of diploma work and specialisation chosen. Students graduate from the Faculty with the degree of `Engineer - Ing.'.

Study Plan: Bachelors Degree

| | |
|---|---|
| Study Major: | Tourism and Hospitality Administration |
| Study Garant: | Department of Tourism and Hospitality |
| Study Form: | Full-time |
| Length of Study: | 3 years |

**Table 9.1: Study plan, bachelors degree**

| **Courses** **Year** | I | I | II | II | III | III |
|---|---|---|---|---|---|---|
| **Semester** | 1 | 2 | 3 | 4 | 5 | 6 |
| 01. Economics I. | 4 | 4 | | | | |
| 02. Economy Mathematics | 4 | 4 | | | | |
| 03. Computer Labs | 4 | 2 | | | | |
| 04. Accounting and Balancing | | | 4 | | | |
| 05. Accounting in Tourism | | | | | | 2 |
| Enterprise | | | | | | |
| 06. Finance and Investment in | | | | | 4 | 2 |
| Tourism | | | | | | |
| 07. Introduction to Law | 2 | | | | | |
| 08. Business Law | | 4 | | | | |
| 09. Introduction to Tourism | | | | | | 4 |
| Marketing | | | | | | |
| 10. Tourism Enterprise | | | 4 | | 4 | |
| Economics | | | | | | |
| 11. Statistics Theory | | | | | 4 | |
| 12. Tourism Enterprise Statistics | | | | | | 4 |
| 13. Tourism Enterprise | | | | | | |
| Management | | | | | | 4 |
| 14. Geography in Tourism | | | | | | |
| 15. 1st Foreign Language | 2 | | | | | |
| 16. 2nd Foreign Language | 2 | 2 | 2 | | 2 | |
| 17. Introduction to Tourism | 2 | 2 | 2 | | 2 | 2 |
| 18. Personal Management in | | 4 | | | | |
| Tourism | | | 4 | | | |
| 19. Service Technology in Hotel | | | | | | |
| and Hospitality Industries | | | | | 4 | |
| 20. Service Technology in | | | | | | |
| Tourism Agencies | | | | | | |
| 21. Introduction to Food-Service | | | | | 4 | |
| Management | | | | | | |
| 22. Practical Seminar | | | 2 | | | |
| 23. History of Art | | | | | | |
| 24. Physical Education | | | | 2 | | |
| 25. Groups of Voluntary | | | 2 | | | |
| Courses | 2 | 2 | | | | |
| | | 2 | 2 | | | 4 |
| Hours a week | 22 | 26 | 22 | 2 | 24 | 22 |

Optional Courses (No.25):
Communication in Tourism, Philosophy, Politics, World Economy, Environment, Psychology, Spa Tourism, Case Studies, Agrotourism, Transportation and Food and Beverage.

Some of the main subjects are taught at both study levels in German, English and French and the practical placement can be provided abroad. Summer and winter sports courses are organised on a volunteer basis for regular students.

Study Plan: Masters Degree
Study Major: Tourism and Hospitality Management
Study Garant: Department of Tourism and Hospitality
Study Form: Full-time
Length of Study: 2 years

**Table 9.2: Study plan, masters degree**

| **Courses** | **Year**<br>**Semester** | IV<br>7 | IV<br>8 | V<br>9 | V<br>10 |
|---|---|---|---|---|---|
| 01. | Economics II. | 6te | | | |
| 02. | Introduction to Tourism | 4te | | | |
| 03. | Tourism Enterprise Economics | 4te | | | |
| 04. | Tourism Management | | 4te | | |
| 05. | Tourism Statistics | | 2te | | |
| 06. | Tourism Marketing | | | 4te | |
| 07. | Tourism Law | 2e | | | |
| 08. | Case Studies | | | 2t | 4t |
| 09. | Managerial Communication | | | | 6te |
| 10. | Computer Labs | | 4t | | |
| 11. | Special Seminar | 2t | 2t | | |
| 12. | Thesis / Diploma / Seminar | | | 2t | 2t |
| 13. | Thesis / Diploma / Practice | | | | t |
| 14. | 2nd Foreign Language | 4t | 4t | | |
| 15. | Voluntary Course | | 2e | 2e | 6te |
| 16. | Groups of Specialisation Courses | | | 12te<br>3 cour | |
| Hours a week | | 22 | 18 | 22 | 18 |
| Exams (e) | | 4 | 3 | 3 | 2+F |
| Tests (t) | | 5 | 5 | 4 | 5 |

Optional Courses (No.15):
Animation in Tourism, *Fuehrungspsychologie, Reisentscheidungen und Konsequenzen fur das Marketing,* Public Relations in Tourism, Service Quality Management in Tourism, Customer Behaviour in Tourism.

**Table 9.3: Specialisation courses**

| **Groups of specialisation courses** | **Year**<br>**Semester** | V<br>9 | V<br>10 |
|---|---|---|---|
| 1. Tourism Management | | 4te | |
| a) Regional Tourism Planning | | 4te | |
| b) Investment Decision-Making in Tourism | | 4te | |
| c) Tourism Destination Marketing | | | 6te |
| d) Public Relations in Tourism | | | |
| 2. Hotel and Hospitality Management | | | |
| a) Lodging Services Management | | 4te | |
| b) Food-Service Management | | 4te | |
| c) Hotel and Hospitality Marketing | | 4te | |
| d) Physical Plant Design in Tourism | | 2t | 6te |
| 3. Travel Agencies and Conventions Management | | | |
| a) Travel Agencies Management | | 4te | |
| b) Meetings and Conventions Services | | 4te | |
| c) Travel Agency Marketing | | 4te | |
| d) Animation in Tourism | | | 6te |
| 4. Spa Resorts Management | | | |
| a) Spa Resort Management | | 4te | |
| b) Balneology and Recreology | | 4te | |
| c) Spa Resort Marketing | | 4te | |
| d) Animation In Tourism | | | 6te |
| 5. Tourism Enterprise Management | | | |
| a) Tourism Services Management | | 4te | |
| b) Tourism Enterprise Financial Management | | 4te | |
| c) Tourism Enterprise Marketing | | 4te | |
| d) Physical Plant Design in Tourism | | | 6te |

The curriculum presented above is very up to date and was developed after discussion with colleagues from Germany, Switzerland, Great Britain and the USA and was adapted to our conditions. In order to provide a clearer understanding of the improvement in tourism education, there follows a presentation of the curriculum in 1990/1991 just after the velvet revolution, which was the beginning of changes in tourism education not only at our faculty, but also in Slovakia as a whole.

| | |
|---|---|
| Study Plan: | Academic Year 1990/91 |
| Study Major: | Economy of Services and Tourism |
| Study Specialisation: | Economy and Management of Tourism and Hospitality |
| Study Garant: | Department of Economy of Tourism and Hospitality |
| Study Form: | Full-time |
| Length of Study: | 5 years |

**Table 9.4: Study plan for the academic year 1990/91**

| Courses Year | I | I | II | II | III | III | IV | IV | V | V |
|---|---|---|---|---|---|---|---|---|---|---|
| Semester | 1 | 2 | 3 | 4 | 5 | 6 | 7 | 8 | 9 | 10 |
| 1. Economics | 4et | 6et | 4et | - | - | - | - | - | - | - |
| 2. Mathematics | 4et | 4et | - | - | - | - | - | - | - | - |
| 3. Statistics | 2et | - | 4t | 4et | 3et | - | - | - | - | - |
| 4. Computer Labs | 4e | 2t | - | - | - | - | - | - | 2t | 2t |
| 5. Finance | - | - | - | 4t | - | - | - | - | - | - |
| 6. Accounting | - | - | - | 4et | - | - | - | - | - | - |
| 7. Law | 2et | - | - | - | - | - | - | - | - | - |
| 8. Introduction to Tourism | - | - | 2t | 2t | - | - | - | - | - | - |
| 9. Management | - | - | 4et | - | - | - | - | - | - | - |
| 10. Introduct. to Ec. of T. and H. | - | - | - | - | 4et | - | - | - | - | 2t |
| 11. Economy and Mngm. of T. and H. Enterprise | - | - | - | - | - | 3t | 5et | P | - | 2t |
| 12. Technology of T. and H. | - | - | - | - | 3 | 3e | - | - | - | - |
| 13. Enterpreneurship in Tourism and Hospitality | - | - | - | - | - | 3t | 3e | - | - | - |
| 14. Information Process in Tourism and Hospitality | - | - | - | - | 3 | 3e | - | - | - | - |
| 15. Social Protocol | - | - | - | - | 2 | - | - | - | - | - |
| 16. 1st. Foreign Language. | 3 | 2 | 2 | 2 | 2 | 2e | - | - | - | - |
| 17. 2nd. Foreign Language. | 3 | 3 | 3 | 2 | 2 | 2e | 2 | - | - | - |
| 18. Special Seminar | - | - | - | - | - | 1 | - | - | - | - |
| 19. Thesis Seminar | - | - | - | - | - | - | 2 | - | 2 | 2 |
| 20. Block of Voluntary Courses | - | - | - | - | - | - | 4e | - | 4e | - |
| 21. Voluntary Ccourses | - | 4e | - | - | 2e | 2e | 2e | - | 2e | 2e |
| 22. Case Studies in T. & H. | - | - | - | - | - | - | - | - | - | 4 |
| 23. Organisation of Managerial Work | - | - | - | - | - | - | - | - | 4e | - |
| Number of Hours/Week | 22 | 21 | 19 | 18 | 21 | 19 | 18 | - | 14 | 14 |
| Number of Exams | 5 | 3 | 2 | 2 | 3 | 5 | 4 | - | 3 | 1F |
| 24. Voluntary Courses | - | - | - | 4e | - | - | - | - | - | - |
| 25. 3rd. Foreign Language | - | - | - | - | 4 | 4 | 4 | - | 4e | - |
| 26. Physical Training | 2 | 2 | 2 | 2 | 2 | 2 | 2 | - | - | - |

P = practical placement;
F = final exam;
e = exam;
t = test.

Voluntary courses (No. 20): Economy and Management of Hotels, Economy and Management of Travel Agencies, Economy and Management of Spas, Economy and Management of Hospitality, Economy and Management of International Tourism.

Voluntary courses (No. 21): Philosophy, Psychology, Sociology, History of Arts, Nutrition, Modelling Economic Processes, Theory of Games, Geography in Tourism, Transportation in Tourism, Recreology, Economy of Food and Beverage, Technology of Food and Beverage, Physical Plant Design in Tourism, Reservation Systems in Tourism, Regional Analysis and planning in Tourism, International Law and Finance in Tourism.

After completing their studies at the Faculty of Economics, graduates were offered higher degree courses in the economics of tourism. Graduates of this programme were awarded the degree of PhD. With a view to changes in both economy and the market for tourism, the faculty also organised short-term courses for qualification and retraining in the tourism field.

To meet the new conditions in the labour market the Faculty has innovated the curriculum outlines and started new subjects. As the changes in society mostly concern the economic sphere, it is obvious that they were strongly reflected in the whole content and system of study at the Faculty. Changes have been made in the areas of school admission policy, systems of evaluation, options, forms of exams and written tests, evaluation of teachers by students, possibilities for study abroad as well as the weekly number of obligatory lessons (maximum of 22), the lower number of exams and engaging lecturers and experts from industry both from our country or from abroad. The aim of these changes is to bring the curriculum more in line with systems of study in countries with developed economies and systems of education and to meet market demand.

The placement of students after finishing their studies is made according to work requirements. Non-academic industry experts take part in sponsoring final projects. The teachers from the faculty are members of commissions that help to choose experts in tourist enterprises. The Department of Tourism does applied research, some granted by the Ministry of Education and used by Department of Tourism of Ministry of Economy (Tourism Market in Slovakia, Marketing Information Systems).

Graduates from the Faculty of Economics who specialised in tourism are able to pursue jobs in various industry sectors, e.g. hotels, restaurants, spa resorts, travel agencies (and also in the educational system and state administration). After completing their studies the graduates can begin their careers at entry level (assistant manager, receptionist, head of a community centre) and then, after having obtained the necessary experience, they can be promoted up to the level of top managers. As it was mentioned above, some of the specialised subjects are taught in English, German or French. Thanks to our wide international contacts and the TEMPUS project started in 1994, we are able to offer a variety of subjects taught in these languages.

In a TEMPUS project under the title "Restructuring of Tourism and Hospitality Study in Slovakia" Universite d'Angers, France, the University of the West of England (Bristol Business School), UK and Fachhochschule Kempten, Germany, are involved. The aim of the project is to develop tourism and hospitality curriculum in a European context. The goal we would like to achieve is to receive accreditation of our Tourism and Hospitality course from the European Foundation for the Accreditation of Hotel School Programmes (EFAH).

As part of the TEMPUS project, 12 Slovak students took part in a three month practical placement, six Slovak teachers took part in a one-month study visit to participating countries and seven teachers from abroad taught at the Faculty in the last academic year.

Together with the University of South Carolina in Columbia, South Carolina, USA our Faculty received a grant from the U.S. government for a three year teacher exchange in 1992 in which five Slovak and five American teachers were involved. For the academic years 1993/94 and 1994/95 the Faculty received an additional grant for a two-year student exchange. Consequently two Slovak students studied in the USA and two American students studied at the Faculty of Tourism and Hotel Management. This project finished in 1994/95.

In cooperation with the Institute of Transport and Tourism in St. Gallen, Switzerland, the Swiss department of Tourism and Hospitality organised Hospitality Management courses for our teachers and for the hotel academy teachers as a part of a Swiss Tourism Programme for Slovakia. Eighty teachers took part in this project over three years. This cooperation continues and the two institutions founded in 1994 the Slovak-Swiss Institute for Tourism Postgraduate Studies. The Department of Tourism and Hospitality also cooperates with other faculties and universities from the Netherlands, Poland, the Czech Republic, Austria, Hungary, Bulgaria, the United Kingdom, Germany, Switzerland, France and the USA.

We hope that the changes in our curriculum as mentioned above, our contacts with industry, universities and institutions from abroad will increase the quality of tourism studies at Matej Bel University and bring benefit to our students and our staff as well as to tourism industry in Slovakia a whole.

# Chapter 10

# University level tourism education in Slovenia

**Franc Pauko**

## INTRODUCTION

As an independent country, Slovenia has created a separate educational national policy concerning the field of tourism. Although recent years have seen a strong stress on tourism development from an economic perspective, we cannot see such an emphasis in the teaching of tourism. This was not only the result of financial shortages, but often a misunderstanding of what tourism theory means for the tourism economy. A lot of leading people in tourism enterprises as well as the clerks and functionaries in the public administration did not recognise for a long time the necessity of having highly educated staff, especially in the field of marketing and modern management. We still can find enterprises rejecting or ignoring young graduates with a relatively good knowledge of tourism marketing and management, which has been taught in our country for years. It seems as if the older generation cannot accept modern marketing and the management philosophy because they are not sufficiently acquainted with these principles.

The Slovene Ministry of Tourism estimated that the tourism industry gave employment to nearly 27,000 people in 1992, just in the statistically traditional tourism sectors, i.e. the hospitality industry and travel agencies. Through the recent process of privatisation this number is actually much higher and may be 40,000 or more if we bear in mind the whole variety of tourism activities, like personal transportation and small business, cultural and sport institutions. We estimate that about 10% of tour operating staff have a university education, but the hospitality industry has much lower percentage of higher educated leading staff. In this respect we estimate that the national need for highly qualified people in the tourism area is at least 5,000 marketers and managers in hospitality, and 2,000 in the travel industry. It is evident that none of the existing university institutions in the country could supply the tourism industry with such a number of specialists in the near future. In my opinion the main problem of a growing tourism economy is the shortage of highly qualified marketers and managers. That's why tourism needs special professional schools at university level.

## TOURISM STUDY AT THE FACULTIES OF ECONOMICS

*School of Economics and Commerce, Maribor University*
When Slovenia established in early 1959 the 'School of Economics and Commerce' in Maribor we began as the first university institution in this country to lecture on tourism. As we began as a typical school for business economy, from the very beginning the main task of teaching was the most representative tourism activities, i.e. travel agencies and hospitality industry. We have carried on these activities for more than 30 years. In 1974 we added to the existing subjects a new course on transport, i.e. the so called (mass)personal transportation with special focus to the tourists' means of travel on road, trails, vertical transport (aerial ropeways, ski-lifts ...), air and water transport. As far as I know no institution in former Yugoslavia or elsewhere in the neighbouring countries (except St. Gallen in Switzerland) has introduced this course into the tourism curriculum, completely covering all the personal means of transportation. We are still improving this discipline, bearing in mind the global importance of personal mobility. In this respect I published in 1987 a manual of the above-mentioned content. In 1984 we changed the title of the course 'travel agencies' into the much more modern concept of 'Integral tourism marketing', which is still on the programme. The course on 'tourism economics', which has been on the programme since the beginning, is a mixture of multidisciplinary views, such as geographical aspects, special investments and its financing, the state tourism institutions and policy as well as the international relations with a special stress on the common future European development and the necessity for cooperation. This course also involves a section on environmental factors due to tourism activities. Certainly, special sorts of the so called integral tourism offer, like mountain-tourism, farm-tourism, spa-tourism, seaside-, lake-, river-tourism, hunting and fishing-tourism and other sorts of Slovenia's perspective tourism markets are also discussed in classes.

If we add to these courses the compulsory business language knowledge of English, German or French, our curriculum is, in fact, the most extensive tourism programme in the country, at present.

### The ITI Project

In 1989 Slovene tourism enterprises expressed the wish to establish a complete tourism course of 8-semester duration which should be oriented to university study, but also to the very practical purposes of tourism enterprises (mainly tour operators). Our Faculty of Business and Economics was selected the prepare the project in close cooperation with the American universities, the so called 'big ten' midwest universities of the USA, united in the consortium 'MUCIA'. The main aim was to create an independent international school of tourism on the basis of bilateral Slovene and American partnership, located at Maribor University. From its very beginnings the project was meant to be financed 60% by Americans and

40% by Slovenes. This 'International Tourism Institute' (ITI) should be an international university institution, established as a separate faculty of Maribor University. Our Faculty of Business and Economics was selected because of its 30-year tradition in tourism education and experience of teaching, modern school-buildings and equipment and supply of administrative staff to facilitate the management of the ITI. The ITI teaching staff should consist of an international group of professors holding university positions. The project was prepared with the help of the University Wisconsin-Stout/Wisconsin and Purdue University, West Lafayette/Indiana. On July 18th, 1989 we signed a 'memorandum' defining the functions of the School in the area of education and training, research, consultancy and publications.

After successfully completing an 8-semester programme of study the students would receive a degree of "bachelor of science in tourism".

The course consisted of basic business, social science and language courses, with compulsory units in management and tourism, together with specialist units in tour operations, travel agency management, lodging management, resort management, food service management, transportation management and non-profit tourism institutions (see Appendix 10.1).

The programme was to be taught in English and students were also required to take a second language. Two six-month placements were built into the course.

**List of the courses in the ITI programme**

Group A: THE BASIC COURSES (obligatory for all the students)
1. sociology
2. psychology
3. social sciences
4. basic economics
5. mathematics
6. statistics
7. computer sciences
8. communication
9. humanities
10. foreign business language group

| Group B/1: THE MANAGEMENT COURSES | credits |
|---|---|
| 1. human resource (personnel) management | 4 |
| 2. financial management | 3 |
| 3. theory of management & organisation | 3 |
| 4. basic marketing | 4 |
| 5. consumer behaviour | 4 |
| | ---- |
| | 18 |

Group B/2: THE TOURISM COURSES (core)

| | |
|---|---|
| 6. introduction to tourism | 3 |
| 7. tourism policy (macro) | 3 |
| 8. economic implications of tourism | 3 |
| 9. tourism planning & development | 4 |
| 10. socio-cultural impacts of tourism | 2 |
| 11. geography of tourism | 2 |
| 12. history of tourism | 2 |
| 13. tourism organisations | 2 |
| 14. international tourism | 2 |
| 15. computer applications in tourism | 3 |
| 16. tourism promotion | 4 |
| 17. marketing research methods in tourism | 4 |
| | ---- |
| | 34 |

Group C: SPECIALISED COURSES (in various tourism activities)

Group C/1: TOUR OPERATIONS

| | |
|---|---|
| 1. tour marketing | 4 |
| 2. packaging | 4 |
| 3. distribution channels | 4 |
| 4. domestic tour operations | 3 |
| 5. international tour operations | 3 |
| 6. tour management | 3 |
| | ---- |
| | 21 |

Group C/2: TRAVEL AGENCY MANAGEMENT

| | |
|---|---|
| 1. travel agency marketing | 4 |
| 2. packaging | 4 |
| 3. travel regulations & organisations | 4 |
| 4. distribution channels | 4 |
| 5. airline reservations systems | 3 |
| 6. travel (destination) geography | 2 |
| | ---- |
| | 21 |

Group C/3: LODGING (TRANSIENT) MANAGEMENT

| | |
|---|---|
| 1. hotel & motel marketing | 4 |
| 2. lodging management & law | 4 |
| 3. convention/meeting planning | 4 |
| 4. property management | 3 |
| 5. front desk operations | 3 |
| 6. housekeeping | 3 |
| | ---- |
| | 21 |

Group C/4: RESORT MANAGEMENT

| | |
|---|---|
| 1. resort marketing | 4 |
| 2. lodging management & law | 4 |
| 3. physical resort development | 4 |
| 4. property management | 3 |
| 5. front desk operations | 3 |
| 6. housekeeping | 3 |
| | ---- |
| | 21 |

Group C/5: FOOD SERVICE MANAGEMENT

| | |
|---|---|
| 1. restaurant marketing | 4 |
| 2. purchasing | 4 |
| 3. food and beverage production (institutional food service) | 4 |
| 4. commercial food and beverage production (for individual sale) | 3 |
| 5. food and beverage control | 3 |
| 6. food service sanitation | 3 |
| | ---- |
| | 21 |

Group C/6: TRANSPORTATION MANAGEMENT

| | |
|---|---|
| 1. transportation marketing | 4 |
| 2. transportation management and organisation | 4 |
| 3. transportation services/facilitator | 4 |
| 4. transportation law | 3 |
| 5. transportation domestic operations | 3 |
| 6. transportation international operations | 3 |
| | ---- |
| | 21 |

Group C/7: NON-PROFIT TOURISM INSTITUTIONS

| | |
|---|---|
| 1. marketing for non-profit institutions | 4 |
| 2. management and organisation of non-profit institutions | 4 |
| 3. attraction planning and development | 4 |
| 4. community leadership in tourism | 3 |
| 5. planning of community festivals and events | 3 |
| 6. information services and tour guidance | 3 |
| | ---- |
| | 21 |

In spite of the eagerness to carry out this project, the Balkan war stopped it. After the war in 1992, the ideas of the ITI-project were shelved as the new government and its ministers for education offered new suggestions in spite of the complimentary reports of the consortium MUCIA that declare this programme to be one of the best in the world.

*Faculty of Economics, Ljubljana University*

Ljubljana offers tourism courses which are included in the study of economy as optional courses in tourism economics and the management of tourism enterprises. Each of the courses has a duration of 90 hours.

## TOURISM STUDY AT THE OTHER FACULTIES

At other non-economic schools tourism is included in the study of geography: at Ljubljana's Faculty of Geography as a single course of 'tourism geography' and at Maribor's Pedagogical faculty as the same course (under the same title of 'tourism geography'), lectured by the same professor. It seems to be more an informative course for future teachers in primary and secondary schools. This is all that Croatia could offer students of tourism management until recently.

## THE PERIOD OF NEW UNIVERSITY LEGISLATION IN SLOVENIA

Recent reforms affecting the entire education system have also brought some novelties in tourism education. We introduced the so-called bimodal study at the highest educational level: professional (technical) schools, and parallel university studies. Because the universities obtained independent status, they can change their programmes. It is up to them which disciplines they introduce if students are interested.

In terms of tourism studies Slovenia decided to follow the existing structures, but complimented it with these higher level courses, especially those in close connection with the tourism economy. That's why several programmes appeared, but they differ one from the other. Let us examine the new courses at the new schools of economics.

*School of Business and Economics, University of Maribor*
Maribor has decided to have tourism courses at both university level and professional school level, lasting 6 semesters plus 1 training semester and a university study which is still not defined at the moment, but which will lead to a masters degree and enable doctoral study.

The programme of the professional school has a lot of options, such as banking, trade, foreign trade and tourism. The first two semesters are common for all the students and include common economic courses, like basic economic theory, mathematics, basic marketing, business informatics, sociology and foreign business languages. Special tourism courses (core) begin in the 4th and 5th semesters with:
- personal (tourism) transportation;
- hospitality marketing;
- ecotropology;
- tourism economics;

- integral tourism marketing;
- management and business languages (with tourism items).

Besides these the students have to take selected courses on business communications and the foreign trade system of Slovenia. The course covers in total 2,460 periods including 1,530 periods of common courses, 390 periods of common tourism courses, 180 periods of selected courses and 320 periods for training in tourism enterprises.

A special stress is placed on foreign business languages and for tourism students two foreign languages are compulsory.

At present the tourism postgraduate study lasts 4 terms (ten courses) and will be approximately the same in the future.

*Faculty of Economics at Ljubljana University*
The Faculty of Economics in Ljubljana also plans to run tourism courses in the framework of the 4-term business school. The following courses run in the 3$^{rd}$-and 4$^{th}$-terms: management of tourism, enterprises, tourism economics, business communication, tourism diploma-seminar and electives.

Total periods per study year are 735-750, but for the entire programme 1,545 - 1,560.

*School of Hoteliery and Tourism in Isola*
The school in Isola was established in 1994 as a professional school, partly privately financed, but linked to the Biotechnical Faculty of Ljubljana University. The two programmes hoteliers and tourism (travel agencies), are technologically oriented in their core courses. The whole study lasts 6 terms plus three months of industrial placements. For the year 1995/1996 they expect just the students who already work and have to pay schoolfees. The courses are shown in Appendix 10.2.

Each study year involves 735-785 teaching periods, giving 2,240 periods in total for the whole study.

If we analyse the programme of the three tourism educational institutions it is evident that: Maribor's School has a typical business programme in tourism with the most developed specialisation in tourism marketing and management; Ljubljana's Faculty of Economics has the same business programme but not so broad as Maribor's and the Isola School of Hoteliery and Tourism concentrates mainly on the hospitality industry and travel agencies with technological approach - in this respect it is a logical continuation of the Catering High School.

This analysis shows that Slovenia offers different programmes in tourism higher education but still lacks certain courses applicable to some important sectors of the tourism industries. A comparison of the current and the desired Slovene-American ITI project illustrates the deficiencies of the current provision.

## CONCLUSION

Slovenia as an independent country devotes much attention to tourism, because tourism should become one of its most important and profitable service industries. For this reason, and due the new education reforms, the universities presently have the opportunity to develop more appropriate and applicable study programmes to meet the requirements of all tourism business. The achievements of the Maribor Faculty of Business and Economics have enabled the school to establish a professional tourism department, which will specialise in tourist business administration. The Faculty of Economics in Ljubljana has started the same programme, but not as broad as the Maribor's. The most recently established school in Isola (near Trieste) has attempted to develop out a detailed technological programme for the catering industry and travel agencies. Both Maribor and Ljubljana provide tourism courses to PhD level. However, an analysis of current tourism education provision indicates that much more remains to be done if a balanced approach covering all sectors of the tourism industry is to be achieved.

## APPENDIX 10.1 THE ITI TOURISM COURSE

A. The basic courses are obligatory for all students.

B. The required courses are divided into two subgroups:
- Required management courses;
- Required tourism courses (core).

C. Courses of specialisation in tourism activities.

D. Grading:
A system of examinations should be used and each student must pass every course with a minimum of a grade 'BC'. ITI accepts the American system of grading, i.e., A-4 points-excellent; AB-3,5 points-very good; B-3 points-good; BC-2,5 points-sufficient.

E. The system of credits:
The study is based on valuation of courses for credit. The importance of the courses is expressed by the number of credits; the lowest number is 2, the highest is 4 credits.

| | |
|---|---|
| The degree program should total | 120 credits: |
| - for A (basic courses) | 30 credits |

| | |
|---|---|
| - for B/1 (management courses) | 18 credits |
| - for B/2 (tourism courses-core) | 34 credits |
| - for C/1 (specialised courses) | 21 credits |
| - for C/2 (specialisation-electives)[1] | 12 credits |
| - for work experience | 5 credits |

F. ITI should required the following language-competencies:
- English is required on the basis of the final exam at a high school level or 550 TOEFL a score (Test of English as a foreign language);
- A second language is required and has to be chosen from among the following languages: French, German, Italian, Spanish, Russian, Japanese. An exam has to be passed before graduation;
- ITI study requires of the students a good knowledge of English in order to understand the foreign professors. There will be no translation in the classes.

G. ITI study requires work experience in tourism enterprises:
Each student has to spend 6 months or two summers in a practicum during the programme of study.

## APPENDIX 10.2 TOURISM COURSES AT THE ISOLA HOTEL AND TOURISM SCHOOL

### Department A: Hoteliery

1. mathematical methods (60 periods),
2. biology with environment (60 periods),
3. food chemistry (60 periods),
4. physics (60 periods),
5. foreign language I (150 periods),
6. foreign language II (150 periods),
7. economics of hoteliery & tourism (75 periods),
8. accounting (60 periods),
9. basic statistics and informatics (90 periods),
10. natural and cultural inheritance (90 periods),
11. arrangement and decoration (60 periods),
12. business administration of hotel- and tourism enterprises (75 periods),
13. business psychology and communicology (90 periods),
14. hotel and tourism law (60 periods),
15. nutrition and dietetics (105 periods),
16. gastronomy (75 periods),

---

[1] electives: students have to earn the following of credits:
A.21 credits of elected specialised courses plus
B.12 credits from any specialisation, i.e. all together 33 credits.

17. technology of the catering industry (105 periods),
18. content and quality of food and beverages (135 periods),
19. hygiene and sanitation (60 periods),
20. tourism sociology (45 periods),
21. tourism marketing (90 periods),
22. optional courses (180 periods).

One study year involves 735 periods, i.e. in total (3 years) 2,255 periods.

**Department B: Tourism**

1. mathematical methods (60 periods),
2. basics statistics and informatics (90 periods),
3. natural and cultural heritage I (120 periods),
4. natural and cultural heritage II (90 periods),
5. ecology (environment) (60 periods),
6. tourism geography (75 periods),
7. foreign language I (150 periods),
8. foreign language II (150 periods),
9. economics of hoteliery and tourism (75 periods),
10. accounting (60 periods),
11. management of hotel- and tourism enterprises (75 periods),
12. business psychology and communicology (90 periods),
13. hospitality and tourism law (60 periods),
14. tourism sociology (45 periods),
15. tourism marketing (90 periods),
16. sports and recreation (60 periods),
17. hygiene and sanitation (60 periods),
18. tourism management (60 periods),
19. animation and entertainment (90 periods),
20. organisation of tours (120 periods),
21. transportation systems (60 periods),
22. training (320 periods),
23. optional courses (180 periods).

# Chapter 11

# Tourism education, issues and perspectives: A UK case study

**David Bowen**

## 1. BACKGROUND

### 1.1. Rationale

The rationale for this article stems from a series of visits to Oxford Brookes University (UK) from colleagues in Central and Eastern Europe as well as from other parts of Europe and the Far East. It is invariably interesting to discover the particular issues facing colleagues in different environments. In most cases, an exchange of information is most useful when jargon and abstract theorising are cast aside - for a moment at least - and the practical realities of setting-up and subsequently managing a tourism course are confronted head-on. Some of the issues that most often materialise in such discussions are outlined here and commented on from the point of view of the Oxford Brookes (hereafter referred to as Brookes) experience. Three key issues have been chosen namely, curriculum matters; assessment; industry visits/visiting speakers/work placements.

### 1.2. Tourism at Oxford Brookes University

An undergraduate Field (area of study) in tourism was introduced to the modular degree programme at Oxford Polytechnic, now Oxford Brookes University, in 1987. This was one of the first such courses of its kind in the UK and there have since been six cohorts of graduates.

Typically, students follow a full-time course of study for a period of three years leading to the award of an Honours degree. The course is composed of 27 modules - units of study which are self-contained in teaching, learning and assessment. The initial period of study - known as Stage 1 - is usually completed in one year. The final two years - Stage 2 - determine the class of degree that a student receives. Most students study 9 modules in each year.

There are various nationally recognised schemes in operation so that credit may be given for prior learning and experience. This reduces the length of the degree. By contrast it is also feasible to study on a part-time basis which increases the length of the degree. One member of the very first cohort of students recently completed her degree after seven years -with, it must be said, several additions to her family along the way.

All the degrees are Joint Honours. There is a range of 40 possible degree combinations. Generally, however, in each cohort of students there will be about 15 combinations with tourism - the most popular are Business Administration, Hotel and Catering Management, Retail Management, Marketing, Geography and various Languages. However, other useful combinations range from Anthropology through to Publishing.

Administration of the degree was initially vested within a body named as the Oxford Centre for Tourism and Leisure Studies (OCTALS) although this body has subsequently concentrated on research and consultancy. Administration now lies with the School of Business - Business is the central theme - although teaching is shared with specialists from the School of Planning and the School of Hotel and Catering Management. OCTALS employs a full-time manager who oversees research and consultancy projects from the initial tendering through to presentation and, importantly, acts as a focus for liaison between the staff who carry out the projects from the three schools. A comparatively small annual fund has been necessary in order to subsidise the various OCTALS activities - absolute financial independence has not been achieved - but it is accepted that there are substantial benefits from OCTALS. The benefits extend beyond client use of findings from the research and consultancy. In particular, teaching is a clear beneficiary as OCTALS work provides vital fresh details and ideas.

## 2. CURRICULUM MATTERS

Some sort of consensus has now emerged within the UK regarding the key components that should be contained within any course in tourism (see Holloway, Chapter 12, this volume). This is not to say that there is complete agreement on a core curriculum. Tourism courses do not all have the same rationale - the Business and Management theme, for example, is challenged by courses that dwell more on Geographical and Anthropological themes.

The core subject areas that emerged from discussions piloted by the CNAA and subsequently by the Tourism Society are listed below (Figure 11.1). Very broadly this represents the minimum core - excluding skills teaching and general Business and Management concepts - that is followed at Brookes.

- The meaning and nature of tourism and its relationship with Leisure and Recreation.
- The structure of the tourism industry; key sectors in the industry and their principal operating characteristics; linkages within the industry.
- The dimensions of tourism - internationally and within the UK - and issues of measurement.
- The significance and impact of tourism - the economic, social and physical environment and issues of sustainable development.
- Marketing - tourism applications
- Planning and Development - tourism applications.
- Policy issues, Management of Tourism, Finance and Organisation.

**Figure 11.1: Proposed minimum common core - tourism elements (CNAA, 1993)**

At Brookes it is the core compulsory modules that provide the structural cohesion and continuity which could so easily be lost within a modular system - yet alone a system that is based on Joint Honours degrees. It is necessary to view the educational process from the student perspective - a perspective that is unavoidably narrow on entry to the system. Students are unlikely, until well into their study programme and despite frequent explanation, to see the broad picture of the course and its progressive, developmental structure. Accordingly, it is imperative that the opportunity is taken to provide some sort of tightness and logicality to the study - and a meaningful compulsory core is one method of doing this.

In Stage 1, the core syllabus, taught in a two term compulsory module known as 'Tourism Concepts', is intended to enable students to research and analyse tourism information; identify the sectors within the industry and the inter-sectoral links; appreciate the scale, extent, and dynamism of the industry and the consequent implications of these for tourism managers; and then, importantly, to describe and analyse the economic, social, political and environmental factors affecting tourism - and conversely the economic, social, political and environmental impact of tourism on a variety of scales (local, regional, national and international). Two parallel compulsory courses exist, not staffed by tourism specialists and geared to Business and Management in general, that introduce basic Business and Management ideas - 'Introduction to Business' and 'Management Concepts'. Ryan suggested that such generalist courses are detrimental to the student understanding of tourism as a whole (Ryan, 1995). From the experience at Brookes, however, the danger of this happening is presently mitigated by the strategic 'Tourism

Concepts' module which is essentially confined to Field students and which generates a strong sense of both academic and social unity.

In Stage 2, the core syllabus is again taught in a two-term compulsory module - 'Tourism Development and Management'. The module framework in Figure 11.2 summarises the subject areas of this core syllabus.

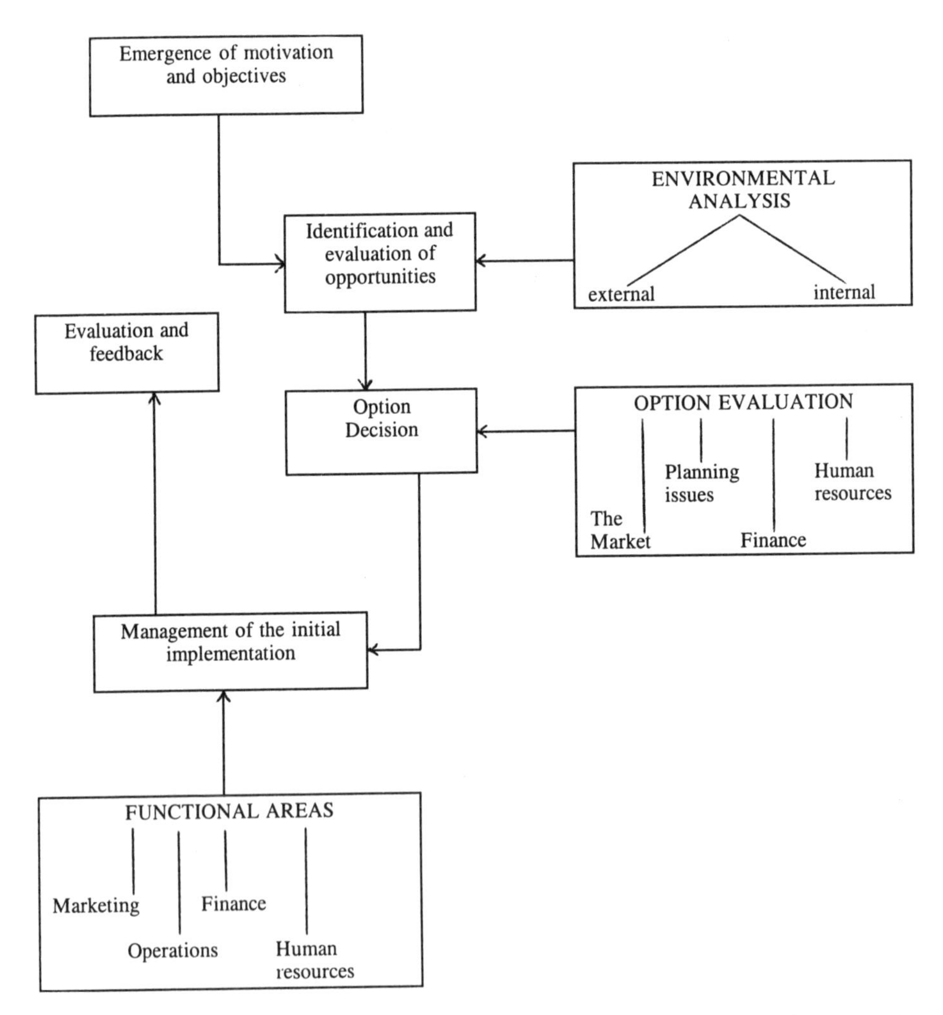


**Figure 11.2: Tourism development and management - Module framework**

Clearly this framework builds on the foundation principles of Stage 1 and is the key module that attempts to fulfil the overall objective of the course - to produce graduates who are able to manage, develop and plan tourism resources. Once again the strategic positioning of this module encourages a sense of academic and social unity.

Greater student choice is a feature of Stage 2 (Figure 11.3).

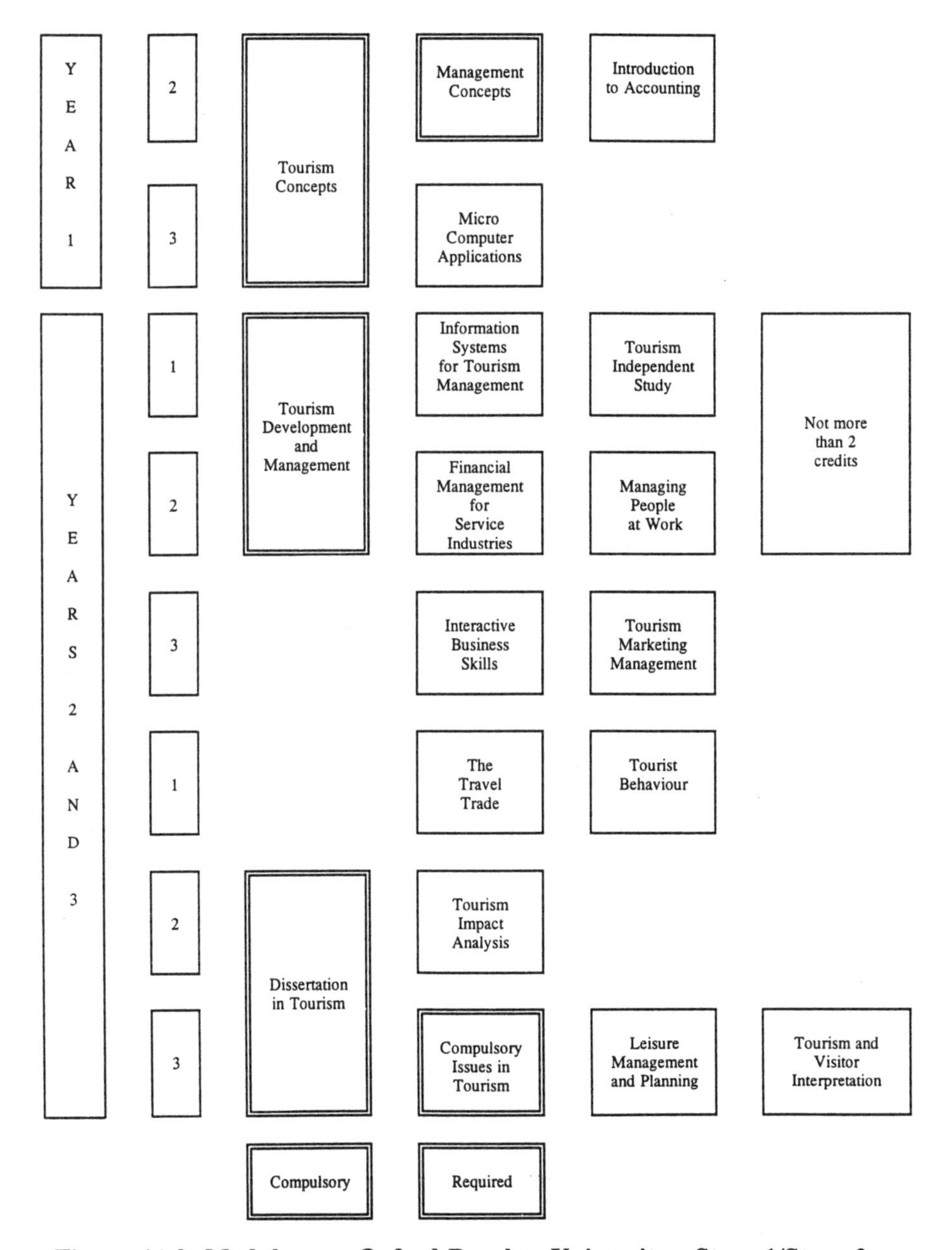


**Figure 11.3: Module map Oxford Brookes University - Stage 1/Stage 2**

Students increasingly develop particular interests which they can pursue via their own choice of modules. These may be drawn from those offered by the Tourism Field and, to a lesser extent, from those offered outside the Field. Advice is offered to students so that there is some sort of logicality in their selections. The limits to choice imposed by the Joint Honours nature of the degree ease the potential for major problems of selection - few students compose particularly strange programmes - although if tourism was ever offered as a double Field it would be necessary to consider the inclusion of key pathways. The 10,000 word Dissertation - a fundamental test of student quality and the arbiter of an Honours classification - is both a further compulsory element and a great opportunity for students to concentrate on a favoured specialism. The only other compulsory element - 'Contemporary Issues' - finally signs off the degree study with an analysis of key contemporary issues. These vary, of course, from year to year.

## 3. ASSESSMENT

Assessment of taught modules is via both coursework and examinations. Each module has its own particular mix of these two methods. The coursework component ranges from 40% of total marks through to 100%.

Coursework assessment is done on an individual basis and in groups of various sizes - 2/4/6. The former method is the most favoured by students although it is costly in terms of staff time and does not necessarily mimic the reality of the workplace. A compromise is, therefore, most often sought.

Coursework is an integrated part of the study programme and aims to both complement and extend the taught programme. A module frequently has a variety of coursework pieces. Just as an example, there are four such pieces in the Stage 1 compulsory module 'Tourism Concepts' - a library exercise which aims to familiarise students with the library resource; an exercise based on a familiarisation tour of Oxford in which students write up their experience in the form of a newspaper/magazine of their choice; an essay style article on a chosen sector of the industry in which students comment on present and future prospects; and a report contrasting the economic, social, environmental and political influences and impacts on tourism in two contrasting destinations.

With regard to examinations, it is preferable to arrange a variety of different types of examination so as to test a range of skills and fit in with the objectives of different modules. At Brookes the so-called 'traditional' examination - unseen essays - is probably still the most common form of examination. These essays test a minimum body of knowledge, an ability to write logically under pressure and also act as a check against the inflation of grades through student cooperation - legitimate or otherwise - on coursework assignments. However, other methods are also employed - 'seen' and 'open book' examinations, oral presentations as a supplement to reports, presentations that form part of an exhibition and so on. Of these it is probably the latter that are the most welcomed by students although this may be to do with their comparative novelty value. The potential tourism graduate must be more than literate and numerate. Presentation skills on a one-to-one and group basis are also necessary. This means that the student must show an ability to inter-relate.

## 4. INDUSTRY VISITS / VISITING SPEAKERS / WORK PLACEMENTS

At least one element of coursework on each module is linked to a group student visit. This adds vital relevancy and focuses student effort both before, during and after the visit. Such visits may involve direct contact with staff at chosen attractions or facilities although this is not always deemed to be a necessity. The location of the visits reflect a balance of module objectives, geographical proximity, previous visits (to avoid plagiarism), and the amenability of staff at attractions/facilities.

Industry visits are therefore, an essential element of the overall course and its assessment. Industry contacts have been gleaned from a variety of sources - OCTALS Board members, network contacts, chance contacts and deliberate targeting of attractions/facilities that meet the location criteria above. Naturally it is most important not to waste the time of the industry contacts. This is done by ensuring that general background concepts are covered in advance of any visit; that the coursework objectives are known in advance to both students and industry contacts - indeed some input is sometimes sought from the latter as the coursework is devised; and that contact is maintained post visit. This is most usefully done by sending a small sample of the best coursework to the industry contact concerned.

The exact amount of direct industry input into the coursework is, of course, variable. There have been no instances within the Brookes experience of total industry involvement in the setting of the coursework and beyond that the running of a module. It is felt that industry personnel would not be interested in such an arrangement. Also as Gunn observed some time ago, good managers do not necessarily make good teachers (Gunn, 1984). Rather, the norm is more likely to be for a manager to give a relatively short talk, followed by a question and answer session, either prior to or immediately after students have gained some familiarity with the product - a relatively straightforward task at, say, an attraction. If this can be backed up with company literature - either that available externally to consumers/shareholders and so on or, for added insight and authenticity, that available internally - so much the better.

It is rather more rare to build in a form of assessment into the information and ideas imparted by visiting speakers - although, of course, this is by no means impossible. As a case in point, a series of visiting speakers can present considerable opportunities for critical analysis by students. Speaker views may be contrasted one with another and also vis-a-vis background literature and then presented in the form of a report or essay. More often, however, it may be sufficient for a student to sit back and absorb the specialist, up-to-date and hands-on views of suitably chosen and briefed visiting speakers without the threat of imminent assessment.

One form of industry contact that is common among parallel institutions but not at Brookes is that of student tourism work placements. Students do have the opportunity to gain experience in the industry and to have such work assessed in the form of the Independent Study. However, the onus on such a choice is placed on the student. Some students choose to take a term or a year out from their formal studies in pursuit of experience but the great majority do not seek to extend the length of time it takes to finish their degree. Experience is, therefore, gained during vacations and/or on a part-time basis during the term time or during the research period of the Dissertation.

The rationale behind such a policy lies in the belief that good work placements are not common enough to justify the necessary input of staff resources. This conforms to some extent with the findings of the CNAA report (CNAA, 1993). For many institutions in the UK the lack of a work placement programme might be seen as a critical weakness. Some graduates who have not taken up any of the non-formalised methods of gaining industry experience have reported some difficulty in obtaining the all-important first job. Generally, however, this has not surfaced as a key issue as suggested by some colleagues in other institutions (Evans, 1993).

## 5. EXPERIENCE

A perspective born out of experience is, of course, two-pronged. It can dull the senses as well as provide the opportunity to offer useful advice. In the context of this article, furthermore, there is the possibility that the value of experience will not necessarily prove to be a good traveller - there are obvious economic, social and political differences between the situation facing a UK example and examples from Central and Eastern Europe.

However, despite the limitations and in the light of the visits and discussions at Brookes by various colleagues from Central and Eastern Europe it is possible to highlight some key learned experiences over the period 1987-1995. Perhaps these can be summarised for prospective providers of undergraduate-style tourism education as follows:

- Establish a core body of knowledge and ideas - relevant on a local, national and international scale - that are progressively introduced.

- On a parallel basis establish an integrated programme of essential, transferable skills -literacy, numeracy computer ability, oral and written ability.

- Organise meaningful student-industry visits via assessed field visits.

- Encourage the integration of relevant, quality visiting speakers into taught modules.

- Develop a range of assessment procedures that both reflect employer requirements and academic standards.

- Research the possibility of creating meaningful student work placements and/or help facilitate other student-led industry contact.

- Seek to develop research and consultancy units alongside the teaching unit.

Of course this list is by no means either all-encompassing or prescriptive. What it represents is a sample of what is considered to be good practice in the delivery of education at undergraduate level with the benefit of experience over the period 1987-1995. Some aspects only emerged as the course was up and running - such as the need to deliver an extended tourism core which excluded non-field students and, therefore, encouraged greater academic and social unity. It is clear that no amount of careful planning can forestall the emergence of problems, both major and minor. Furthermore, circumstances do also change and today's model may be moribund with the changed circumstances of five or ten years' time. One would hope, however, that most of the basic tenets proposed here would still be considered fundamentally sound.

## References

CNAA (1993). *Review of Tourism Studies Degree Courses*. Council for National Academic Awards, London.

Ryan, C. (1995). 'Tourism Courses: a new concern for new times?' *Tourism Management*, 16, pp. 97-100.

Gunn, A. (1984). 'Tourism Education: filling the void'. *Tourism Management*, 5, pp. 234-235.

Evans, J., (1993). 'Tourism Graduates: a case of over-production'. *Tourism Management*, 14, pp.243-246.

# Chapter 12

# The tourism core curriculum: a role for behavioural studies?

**Chris Holloway**

## INTRODUCTION

In this chapter I will look at the historical development of tourism programmes and their curricula within the higher education sector in the UK, and the tension which emerges from efforts to provide academic rigour within a curriculum that strives for vocational relevance. A feature of higher education over the past decade has been the rapid growth of tourism programmes, without a commensurate increase in jobs which are seen as 'suitable for tourism graduates' in the marketplace; and with this expansion academics have come to recognise that the present confused and ad hoc development of post-compulsory education cannot continue. Many of those involved with tourism education would agree that there is now a clear need for a core curriculum for the study of tourism which is capable of maintaining the necessary academic rigour without losing its credibility with employers as a foundation programme for work in the industry. However, inevitably some academics fear that 'relevance' will be interpreted by those employed in the industry as providing job-specific or transferable business skills, rather than knowledge and understanding. This concern becomes greater as the National Council for Vocational Qualifications (NCVQ) presses for their tests of competence to be integrated with qualifications in the higher education sector. Compromises are essential, and the paper makes the case for the academic study of behavioural studies as one means of integrating a well-established body of knowledge within a more broadly based programme of study suited for entry to the travel and tourism industry, while examining the extent to which this is already implemented in existing vocational tourism degrees.

This is a message that should not be lost on countries such as those in Central and Eastern Europe which are currently re-evaluating the direction of their vocational education and training for the tourism industry. These countries share a strong tradition of formal 'classic' higher education and a respect for the academic rigour that such study entails. Elitism in education is not easily lost, regardless of the political hue of the government of the day, and the rigid divisions between the old humanities-based courses and the suspect developing vocational education is as strong in these countries as anywhere in Europe. Vocational education must gain and retain the respect of the society in which it is developing, if it is to flourish.

## CURRICULUM DEVELOPMENT: THEORY AND PRACTICE

Curriculum development, which has engaged philosophers of education at the compulsory school level (and in the education departments of higher education institutions) for many years, is now becoming a subject of focus in British higher education, as pressure grows to vocationalise the curricula of post-compulsory schooling. Tourism as a subject of study has already been a feature of the General Certificate of Secondary Education (GCSE) (16 years +) curriculum for some years, and developments to introduce the subject at Advanced (A) level (18+, university entrance qualification) in secondary schools are already well advanced, gaining the subject a greater measure of academic respectability. Meanwhile, there is confusion as the distinction between further and higher education becomes blurred, as colleges of Further Education (FE) introduce vocational degrees into their institutions, while universities are seeking to raise income through broadening their markets and developing sub-degree and in-service short course programmes. The old divisions between vocational education in the further education sector and an academic education 'for its own sake' in the universities no longer hold true.

As the segregation of work and leisure has increased in society, so has that between vocational and 'humanistic' education. Humanistic education has been defined as containing two essential ingredients; personal development and social consciousness (Saylor, 1977). Arguably, in vocational education, 'personal development' has been seen all too frequently in purely instrumental terms, as a means of ensuring that the graduate offers employable skills such as communication, rather than in terms of the development of the inner self.

The problem of obtaining balance in the curriculum is not a new one. As Wiles (1977) points out, curriculum design has always concerned itself with the need to ensure a balance between subjects. The discourse becomes more complex as what is seen by society as pertinent knowledge becomes more diverse and confused, and as vocational courses attempt to bridge the humanities and technical subjects. As Charity James (1965) put it, "in the knowledge explosion, it is in the areas between subjects that the great advances are being made". Educationalists share a reluctance to educate merely to meet the needs of the workplace, and if success in education is to be measured only by numbers employed and the type of job secured, many would argue that this is an abuse of the purpose of higher education. Certainly, where tourism is concerned, reports produced in the UK reflect increasing concern with the failure to match supply of, and demand for, graduates (CNAA, 1993), which suggests that the observer's view of vocational tourism degrees has little to do with personal development and social consciousness. However, it must also be recognised that academics have to a great extent been hoist by their own petard, in claiming that their newly developed tourism degrees reflect growing demand for jobs in the industry. The fact is that many graduates from tourism programmes will be expected initially to work at routine clerical or customer servicing positions. On the one hand, cynical educationalists would argue that the purpose of vocational education in this framework is to fit the employee to the job, "to liberate his (sic) mind, but make him a productive citizen, willing to work at meaningless, absurd jobs" (Peterson and Park, 1977). An alternative explanation which would place more value on a liberal-vocational education might be to suggest that an in-depth knowledge of behavioural studies would enable the graduate employed in even the humblest customer relations job to fulfil their tasks in this area far more effectively than they are currently doing. Empathy and understanding for the consumer do not come easily to young people working in the travel industry - yet arguably it is precisely these young people who can ensure product differentiation in what has become an increasingly homogeneous product. A sound understanding of the psychology and sociology of the consumer and of the tourist satisfies both the need for academic depth and vocational relevance.

## HISTORICAL DEVELOPMENT OF TOURISM PROGRAMMES IN THE UK

The definitive history of tourism education in the UK has yet to be written, although a number of prominent educationalists over the past twenty years have made useful contributions to the subject (Airey, 1988; Airey *et al.*, 1993; Cooper *et al.*, 1992; English Tourist Board, 1988; HM Inspectorate, 1992; Lawson, 1974). Many of these contributions, however, reveal significant gaps in analysis. There have been few attempts, for example, to relate the development of degree programmes to the expansion of further and higher business studies qualifications at sub-degree level, or to comment on the lack of focus on liberal and humanities studies within such programmes, still less to examine these developments comparatively with other European countries (Airey, 1995). These are significant omissions, given the importance attached to the liberal arts in tourism education on the continent. Few tourism degrees in other European countries fail to include at least one module which can be positively identified as a liberal studies subject, typically such subjects as architecture, archaeology, history or fine arts. In some countries, notably France, the native language is also included as a compulsory element in the course.

In Britain, tourism programmes at undergraduate level can be traced to the introduction of option modules in tourism on hospitality management programmes at the Universities of Surrey and Strathclyde in 1964, with postgraduate courses leading to the Diploma/Msc in Tourism Management launched at these institutions in 1972. These were themselves developments from lower level courses offered earlier for the training of technician level staff in the hotel and catering industry. However, post A level courses in tourism have their origin earlier, in the Higher National Diplomas in Business Studies (Tourism) offered at Bournemouth and Ealing colleges of further education from as early as 1967 and 1968 respectively. These in turn were developed from the lower level Ordinary National Diplomas in Business Studies which had flourished in the expansion of business education during the early 1960s.

Thus, tourism as a field of study was one developed ‘bottom-up’ in the UK, and like other courses seeking academic respectability through higher level qualifications, it has generally been viewed with suspicion by academics from older established institutions, secure in their single subject disciplines and reluctant to embrace the new opportunities provided by the expansion of vocationally relevant programmes that were developed to meet the government’s objectives in the aftermath of the Robbins Report of the early 1960s. Such programmes failed to gain the advantages that could have been offered by ‘top-down’ course development, where curriculum planners would be reluctant to abandon traditional core subjects of a liberal education. Furthermore, tourism as a field of study derived almost entirely from hospitality or business and management courses, themselves interdisciplinary by nature. Only where tourism has arisen largely as an extension of the discipline of geography can one find alternative routes to academic rigour, in fields such as planning, heritage or conservation studies.

Airey (1995) has argued that tension should not arise between vocational relevance and academic rigour; what he sees as essential is that the content of vocational courses reflects their aims and objectives. In his view, the necessary rigour has been demonstrated in vocational programmes, as exemplified in HMI reports on extant degree programmes. However, it is my contention that such courses face three threats which would severely undermine the academic value of higher education:

1. the extension of tourism programmes to encompass leisure, sports studies, hospitality or other fields of study is resulting in shallower, not deeper, study of the subject of tourism;

2. the practice of modularisation of degree programmes, leading to a "pick ’n’ mix" approach to tourism studies, adds to the danger of superficiality in studies. One result of this approach has been that students select those modules which are seen as non-numerate or less demanding. Sadly, the study of tourism itself is too often perceived in this light;

3. the emphasis on vocational orientation to the exclusion of the study of subjects for their own sake is leading to students adopting a narrowly focused view of higher education, reflected in the superficiality of their studies.

We are therefore facing a situation in which students are entering programmes which many feel have become increasingly shallow and diverse in approach, less structured, and still insufficiently meeting the criteria for vocational relevance established by employers in tourism.

## THE DEVELOPMENT OF A CORE CURRICULUM FOR TOURISM

Against this background, the Council for National Academic Awards (CNAA), shortly before its demise in 1993, published its Review of Tourism Studies Degree Courses (CNAA, 1993), arguing the case for a common core tourism curriculum in first degrees and postgraduate programmes. In the words of the report:

> Without agreed core concepts, to give the study a shared vision and academic integrity, there is a danger that "tourism" could mean whatever tutors wish it to mean .... Growing diversity would increase the existing levels of confusion among prospective students and employees (para 8.5).

The review concluded that there was a strong case for defining a minimum core curriculum for those programmes whose objectives were to provide vocationally relevant tourism education.

With the establishment in the UK of the National Liaison Group (NLG) for Higher Education in Tourism at the end of 1993, this objective was taken up. The NLG was created as a means of continuing the work of the CNAA in relation to tourism education, in the vacuum which followed its termination. Through a process of consultation with academics and employers, broad agreement was reached on the key material forming the body of knowledge with which it was expected any tourism graduate should demonstrate familiarity. In drawing this up, the NLG also took into account the variations in core curriculum to be found in tourism programmes taught in other countries, especially those within the European Union. This resulted in identifying seven distinct 'areas of knowledge' which should form the foundation for any tourism degree programme:

**Core curriculum for tourism studies:**
1. The meaning and nature of tourism
2. The structure of the tourism industry
3. The dimensions of tourism and issues of measurement
4. The significance and impact of tourism
5. The marketing of tourism
6. Tourism planning and development
7. Policy and management in tourism.

## THE APPLIED BEHAVIOURAL STUDIES RESEARCH EXERCISE

Given that any tourism degree will be by definition interdisciplinary, and that most employers (CNAA, 1993) and many academics judge business and management studies to be the logical framework with which to underpin its study, are suitable alternatives available which can be judged both academically respectable and vocationally relevant?

One likely candidate was thought to be the social sciences, in particular psychology and sociology. These subjects do not generally appear as 'pure' social sciences in tourism degrees, but most programmes do include some study of the applications of these disciplines, with some, albeit limited, study of general theory. Knowledge of the application of these disciplines to tourism is certainly vocationally relevant, for those involved with marketing and planning for tourism, as well as those dealing with tourists face to face; and both are valuable as subjects worthy of study for their own sake, while stretching students academically. Both subjects were thought ideal as elements of a tourism curriculum, whether within a business framework, or as stand-alone disciplines. As a starting point for discussion, it was thought useful to see the extent to which the subjects already appear in tourism degree programmes in the UK.

A research programme was undertaken to establish academics' views on the role of behavioural studies applied to tourism. Specifically, the research set out to discover the extent to which Applied Behavioural Studies as a field was being taught on degree courses in the UK previously identified as vocationally-oriented. Thus the study was carried out within the constraints imposed by this definition, and by implication, this relates largely to courses which are business studies oriented, while other courses which have developed around a core of social science theory (such as Roehampton Institute of Higher Education's Sociology and Anthropology of Tourism) and whose objectives are not defined in vocational terms might still be seen as having a useful role to play in many sectors of the industry. For the purposes of this research, 'Applied Behavioural Studies' was defined as the psychology and sociology of travel and tourism, or any closely related disciplines such as the anthropology of tourism. The economics of tourism was specifically excluded.

Twenty-two institutions identified by the NLG as offering vocational degrees in tourism were circulated with a questionnaire. Eighteen replies were received, 13 of which came from universities and five from institutes of higher education. In all, these institutes offered 21 first degrees in tourism and five postgraduate qualifications.

Questions were included which would establish which institutions included Applied Behavioural Studies (hereafter referred to as ABS) as a field of study within their degrees, how the topic was integrated into the curriculum and the importance the institution attached to the subject; to determine the extent to which the institutions viewed the content of the syllabus as academic or vocational, and to solicit their views on their students' perception of the subject; and to explore the relative weighting given to theory and practice in the syllabus.

In spite of the directives offered on the meaning of the term, clearly many academics had difficulty in interpreting the scale of ABS material within their syllabi.

Nine of the 21 tourism programmes at first degree level included ABS as a stand-alone module within the programme, and six of these also included it as elements in other modules; a further nine programmes incorporated it into other modules. Of the five postgraduate qualifications, only one included a stand-alone module in ABS. Only one university did not offer any input of ABS on their undergraduate programme; significantly, this was one where industry has played a major role in the development of the curriculum.

A question devoted to determining the amount of time spent in teaching the subject proved difficult for some institutions to answer, depending to some extent on individual interpretations of ABS. However, responses indicated that tutors perceive ABS as falling into two categories; that in which considerations of management are paramount, and which involve the study of the tourist as consumer; and that in which the nature of the tourist, and their interaction with hosts and other tourists, is the focus of study.

It was clear that a number of tutors interpreted organisational behaviour, or 'people at work' as being included in this subject, although this had been deliberately excluded in the research design and efforts had been made to ensure the topic under study was to be applied to tourists only, not employees. Clearly, however, it is difficult to distinguish between the two in some instances - for example, in studies of the interaction between tourists and tour guides.

A question on module titles and the hours devoted to teaching the subject drew widely differing replies (see Appendix 12.1). There was considerable variation between the number of hours allocated in different institutions to the subject, ranging from a low of about 13.5 hours to a high of 195 hours on undergraduate programmes. In postgraduate programmes, input appears to fall around the norm of 40-45 hours, which would represent about 13-15% of the teaching time recommended by the NLG to be devoted to core curriculum studies, and here the focus of investigation is the manner in which the tourist impinges on the management of organisations.

To a question on whether teaching of ABS depended upon some prior knowledge of social science theory, only six institutions had this prerequisite, while nine did not. Two out of the three postgraduate courses responding to this question indicated that no prior knowledge of general theory was required.

What becomes clear is that many distinct approaches are being taken to the teaching of ABS on tourism degree programmes. Some develop their programmes in the belief that social sciences applied to tourism should be taught as a distinct entity, while others see it as permeating many modules of the programme. Some modules approach the teaching of ABS from a base of general theory within the module, others deliver the groundwork in other modules and apply it only within the tourism module.

Because detailed syllabi were not examined, it is not possible to discover the full extent to which commonalities in approach exist, although it is apparent that there is a growing body of knowledge which is beginning to form a commonly accepted core for ABS syllabi (see Appendix 12.2). Doubtless this content is becoming increasingly focused as new textbooks appear, specialising in this field. However, individual syllabi are always subject to the interpretation given to them by the tutor assigned to teach them, and, as Burgoyne (1984) recognises, "the need to satisfy multiple stakeholders can mean that the curriculum as taught may differ from that spelled out in official documents".

Notwithstanding the limited research into syllabus detail, it is still clear that substantial differences in approach to the teaching of ABS remain. Further research will be needed to be certain of whether an underpinning of theory is delivered before its application to the subject of tourism in degree programmes, although the findings tentatively suggest this is not always the case. In terms of academic rigour, this might give grounds for concern among some educationalists, particularly social scientists. However, there are grounds for claiming that, while a common core for ABS is a long way from realisation, some commonality of topics is emerging in degree programmes. Features such as myth, image, 'staging', culture and national identity related to tourism are evident in many syllabi, while the influence of consumerism on tourists, in respect to issues such as decision-making and choice, is also a frequent subject of study. In areas of organisation and management studies, one finds a focus on crowd behaviour, queuing theory and management, the psychology of the visitor experience, group dynamics, leadership styles and the management of people, staff and customers.

Respondents were asked how far they saw the subject as theoretical versus practical. Twelve institutions - two-thirds of those replying - felt that there needed to be an equal mix between the theoretical and practical in undergraduate programmes. None saw the subject as predominantly practical, and only one as predominantly theoretical. It is interesting to note, however, that one of the three postgraduate programmes identified the subject as predominantly practical.

Asked to define the main purpose behind the teaching of ABS, six undergraduate tutors (and two postgraduate) saw the subject as enabling students to function more effectively in their future careers. A further six undergraduate, and one postgraduate, tutors saw it as predominantly designed to develop students academically, while two saw both functions as of equal importance. Asked their perception of the way their students perceived the ABS input, ten felt that the subject was seen by students as a means of improving their work performance, while only four thought that students viewed it as a subject of interest for its own sake. All three postgraduate tutors replying to this question felt that students treated the material mainly as a means of improving their job performance. However, some tutors expressed caution in their interpretation of students' views, claiming that while students may well have a very practical orientation towards the material in the initial stages of the programme, they come to see it over time as a means of self-development. It would be interesting to know to what extent this is also true of other subjects in the tourism syllabus.

Asked to judge the importance of ABS as a component of a vocational tourism course, the respondent tutors clearly see the subject as an integral element. Eleven thought it essential or very important in undergraduate programmes, and only one thought it to be of little importance. Two of the postgraduate programme tutors also rated it very highly.

Four respondents took the view that ABS should be taught as a distinct module in an undergraduate tourism degree programme, while four others felt it should be taught as a compulsory element in other modules. A further five recommended it highly as an option in the programme.

Respondents were asked to elaborate on their reasons for the relative importance they attached to ABS in their curricula. Comments reflected their views on the significance of tourism as a 'people business' and the importance of the subject for the operation of a successful business. Statements included:

> "It's a people business"
> "The international context requires behavioural studies"
> "Competition and diversification require a better understanding of motivation"
> "Business must be responsive to ethical concerns"
> "We can't provide appropriate facilities and managed experiences unless we understand our clients"
> "It is essential for tourism planning and marketing".

However, one or two respondents questioned the role of ABS in a business related course. It was recognised that it could be difficult to cater adequately for an ABS input in an already crowded business curriculum.

To conclude, there is generally recognition among academics responsible for tourism degree planning and teaching that ABS has an important role to play in any vocational tourism degree. Getting the balance right in its delivery is problematic, however. Given that tourism is in itself a multi-disciplinary subject and also tends to be taught within the framework of a subject which is itself multi-disciplinary, the extent to which a sound underpinning of general theory in the social sciences can be delivered is problematic.

The research did not set out specifically to find out academics' attitudes towards the concept of an applied social science degree as an appropriate framework for employment in the tourism business, but this would be a useful project for future investigation, as would a study of employers' attitudes to such a course.

**References**

Airey, D. (1988). Tourism Teaching in the United Kingdom. Paper presented at *Teaching Tourism into the 1990s, International Conference for Tourism Educators*, University of Surrey, 19-22 July.

Airey, D. (1995). *Tourism Degrees - Past, Present and Future*. Inaugural lecture, Nottingham Business School, Nottingham Trent University, 31 Jan.

Airey, D., A. Ladkin and V.T.C. Middleton (1993). *The Profile of Tourism Studies Degree Courses in the UK 1993*. London, National Liaison Group for Tourism in Higher Education.

Burgoyne, J. (1994). Curricula and Teaching Methods in Management Education. In: Goodlad, S. (ed.). *Education for the Professions - Quis Custodiet?* Guildford, Society for Research into Higher Education and NFER-Nelson, pp. 141-7.

CNAA (1993). Committee for Consumer and Leisure Studies, *Review of Tourism Studies Degree Courses*, Feb, par. 6.15.

Cooper, C., R. Scales, and J. Westlake, (1992). The Anatomy of Tourism and Hospitality Educators in the UK, *Tourism Management*, June, pp. 234-47.

HM Inspectorate (1992). *Higher Education in the Polytechnics and Colleges; Hotel Catering and Tourism Management*. London, Department of Education and Science.

James, C. (1968). *Young Lives at Stake: a Reappraisal of Secondary Schools*. Glasgow, Collins.

Lawson, M. (1974). *Teaching Tourism*. London, Tourism International Press.

Peterson, J. and R. Park (1977). Values in career Education: Some Pitfalls, in Hass, G. (ed.). *Curriculum Planning: a New Approach.* Boston, Mass, Allyn and Bacon.

English Tourist Board (1988). *Education and the Tourist Industry*. London, ETB.

Saylor, J.G. (1977). Humanistic Education: the Minimum Essentials. In: G. Hass (ed.). *Curriculum Planning: a New Approach*. Boston Mass, Allyn and Bacon, 13-6.

Wiles, K. (1977). 'Seeking Balance in the Curriculum'. In: G. Hass (ed.), *Curriculum Planning: A New Approach*, pp.247-251.

## Appendix 12.1

Titles of modules including ABS, and hours devoted to its teaching.
NB: hours shown are hours devoted to ABS within the module, as defined by the respondent.

| Institution | title | hours | total hours |
|---|---|---|---|
| 1. | Socio-cultural impacts of tourism | 28 | 84 |
| | Anthropology of tourism | 56 | |
| 2. | Consumer service management | 6 | 36 |
| | Current issues in leisure | 10 | |
| | International tourism | 20 | |
| 3. | People, work and tourism | 60 | 120 |
| | Human resources management | 60 | |
| 4. | Sociology and anthropology of tourism | 60 | 90 |
| | International travel and tourism development | 24 | |
| | Travel and tourism business environment | 6 | |
| 5. | Consumer behaviour in leisure and tourism | 40 | 140 |
| | Current issues in tourism and leisure | 30 | |
| | Introduction to leisure | 40 | |
| | Human resource management | 30 | |
| 6. | Leisure management | 12 | 42 |
| | Service sector marketing | 24 | |
| | Introduction to leisure and tourism | 6 | |
| 7. | Management, marketing and strategies for tourism and social responsibility | 45 | 45 |
| | Meaning and significance of social responsibility | | |
| 8. | Planning and development | 4 | 24 |
| | Management studies | 8 | |
| | Visitor attraction and leisure management | 4 | |
| | Welcome host training | 8 | |
| 9. | Functional management | 40 | 40 |
| 10. | Human resource management | 12 | 18 |
| | International marketing | 6 | |

| Institution | title | hours | total hours |
| --- | --- | --- | --- |
| 11. | Personal development | 36 | 162 |
| | Managing people | 36 | |
| | Introduction to tourism | 24 | |
| | History of tourism | 24 | |
| | Social anthropology of tourism | 42 | |
| 12. | Tourism behaviour | 45 | 65 |
| | Tourism research methods | 20 | |
| 13. | Tourism behaviour (option) | 13.5 | 13.5 |
| 14. | Behavioural Studies in tourism | 66 | 66 |
| 15. | Customer in leisure/food industries | n/a | n/a |
| | Operations management | n/a | |
| | Management strategies | n/a | |
| 16. | Leisure in society | 50 | 195 |
| | Tourism frameworks (option) | 30 | |
| | European tourism (option) | 25 | |
| | Tourism planning (option) | 30 | |
| | Tourism marketing (option) | 30 | |
| | International tourism (option) | 30 | |
| 17. | Behavioural studies/psychology | 60 | 180 |
| | Cultural studies and language | 60 | |
| | Cultural tourism studies | 60 | |
| 18. | Tourism framework | 30 | 138 |
| | Tourism facilities management | 15 | |
| | European tourism | 25 | |
| | Tourism development | 8 | |
| | Tourism marketing | 30 | |
| | International hospitality management | 30 | |
| 19. | People and hospitality management | 66 | 119 |
| | Human resource management | 44 | |
| | Hospitality advertising and consumer response | 3 | |
| | Tourism management | 3 | |
| | International tourism | 3 | |

## APPENDIX 12.2

Syllabus content of ABS material (as communicated by respondents).

| Institution | Syllabus includes: |
|---|---|
| 1. | the individual and society<br>motivation<br>group dynamics<br>anthropological implications of travel and tourism<br>changing leisure patterns<br>personality, attitudes, behaviour<br>tourism and myth<br>guided tours and 'staging'<br>culture and national identity<br>understanding, impact. |
| 2. | human resource management<br>selection of service employees |
| 3. | sociological aspects of tourism<br>management of people, staff and customers |
| 4. | crowd behaviour<br>queue management<br>psychology of the visitor experience<br>soccer hooliganism<br>holidaymakers and behaviour |
| 5. | introduction to psychology and sociology<br>behavioural studies<br>organisation behaviour and group dynamics |
| 6. | attitudes<br>culture<br>theories of consumption<br>research methods<br>race, gender, class, age<br>post-modernism<br>social theory<br>social stratification<br>life cycle<br>the role of the State<br>organisational behaviour, leadership and motivation |
| 7. | tourist behaviour, decision-making |
| 8. | basic theories and concepts of anthropology and sociology |
| 9. | psychology, sociology and general theories |
| 10. | choice, perception, social/demographic framework,<br>social stratification, equality, community<br>(mainly integrated through the modules) |

APPENDIX 12.3

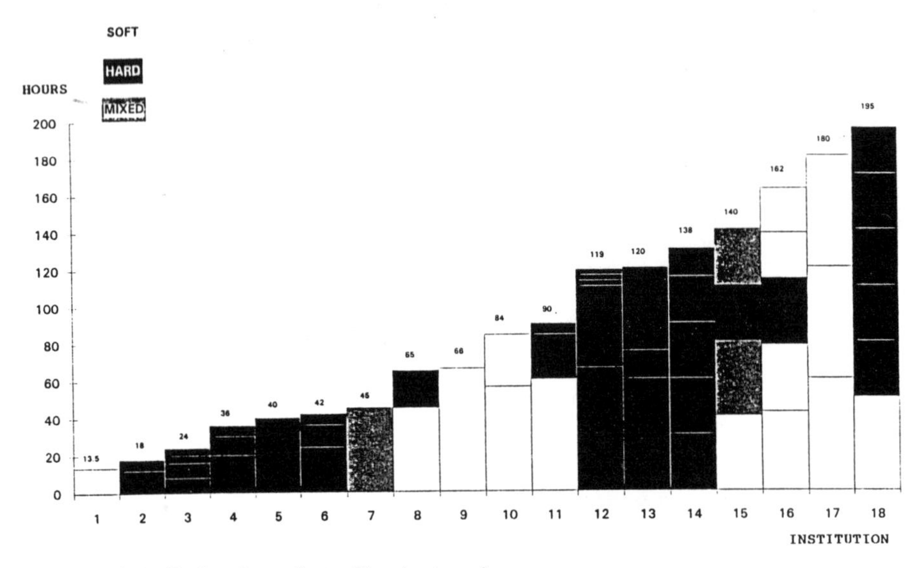


**Figure 12.1: Behavioural studies in tourism**

# Chapter 13

# Towards the development of sustainable rural tourism in Eastern Europe

**John Swarbrooke**

## INTRODUCTION

Rural tourism is a well established phenomenon in Western Europe. Furthermore, the market for rural tourism is growing amongst Western Europeans as they seek to enjoy holiday experiences that are very different to their everyday lives in the relatively highly urbanised and industrialised countries of Western Europe.

This is taking place at the same time as a rural crisis is sweeping across Western Europe which is threatening the future of many rural regions. The crisis is a result of changes in agricultural practice, the power of food manufacturers and retailers, and changes in the Common Agricultural Policy, and the GATT Agreement, amongst other reasons.

Increasingly, therefore, people are looking to tourism as a way of helping give these regions a sustainable future. The alternative would be to simply let the economic and political forces now take over, and see rural areas become urbanised or derelict. However, in most Western European countries this is not acceptable. Rural areas are highly valued because these areas hold a very important place in the nation's culture and history. They are where the food is produced and the places where its citizens go to seek relaxation, peace, and active recreation in their leisure time. They are also the places where many urban families have their roots, the birthplaces of either themselves or their parents. Therefore, action is being taken to try to halt the decline of rural regions across Western Europe.

Clearly the situation in Eastern Europe is different, but the countries of Eastern Europe are increasingly being influenced by the same factors that are affecting the countries of Western Europe. This is particularly the case for those countries which are aspiring to become members of the European Union in the not too distant future.

The aim of this chapter is to offer some ideas based on the Western European experience that might, with suitable modification, help colleagues in Eastern European countries to develop their own rural tourism sectors in a sustainable manner.

Due to the lack of space it is only possible to talk about Eastern Europe in general terms. However, the author recognises and gladly acknowledges that the countries of Eastern Europe are very different in many ways, and face different challenges in the development of rural tourism.

**The potential benefits of rural tourism for Eastern Europe**

The main potential benefits of rural tourism for Eastern Europe include the following:

1 At the national level, a range of economic benefits including the creation of jobs and an influx of valuable foreign currency.

2 Tax revenue for central and local government through sales taxes, airport taxes, corporate taxation, and taxes on employees salaries.

3 Revenue for central and local government arising from their ownership of key elements of the tourism product, such as museums.

4 Rural tourism would provide a stimulus for infrastructure development and could also provide some of the money needed to fund these improvements. Such infrastructure might include regional airports, rail services, and the local road network. This infrastructure could then be used to facilitate the growth of other industries in rural regions.

5 The growth of tourism in rural areas might also provide both an incentive and funding for conservation work. In other words, the fact that rural landscapes, flora and fauna are the key resource base of the rural tourism product might persuade decision-makers of the importance of rural conservation, for any failure to conserve could result in the loss of the economic benefits of tourism. However, tourism could also generate revenue that might be used to fund conservation through a tourist tax perhaps, or even voluntary donations.

These types of benefits could equally be talked about in relation to forms of tourism in other milieus such as coastal resorts and urban areas. However, there are also some benefits of rural tourism which are specific to rural areas. These are outlined below:

- helping maintain and improve the economic and social viability of farms and rural communities in a range of ways, including:
- increasing farm income by offering accommodation services and meals at the farm;
- providing an outlet for the direct sale of farm produce to visitors;

- providing a rationale for the conservation of traditional foods and drinks because of their appeal to tourists;
- acting as a catalyst for the development of small businesses in local areas which would be set up to service the needs of tourists;
- offering opportunities for social interaction for local people who can live isolated lives in farming communities.

These few examples show how tourism might help prevent what can be one of the worst problems in rural areas, namely, migration, which can leave villages de-populated and lead to the desertification of farming landscapes. Tourism can encourage the more entrepreneurial people to stay rather than leave and go to urban areas. Thus, tourism can play a part in achieving a sustainable future for the rural regions of Eastern Europe.

However, as we will see later, rural tourism can bring costs too, if it is not well managed. Therefore we will now move on to look at some principles that should guide the development of rural tourism to ensure that it brings benefits rather than costs to the host community.

## TOWARDS A MODEL OF SUSTAINABLE RURAL TOURISM IN EASTERN EUROPE

There is no universally agreed definition of sustainable rural tourism. In this context it is taken to mean tourism which contributes positively to the economic and social viability of rural communities, while not damaging the social fabric of these communities, and the physical environment in which they are situated, both today and in the future. This definition puts communities and people at the centre and recognises the importance of the economic dimension to rural areas, as well as simply being concerned with the physical environment in isolation from the people who reside in this environment.

Before going on to look at the guiding principles that might underpin a model of sustainable rural tourism in Europe, perhaps we should briefly define two crucial terms, namely, rural areas and rural tourism. Rurality is a difficult concept to define as it is both a factual matter and an emotional matter. However, it is generally accepted that rural areas are characterised by a relatively high proportion of the population being employed in agriculture and a relatively low percentage of people living in urban communities. However, because the level of industrialisation and urbanisation varies dramatically between European countries it is a relative term, at best. In other words, what is considered rural in the highly urbanised Netherlands, is very different to what would be considered rural in sparsely populated regions such as Northern Scandinavia. Similar differences can be seen in Eastern Europe, although perhaps not to the same degree, as overall, Eastern Europe is more rural than Western Europe in spite of the high level of industrialisation and urbanisation in certain regions of Eastern Europe.

Turning to the second term, rural tourism involves the use of rural areas for leisure and recreation purposes, and to a much lesser extent, business purposes, largely by urban dwellers from the same country or a foreign country. However, there are different types of rural tourism that exist under this broad umbrella definition. These include:

- a long holiday to a destination in another country thousands of kilometres away or a half-day visit to a rural attraction just a short journey away from one's home;
- rural holidays can be active (cycling, riding, and walking for example) or passive, such as relaxation;
- some holidays in the countryside are based in one place while others involve touring around a number of destinations;
- visits to friends and relatives who live in a rural area.

In relation to rural tourism development in Eastern Europe, a sustainable approach will have two aspects, depending on the local situation, as follows:

- a focus on visitor management in areas where tourist numbers are great, and the aim is to protect the physical environment and the host community from the negative impact of over-use by tourists;
- an emphasis on the development of tourism and the attraction of more tourists to increase the social and economic benefits of tourism, particularly in rural areas which have fairly serious problems such as depopulation, landscape degradation, high unemployment, and low incomes.

It is now time for the author to set out what he considers to be some useful principles that might underpin the development of sustainable rural tourism in Eastern Europe. This is thought to be more helpful than trying to offer a single model of sustainable rural tourism that would clearly not be relevant given the great national differences in the situation between different Eastern European countries. The suggested principles of sustainable rural tourism are listed below:

(1) Wherever possible, the development of rural tourism should be controlled and managed by the local community as a whole, rather than by outside agencies or entrepreneurs. This should help to ensure that the major benefits of tourism are principally enjoyed by the indigenous population.

(2) The types of tourism developed need to be based on, and sympathetic to, the unique history, social structure, culture and physical environment of the area, rather than being insensitive to, and harmful to, the different heritage of each specific place.

(3) Ensuring that where culture and heritage is the core element in the tourism product that is offered to visitors, that it is authentic rather than synthetic. There are a number of implications of such an approach including the idea that local people should decide which stories they wish visitors to be told about their community, and how these stories should be told.

(4) The volume of tourists should be appropriate to the ability of the area to absorb them without adverse effects on the local society and environment.

(5) Encouraging social contact between visitors and their hosts, including opportunities for tourists to meet local people who are not involved in the tourism industry in their everyday life. Furthermore, this contact should be based upon mutual respect and informal rather than formal contacts, avoiding helping the 'master and servant' relationship which is often seen in hotels in coastal resorts, for example.

Furthermore, this contact should be used to help visitors understand the realities of modern rural life and the area in question, helping to dispel some myths about rural life that can exist, such as the idea that rural life is somehow 'unchanging' and 'picturesque'.

(6) Pricing the product so that visitors pay the full cost of the experience they enjoy, rather than expecting part of the cost to be met by local people who may not even be involved in the tourism industry at all.

(7) Likewise, given the aims of sustainable rural tourism to generate economic benefits and the fact that the capacity of rural areas to accommodate tourists is limited, it could be argued that rural tourism products should be priced relatively highly to maximise the economic benefits and restrict demand.

(8) The benefits of tourism should be spread as widely as possible amongst the resident population of the area, particularly to those people who are the most economically and socially disadvantaged.

(9) Attempting to guide tourists away from so-called 'honeypot' areas, which are already heavily developed for tourism, and from the more affluent regions, towards less developed areas which are most in need of the economic benefits of tourism.

(10) Finding ways of integrating second-home owners and in-migrants into the community, and increasing their commitment and contribution towards the life and future development of the community.

(11) The development of partnerships between state tourism agencies and private enterprises, and the local community, which should encourage these agencies and enterprises to behave responsibly and make a long term commitment to the area.

(12) The existence of mechanisms to ensure that the quality of product is maintained and that the tourists holiday experience is enhanced by the development of a sustainable form of tourism. This is important because tourism can only ever be possible if customers want to continue to buy the product which is on offer, and believe that it offers good value for money.

(13) Recognising that ideas on sustainable tourism cannot stand still. They have to be continually developed to take account of changes in tourism management theory, rural life, concepts of sustainability, and tourist consumer behaviour.

As we shall see later, it is the author's belief that the achievement of such a form of rural tourism will require a market-led approach rather than relying purely on state policy and regulation. This is because the current political and economic situation in most Eastern European countries makes the latter unattractive or unacceptable. As countries move towards a more market-based economy it is logical that approaches to tourism management must reflect this trend.

Before we go on to look at how this form of tourism could be developed in practice, we will look at the current situation of rural tourism in Eastern Europe, as a background for the rest of the chapter.

## The current situation in Eastern Europe

Carrying out a current situation analysis in respect of rural tourism in Eastern Europe is a difficult task. There are differences in data collection methodologies between the different countries in the region, and the statistics that are available are usually some two years out of date. This is a particular problem in Eastern Europe where the situation changes so rapidly.

A major difficulty in relation to the subject of this paper is that the data that are available, in English language publications at least, do not usually separate rural tourism from other forms of tourism. Where particular types of data are isolated from the general picture they tend to relate to matters such as business tourism, and occupancy rates in major hotels, for example. This perhaps reflects the relatively low priority that is generally being accorded to rural tourism currently in Eastern Europe.

However, it may also be due to the fact that most of the widely available published data appear to focus on the international flow of tourists to Eastern European countries. It is, the author suspects, the case that rural tourism is quite heavily developed in domestic markets through the ownership of second homes, for example. Rural tourism also seems to play a significant part in the movement of tourists between certain Eastern European countries, particularly in terms of well-known upland areas like the Tatra Mountains of Southern Poland and the North of the Slovak Republic.

As yet, the Eastern European rural tourism product is hardly being marketed as such to Western tourists, with the exception of cultural holidays to places like the Rila Valley in Bulgaria, with its famous monasteries, or for activity holidays such as walking or skiing in the mountains of Bulgaria and Romania.

Some more controversial holidays have also been targeted at Western tourists such as hunting trips to hunt animals which are either non-existent or are protected by law in the tourists' own country.

This overall relative lack of marketing of the rural product to Western tourists may reflect a belief that it does not offer what these tourists seek, which as we shall see later is probably not true. However, it may also be due to a belief that there is not yet an adequate infrastructure to support rural tourism in many Eastern European regions. This may again be a result of a partial misunderstanding that adequate infrastructure means modern hotels, good roads, and organised excursions for example. For some Western tourists the existing situation would attract them because of the lack of such infrastructure, while the development of new purpose built hotels and the creation of organised excursions would take away this attraction. Market research therefore, is needed in key target markets before decisions are taken about the development of Eastern Europe's rural tourism infrastructure to ensure that it will meet the desires of consumers.

The potential results of trying to attract tourists to the rural regions of Eastern Europe are not difficult to imagine. Even if we discount the large number of new tourists who would be attracted by the marketing of rural tourism products, the existing international market alone in Eastern Europe gives some idea of the potential economic benefit that could be enjoyed by rural areas.

According to the World Tourism Organisation, approximately 49.1 million international visitors from outside Eastern Europe took holidays in the region in 1992, some 95% of whom were drawn from the rest of Europe. These tourists spent an estimated US $ 3,270 million (ECU 3,300 million), an increase of a third over the 1991 figure. However, Hungary alone accounted for some 40% of these international arrivals and 35% of the expenditure.

In addition, there are the millions of tourists who each year travel between the different countries of Eastern Europe.

Then, finally, there is the market of Western tourists who currently buy rural tourism products in Western Europe. Some of these tourists could be attracted to Eastern Europe by the lower prices, novelty value and fascinating rural lifestyles found in the East.

The potential of this market can be seen if we look at Western Europe's leading rural tourism destination, France, where in 1990, British tourists alone took well over 500,000 rural holidays, spending approximately FFR 1.5 Billion (ECU 245 million). This figure is an underestimate as it excludes many touring holidays that may have involved staying in the countryside, and there were 1.4 million of these taken in France by Britons alone in 1990 (Ministére du Tourisme, 1991). France also enjoys substantial flows of rural tourists from Germany, the Netherlands and Belgium, for example.

There are also growing numbers of Western European tourists enjoying rural holidays in Spain, Portugal, Ireland, and Greece, for instance. These are all potential consumers for the rural tourism products of Eastern Europe.

While international tourism to Eastern Europe is, as we have seen, at an early stage of development, the potential is clearly recognised. For example, Mazaraki (1993) outlined a number of rural products that offered the prospect of growth in Ukraine including health tourism in Transcarpathia and recreational activities in the forests of the Carpathian mountains.

The reports of the Economist Intelligence Unit (1992; 1993; 1994; 1995) on individual Eastern European countries have also illustrated the potential of rural tourism in each country as follows:

- Golf, riding, walking, skiing, and spa tourism are all seen to offer growth potential in the Czech Republic and Slovakia, as do the ancient castles, either as visitor attractions or luxury hotels.
- In Hungary, golf and riding were highlighted, as well as big game hunting in the Pilis Mountains, wine tours, and the re-launching of old spa resorts.
- Special interest holidays in the Bulgarian countryside including themes such as folklore events, ancient monasteries, wine, and hiking, while the potential for rural campsite based tourism was also identified.
- Activity holidays in Poland based on walking, camping, boating and skiing as well as visits to historic buildings such as the Jasna Gora monastery.

The clear point to emerge here is that while there is potential, the types of products are often similar, so that competition may be intense between Eastern

European countries.

We have now discussed the concept of sustainable rural tourism and briefly explored the current situation in Eastern Europe. It is now time for us to look at how sustainable rural tourism might be developed in Eastern Europe. The ideas that follow are based on the Western European experience so that some may be inapplicable to Eastern Europe, while others may require modification to make them appropriate to the regions of Eastern Europe. Nevertheless the ideas should at least stimulate debate which should result in decisions being taken in a more informed manner.

The author will argue that the most appropriate approach that should be taken to achieve sustainable rural tourism is a marketing one. However, the role of planning and regulation will also be briefly examined toward the end of the paper.

## A MARKETING APPROACH

A marketing approach, rather than a reliance on state control and regulation only, appears to be appropriate for Eastern Europe, for several reasons, notably:

- the move towards a market economy which is taking place across the countries of Eastern Europe albeit at varying paces and in different ways in different countries;
- the growing power of the tourism industry internationally;
- the increasing sophistication and higher expectations of tourists, particularly those who are the most experienced travellers and the highest spenders, and who form a clearly identifiable market segment.

These three trends all point to the relevance of adopting a marketing approach. However, it must be recognised that here we are talking about social marketing, in other words, marketing where the objectives are social rather than commercial. The aim is to use rural tourism to aid rural development rather than simply to make profits for individuals.

## UNDERSTANDING THE CONSUMER

In line with the modern concept of consumer-led marketing we should start by considering the consumer and their motivators, and the factors that determine the type of trips they will take. We must recognise that if consumers do not find a tourism product attractive they will not buy it, and as a result tourism will not develop at all, let alone become sustainable in the longer term.

In this discussion we will focus on the international market outside Eastern Europe, because that is the market the author knows best and it is one which is attractive to Eastern European countries because, for example, it brings foreign hard currency earnings.

The Western consumers who, in the author's opinion, are most likely to purchase the type of sustainable rural tourism outlined in this paper, will probably be those who are motivated by factors which mean they seek a holiday which provides opportunities to:

- live in an environment which is a contrast with the urban areas in which they live;
- relax;
- indulge in some physical exercise such as talking or cycling;
- observe cultures which are different to those with which they are familiar;
- learn a few words of a new language;
- make new friends amongst the local population;
- see new sights;
- try new food and drink.

As well as these general motivators, other groups may be attracted to rural Eastern Europe, for specific reasons, including:

- visiting friends and relatives;
- indulging in special interest holidays such as skiing, mountaineering, hunting, or painting, for example;
- health, in relation to rural spa resorts.

Destination marketers must take these motivators into account when designing rural tourism products. However, they also have to recognise that the holiday tourists purchase only partly reflects their motivations, they are also influenced by determinants. These are factors that influence the nature of a trip that a tourist actually takes. There are a number of different determinants, including:

- disposable income;
- available time;
- health;
- word of mouth recommendation;
- media images of destinations;
- availability of suitable tourism products;
- preferences for particular modes of transport and types of accommodation.

This list is only selective but it does indicate that whereas some determinants are incapable of being influenced by destination marketers, some can be influenced by the activities of marketers.

As far as the promotion of rural tourism destinations is concerned, it is necessary to divide the total market up into sub-groups or segments which share similar buying characteristics. These segments can then be targeted with appropriate messages. A number of criteria can be used to segment the overall market, including the following:

- the country of origin of the tourist;
- age;
- sex;
- stage in the family life-cycle;
- lifestyle;
- personality.

However, this requires sophisticated market research which is often beyond the means of most destination marketing agencies. We must also recognise that consumer behaviour is not easy to record or predict. Tourists can claim to behave in a certain way but in reality they may behave differently. Likewise, consumer behaviour changes over time with changes in personal circumstances and attitudes.

Overall, nevertheless, we can identify some market trends in the Western market which Eastern European countries should seek to exploit if they wish to develop sustainable rural tourism effectively. These include:

- the demand for more flexible types of holiday packages and a growth in independent travel;
- the desire by more and more people to use their holiday as an opportunity to learn something or develop a new skill;
- a wish to gain status by enjoying experiences which have not been experienced by many other people in their own country.

Again these, and the other trends, need to be taken into account by marketers seeking to attract international tourists, when they develop their marketing plans.

## THE MARKETING MIX

We will now consider the role of the Marketing Mix in the development of sustainable rural tourism. Destinations may manipulate the Marketing Mix to achieve their objectives. The Marketing Mix covers the following four elements:

1 The Product, both in terms of the individual elements of the product such as attractions and accommodation, as well as the way in which these elements are combined in packages.

(ii) Pricing policies.

(iii) Place, or rather distribution.

(iv) Promotional techniques including advertising and promotional literature.

## THE PRODUCT

At the moment there is a need to develop elements of the rural tourism product in Eastern Europe. These elements are presented in figure 13.1.

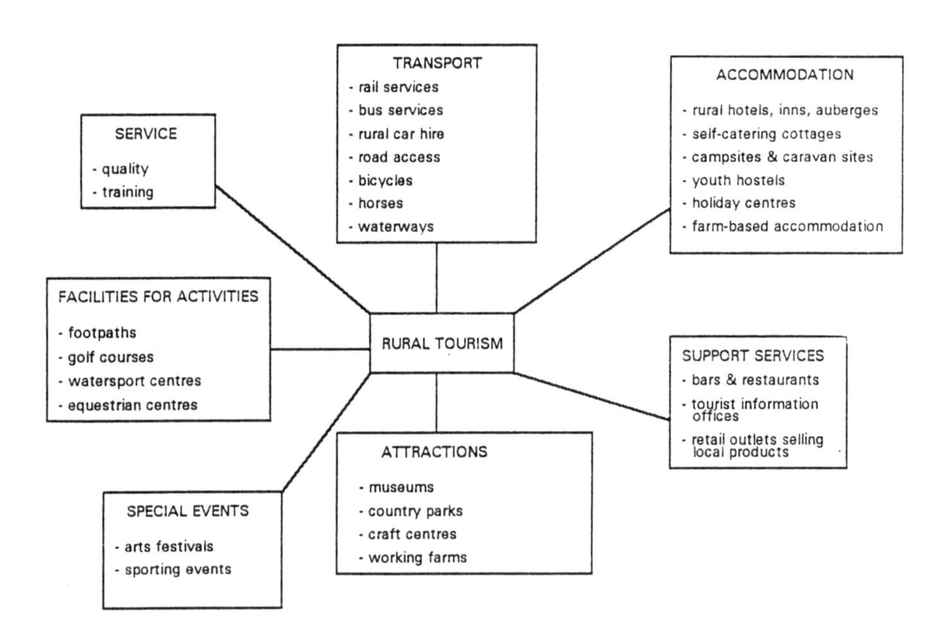


**Figure 13.1: Rural tourism product development**

As most rural areas are still based on an agrarian economy most product development should, wherever possible, be based on farms. In this respect lessons could be learned from the French experience where agro-tourism is highly developed. In France there are *gîtes* (derelict farm buildings converted into holiday cottages), *fermes-auberges* (where farmers provide meals based on the produce of the farm), *chambres d'hôtes* (bed-and-breakfast accommodation on working farms), and direct sale of products to tourists like cheese, charcuterie, and wine, for example. Rural crafts are also conserved and promoted by the French as a tourism product, while *Ecomusées* have been developed to

interpret, in an authentic manner, the economic, social, and ecological history of an area.

However, in order to maximise the benefits, these elements have to be combined into packages which can be purchased easily by consumers. This has been the role of the publicly-owned Loisirs Accueil agencies in France.

One type of package that could be developed in Eastern Europe could be termed, "Discover the Real Countryside Holidays", which would be in line with the principles of sustainable tourism. These holidays could contain a number of elements including:

- visiting rural workplaces such as craft centres, farms and small factories to see how people live in rural areas. These could develop so that visitors might participate more actively, perhaps by trying to make simple craft products. In any event, opportunities should exist to sell products directly to visitors;
- taking part in everyday leisure activities such as traditional games, and more controversially hunting, for instance;
- trying local food and drink products and learning how to cook traditional dishes;
- listening to older residents talking about life in the area in the past, and talking to local people about what rural life is about today;
- wherever possible, eating and sleeping in people's homes, as a family guest, rather than in hotels;
- travelling on more environmentally friendly forms of transport such as horse and bicycle.

For this product to contribute positively to sustainable tourism it should follow some simple guidelines as follows:

- it should be locally managed and marketed;
- numbers should be limited to ensure the exclusivity and status value of the product for customers, and to protect the host community from the problem of overcrowding;
- the product should be authentic rather than be created for the market;
- it should be offered by those communities which are most in need of the benefits which tourism can bring;
- each product must be different from that offered by other destinations, so that consumers can be encouraged to make repeat purchases of such holidays as they will know that a holiday in another area will be different;
- host-visitor relationships should be informal and based on mutual respect;
- holidays should be of short duration, perhaps a weekend break;
- it should involve as many local people as possible;
- the organisation of the holiday should be loose and flexible so that it

does not feel like a 'package holiday'.

Other types of sustainable tourism packages might include:
- activity holidays that utilise the areas physical environment but which involves education for visitors to show them how they can help them conserve the environment while enjoying it;
- special interest holidays including language courses and cooking holidays;
- offering day trips specifically for second home owners or people staying with friends and relatives to help them find out more about the area, as well as to encourage them to spend money. This is important as such people can contribute only limited economic benefits to the area because they do not pay accommodation charges to local suppliers.

**PRICE**

The price which is charged for the rural tourism product is important because it determines the level of economic benefit which the host community will enjoy from tourism. As no charge is usually made for using rural footpaths or visiting traditional events, for example, many people are able to use rural areas without making any real financial contribution towards their upkeep.

However this does not mean that there is no cost involved in providing the facilities and services which tourists require, including car parks, information offices and park rangers. Often therefore, the tourist enjoys the benefits of being a tourist in an area without paying the full cost of this experience. The balance of the cost is met by local taxpayers who may not even make any income out of tourism. This is clearly unfair, particularly when the tourist is more affluent than the local resident.

We need to develop pricing policies, therefore, to ensure that the consumer pays the full cost of providing the product, but also that they contribute extra economic benefits for the host area. This can be achieved in a number of ways, namely:
- reflecting the exclusivity and rarity value of many of these products, such as the "Discover the Real Countryside Holidays" in high 'premium' prices;
- a seasonally sensitive pricing policy so that demand can be spread more evenly over the year;
- tourist taxes or levies which could be ploughed into product improvements and training that will in turn enhance the quality of the tourist experience, while ensuring that the burden of paying for these things does not fall on the local population;
- 'adding value' to the rural resources which are offered at no cost to

tourists, so that a charge can be made. For example, while walking on a footpath is free, guided walks on the same footpath, using volunteer guides, could be offered for which visitors would pay, so that revenue would be generated. Whatever price is charged, however, the tourist must feel they have received good value for money or the areas reputation in the market may be harmed.

## PLACE

Distribution of the rural tourism product might be handled by a local agency which offers consumers the chance to buy the product from one supplier only, on a 'one stop shop' basis rather than having to contact a number of different suppliers who all offer just one element of the product. The product could be sold either directly to tourists or through partnerships with selected intermediaries in other countries. Whichever approach is adopted the process of buying the product must be made as easy as possible, particularly for consumers who speak another language.

## PROMOTION

Promotional techniques have to be designed so as to encourage people to pre-book and purchase the types of product discussed in this paper. The most effective promotional methods, that are complementary to the concept of sustainable tourism, might include:

- informative but honest brochures that offer true visual images and do not make unrealistic promises;
- the use of press releases and press representative familiarisation visits to ensure that favourable free editorial coverage is obtained in foreign media;
- direct mail marketing to people who are identified as being in the target market for what individual Eastern European rural regions offer;
- using modern technological development such as multi-media systems like CD-ROM to show potential visitors images of the region.

## COMPETITIVE ADVANTAGE STRATEGIES

The international tourism market is very competitive, particularly in terms of the destinations which are seeking to attract higher spending so-called 'quality' tourists. This is the very market segment which Eastern European countries might wish to attract if they are to develop sustainable rural tourism.

Michael Porter (1985) has outlined three approaches which can be taken to achieve competitive advantage, and they are relevant to rural tourism in Eastern Europe.

They are as follows:

1. Cost Leadership. This means producing the product cheaper than competitors so one can either sell at the lower price and gain more customers because of the price advantage, or sell at a normal price and increase profit margins. Interestingly, this is the potential advantage which many destinations in Eastern Europe have over most of those in Western Europe. However, this is often a short-lived advantage as other destinations come on to the market with even lower cost bases. Furthermore, cheapness neither delivers the full potential economic benefits of tourism for the community or maintains a quality image for the product.

2. Product Differentiation. In other words, differentiating the product you offer from that offered by others so that people buy it because it is different rather than because of the price. This fits in better with the idea of sustainable tourism and rural development, through the emphasis on quality rather than price and on exploiting local uniqueness rather than aiming for standardisation which is often the basis of cost leadership.

3. Market Focus. Here, the focus is on the market rather than the product. The area or region sets out to become the acknowledged leader in a particular market segment, for example, environmentally sensitive people, those concerned with healthy lifestyles, or those who enjoy particular activities. From our perspective this approach has two advantages. Firstly, people with particular interests like these are often not too price sensitive and will pay a premium price for their desired experience. Secondly, once identified they can be targeted quite easily in promotional campaigns, for example, through their readership of specialist journals, hence marketing costs are relatively modest.

In addition to the Porter model, there is the idea that increasingly organisations are marketing their corporate values and ethics as well as their products. This has been seen in the case of successful organisations like the Body Shop, for example. Therefore a destination that takes a strong stand on sustainable tourism and makes its mission the development of socially responsible tourism, and promotes this mission as part of its marketing efforts, may find that it reaps a reward of increased popularity as a result.

## MARKETING ORGANISATION

Marketing theories and ideas are important but ultimately marketing is an activity with measurable results. The success of marketing often lies, not only in creative, imaginative ideas, but in how effectively marketing activity is organised.

The success of an approach to rural tourism like that outlined in this chapter would also depend on the quality of marketing organisation.

As we noted earlier, there needs to be a central agency in each area co-ordinating the efforts of individuals and communities. A co-operative rather than state-controlled structure might be more in keeping with the spirit of sustainable tourism. This organisation would have to package the product and promote it to customers, but it would also need to liaise with outside organisations that would continue to play a part in the area such as tour operators.

It might be possible to form marketing consortia linking these agencies together to give them more power within the tourism market and industry. The agency might also develop partnerships with government bodies, for example.

Another aspect of marketing organisation is the budget. Tourism marketing is expensive and an adequate budget for the task would require a co-ordinated approach to raising the funds. Sources of finance might include tourist taxes, income from products sold and merchandising, membership fees from local businesses, government grants, and sponsorship.

Finally, successful marketing requires constant monitoring and evaluation to ensure that objectives are being met efficiently and cost-effectively. This requires performance indicators or targets against which performance can be measured. Such indicators might include jobs created, income earned that could be used for community purposes, and the number of local people involved and receiving some form of benefit from tourism.

## DE-MARKETING

If sustainable rural tourism is to be developed, it has to be recognised that we must discourage some aspects of tourism demand through de-marketing. This is a relatively new concept and a difficult one to implement. However, in the context of this paper, de-marketing might be used to:

- discourage certain types of tourist from visiting rural areas in Eastern Europe such as those who spend little money and are simply seeking a cheap holiday;

- divert demand away from areas which are already overcrowded to places where tourists might be more welcome, and their economic benefits may be more needed;
- reduce visitor numbers at peak times and try to stimulate off-peak demand instead.

## THE BENEFITS OF A MARKETING APPROACH

The benefits of the approach outlined in this paper would take a number of forms. Benefits would be distributed more widely throughout the community than is usual and the benefits would spread to areas where the need was greatest. It would ensure that the destination continued to evolve in response to changes in demand and that visitors received a quality experience. The economic yield from visitors would be increased while the economies of areas and regions would be diversified to help them withstand the effects of agricultural change for example. In a wider sense, this approach would provide a catalyst for community development and self help.

## THE POTENTIAL PROBLEMS WITH A MARKETING APPROACH

However, there are potential problems with a marketing approach, particularly the danger that the desire to attract more tourists would lead to a trivialisation of the area's heritage, to make it more picturesque and less difficult for tourists to understand.

In the longer term, this could devalue the product and harm the self-respect and pride of the community. The second major potential problem is that given that, in the early days at least, the skills required to implement this approach are likely to be in short supply in most rural communities, the lead could be taken by a small number of experts within, or outside, the community. This could alienate the majority of the population of the area.

## THE ROLE OF THE PUBLIC SECTOR

So far this paper has focused on marketing and local community action as a way of achieving sustainable rural tourism in Eastern Europe's rural regions. However, there is an essential role for public sector organisations in both central and local government in the development of sustainable rural tourism. There are two aspects to the role of the public sector in rural tourism, in that it can pro-actively encourage positive developments, while preventing negative things from happening. We will now consider the role of the public sector under five headings:

(1) Planning. Successful tourism development in any country, it could be argued, requires a degree of economic planning that ensures that tourism receives an adequate share of resources to allow it to be developed. Sustainable rural tourism also requires a physical planning system that prevents developments which harm the physical environment of rural areas, and ensures that new buildings blend into the landscape rather than detracting from its aesthetic quality.

(2) Policy. A range of government policies are relevant to sustainable rural tourism, including, for example:

- border control policies, in terms of how easy it is for foreign tourists to enter the country;
- policies on taxation which influence domestic demand, together with the tax burden on private enterprises;
- agricultural policies given that mixed farming areas with smaller family farms are generally more attractive to tourists than those based on monoculture (except wine) and large 'industrial' farm units;
- policies on environmental protection in relation to landscapes and wildlife;
- policies on rural development and whether the government wishes to maintain the viability of its traditional rural economies or see its rural regions develop and become more industrialised and urbanised;
- attitudes towards small businesses and co-operatives.

(3) Funding. In most countries, there is a need for some government funding to help develop sustainable rural tourism. Financial assistance is often required to fulfil a 'pump-pricing policy' in relation to capital projects such as the creation of museums and the conversion of derelict farm buildings into tourist accommodation.

Likewise, public money may be required in terms of revenue expenditure to support tourist information services, for example. Current thinking, however, is in general that the state should not provide all the funding that is required, but instead should enter into partnership with private companies and voluntary bodies, based on sharing the costs of initiatives. It should be noted that state funding and rural tourism is not all one-way, for rural tourism can bring revenue to the public sector through employee tax contributions and sales taxes, for example.

At the same time we should recognise that state funding is required for areas other than tourism if sustainable rural tourism is to be developed. Perhaps the most important example of this point is the financial assistance which is made available to support farmers in marginal farming areas. Tourism income can help in this respect but here may still be the need for some state aid for farms.

(4) Training. Given the fact that the idea of a market economy is still relatively new in Eastern Europe, and that the type of rural tourism outlined in this paper is at an early stage of development, there is a major role for the state in training in Eastern Europe. This training will need to cover business skills such as marketing together with customer care. There will also be a need for some training in tourism planning and management. Given that many of those requiring training will be in employment, and unable to attend full-time courses, alternative methods of delivering this training might need to be developed, including part-time courses and distance - or open - learning programmes.

(5) Regulation. Some government regulation will be needed to ensure that rural tourism does not develop in ways which compromise the principles of sustainability. This regulation will need to cover issues such as quality control and consumer protection. Countries might even find it advantageous in terms of competitive advantage in the international tourism market if they were to develop a system of labelling for sustainable rural tourism products that meet certain standards. These labels themselves would then need to be protected by regulations.

The public sector therefore, has a crucial role to play in developing sustainable rural tourism in Eastern Europe. However, it can only create the climate in which such tourism can flourish. Ultimately, success will depend on local enterprises and voluntary bodies creating and marketing products that are both attractive to consumers, and sustainable.

## IMPLEMENTATION ISSUES

It is well known that it is usually easier to develop a strategy than it is to ensure that it is implemented. Perhaps, therefore, we should say a few words about key implementation issues and the problems that would be faced by any attempts to develop sustainable rural tourism in Eastern Europe. However, it is also true to say that most of these issues and problems would also be relevant to such an undertaking in most countries of the world. The author has listed some of the most important of these issues and problems below:

(1) The co-ordination of the actions of all the relevant players including local communities and farmers organisations, transport operators, accommodation suppliers, attractions, governmental agencies and organisations in other countries such as tour operators.

(2) The need to gain community commitment to the concept of sustainable rural tourism when poverty can make people, quite understandably, want to concentrate on short-term economic gain rather than taking a longer

term perspective.

(3) Reconciling the traditionally individualistic nature of most rural dwellers with the need for collective action which has been advocated in this chapter.

(4) The availability of funding to invest in rural tourism in terms of how much money is available, where it comes from, and what conditions are attached to its use.

(5) The need to balance the needs and desires of local people with outsiders such as the tourists, government agencies, and the tourism industry.

(6) Resolving controversial issues such as hunting, which is a traditional rural activity that can be an attraction to tourists. There are both moral questions about hunting and the ethical dilemma as to what extent you should allow foreign visitors to do things in your country which are illegal in their own country. Likewise allowing hunting by tourists may attract some tourists but put others off visiting the country because of their opposition to hunting.

(7) Recognising that some areas may not have the physical and cultural resources to allow them to provide an offer that will satisfy consumers, and that effort and money should not be expended on rural tourism in these areas. This does not mean abandoning these areas, but simply developing different approaches to their development which do not involve tourism.

(8) The availability of market research data that allows Eastern European destinations to ensure that their product evolves in response to changes in consumer tastes in their target markets.

(9) An awareness of what competitors are doing so that an areas product can be differentiated from that of its competitors.

(10) The provision of advice, training, and education, to help local people develop the skills which are necessary to allow them to play a full part in the development of sustainable rural tourism.

(11) Developing democratic decision-making mechanisms so that everyone in the community has an equal voice in debates over tourism development in rural areas.

(12) Maintaining an area's clear identity and resisting the usual tendency towards standardisation and homogeneity, for it is the differences

between areas, which produce any destination's "Unique Selling Proposition".

However, perhaps the greatest overall challenge to rural tourism in Eastern Europe is the development of the infrastructure and the product which is on offer to tourists, if the aim is to attract high-spending foreign tourists, as well as domestic tourists.

## THE DANGERS OF TAKING NO ACTION

Clearly, developing sustainable rural tourism in Eastern Europe, as anywhere else, will be difficult. However, there are enormous dangers if we decide it is too difficult and instead choose to take no action. This would be detrimental in two ways, namely:

1 Some areas will become over-developed for tourism and the volume of tourists will overwhelm the capacity of the local area.

2 Other areas, where farming is no longer viable, will become de-populated and farmland will become derelict and degraded.

It is the author's contention that both eventualities are unacceptable in social, economic, environmental, and political terms, and that action has to be taken to prevent them from happening.

## CONCLUSIONS

This paper has discussed ways in which a community-led marketing-oriented approach might be adopted to achieve a form of sustainable rural tourism in Eastern Europe, that will underpin future rural development and regeneration. It may seem ironic to think of using tourism, which many have argued has done so much to damage rural areas in some parts of the world, to help conserve and develop rural areas in Eastern Europe. However, tourism does have the potential to play a positive role and, in any event, tourism is a major international phenomena that is already developing rapidly in Eastern Europe. The tourist will arrive in the rural regions of Eastern Europe in ever growing numbers whether we like it or not. We should, therefore, seek to manage tourism so that it is a positive rather than a destructive force. Tourism is not in itself bad, it is only detrimental when it is badly managed or unmanaged.

Perhaps the greatest dilemma for Eastern European countries is how to manage rural tourism, in terms of the balance between state control and private and community enterprise. In some countries the balance may be too strong currently in terms of the former because of the resilience of old attitudes from the previous political system. On the other hand, in other countries, a headlong rush towards a market economy has put too much emphasis on private enterprise and has swept away some elements of state influence that are necessary for sustainable rural tourism. Individual Eastern European countries need to find the balance that suits their needs best.

This highlights a general point about this chapter - by necessity it has focused on the regions of Eastern Europe as a whole. However, as we know, Eastern Europe is not homogenous. It consists of a number of countries which differ greatly in terms of a number of characteristics, including:

- levels of economic development;
- political systems and political stability;
- types of agriculture;
- patterns of rural settlement;
- religion;
- language;
- history.

It is important, therefore, that in order to make progress in this debate we disaggregate Eastern Europe into individual countries and regions, and consider each one on the basis of its own particular situation. The development of local, place-specific approaches rather than standardised models would appear to be the appropriate way forward.

However, before we commit ourselves to action we must be sure that what we plan to do is ethically correct, in the widest sense. For instance, is it right to interfere with the process of agricultural change and urbanisation which appears to be taking place in much of Europe, or should we not simply allow this process of 'evolution' to continue? We must always remember that the landscapes and rural cultures we treasure today are the result of change in the past.

Secondly, are we convinced that our desire for rural area conservation is not merely a self-indulgent mixture of nostalgia and self-interest on behalf of urban tourists and decision-makers, rather than being in the interests of the rural areas and their communities? The author believes the way of resolving this latter dilemma may be to ensure that we use sustainable tourism as a means to the end of rural development rather than as an end in itself. This means putting the needs of local people above those of the tourists.

There is no doubt that the pressure on rural areas in Eastern Europe will grow in the future, through changes in agricultural technology and the need to develop agricultural production so that it can make a greater contribution to the exports of Eastern European countries. This may result in a move towards forms of agriculture which are probably not sustainable in terms of their impact on the physical environment.

Tourism could play a vital role in developing a more balanced economy for rural areas in the future, so that they do not need to become industrialised 'food factories' to survive.

However, in an era when the emphasis is on seeing agriculture as just another activity to be left to market forces, there needs to be a change of philosophy in both Eastern and Western Europe. We might need to see rural areas not as places where inefficient farms produce over-priced food. Instead, we should see rural regions as places where farmers and rural dwellers produce wholesome fresh food, conserve treasured landscapes, remind us of our past, and manage a leisure resource on behalf of everyone, efficiently, at a relatively low cost.

Interestingly, from a marketing point of view, these four areas are all ones which are growing in popularity amongst many European consumers, namely, healthy eating, conservation, heritage, and leisure. Perhaps, therefore, trends in consumer behaviour may well now be compatible with the aims of sustainable rural tourism and good practice in rural development.

By necessity, this chapter, which has sought to discuss a massive subject in just a few thousand words, has been selective and superficial. It has had to make generalisations without the opportunity to look in detail at the exceptions to these generalisations. There is therefore a need for more debate and detailed research about different forms of tourism and the different types of rural regions which exist in Eastern Europe.

Nevertheless, the author believes that a market-led approach complemented by appropriate state intervention, might create a form of sustainable rural tourism that could be developed in at least some Eastern European regions that would help to ensure the long term future of rural economies and societies.

Whereas, in the past, marketing has been blamed for causing the standardisation of products, places, and consumer behaviour, the author is saying that in this instance, taking a marketing approach could be the means of resisting standardisation and conserving local uniqueness. This local uniqueness is very important as it is what local residents take pride in, and it is also what tourists come to experience. Both groups therefore will suffer if it is lost, as the countries of Eastern Europe strive to develop economically, socially, and politically.

Therefore we may have to reverse the clarion call of global marketers, so that in the case of sustainable rural tourism marketing, we may have to "Think locally, act globally". For it is the individual local area that is important but its future success will mean influencing consumers and organisations nationally and internationally.

Finally, it has to be said that this paper has been written from a Western European perspective. It is for colleagues in Eastern Europe to evaluate its relevance to the regions where they work. The author hopes that they will find at least some of its ideas worthy of further consideration and looks forward, hopefully, to engaging in mutually beneficial discussions with these colleagues.

## REFERENCES

Bouquet, M. and M. Winter (eds.) (1987). *Who From Their Labours Rest?* Conflicts and Practices in Rural Tourism. Aldershot: Avebury.

Bramwell, B. and B. Lane (eds.) (1994). *Rural Tourism and Sustainable Rural Development.* Clevedon: Channel View Publications.

Buller, H. and K. Hoggart (1994). 'The Social Integration of British Second Home Owners into French Rural Communites'. *Journal of Rural Studies*, 102: pp.197-210.

Centre National de Ressources du Tourisme en Espace Rural. *Annual Proceedings of the Annual Tourisme Rurale Université d'Été.* 1991 (Super Lioran), 1992 (Contrexéville), 1993 (Rodez), 1994 (Autun). Lempdes: ENITA.

Economist Intelligence Unit, (1995). 'The Czech Republic and Slovakia'. *International Tourism,* 1: pp.39-57.

Economist Intelligence Unit, (1994). 'Hungary'. *International Tourism Report,* 3: pp.5-24.

Economist Intelligence Unit, (1993). 'Bulgaria'. *International Tourism Report,* 2: pp.21-39.

Economist Intelligence Unit, (1992). 'Poland'. *International Tourism Report,* 2: pp.65-89.

English Tourist Board, (1991). *Tourism and the Environment: Maintaining the Balance.* London: English Tourist Board.

Grolleau, H. and Ramus, A. (1986). *Espace Rural, Espace Touristique: Le tourisme à la campagne et les conditions de son développement.* Paris: La Documentation Française.

Hall, D.R. (1991). *Tourism and Economic Development in Eastern Europe and the Soviet Union*. London: Belhaven.

Hunter, C. and H. Green (1995). *Tourism and the Environment: A Sustainable Relationship?* London: Routledge.

Keane, M.S. and J. Quinn (1990). *Rural Development and Rural Tourism*. Galway: University College.

Kotler, P. (1994). *Principles of Marketing*. Sixth Edition, Eaglewood Cliffs.

Mazaraki, A. (1993). 'Prospects for Tourism in Ukraine', *Tourism Management 14*: pp.316-317.

Middleton, V.T.C. (1994). *Marketing in Travel and Tourism*. Oxford: Heinemann, Second Edition.

Ministère du Tourisme (1991). *Memento du Tourisme*. 11th Edition. Paris: Ministère du Tourisme.

Murphy, P.E. (1985). *Tourism: A Community Approach*. London: Methuen.

O.E.C.D. (1993). *What Future for our Countryside: A Rural Development Policy*. Paris: OECD.

PA Economic Consultants (1987). *A Study of Rural Tourism*. London: Rural Development Commission and English Tourist Board.

Porter, M. (1985). *Competitive Advantage*. New York: Free Press.

Pritchard, G. (1990). *Farm Holidays in Austria, Denmark, and France*. London: British Travel Education Trust.

Sharpley, R. (1994). *Tourism, Tourists and Society*. Huntingdon: Elm.

Swarbrooke, J. (1992). 'Towards Sustainable Rural Tourism: Lessons from France'. *Insights*, November 1992: A65-A70.

Swarbrooke, J. (1992). *The Role of the Media and Marketing in Rural - Tourism*. Paper presented at the 'Envirotour '92 Conference', Vienna. November 1992.

Tourism Eco (Journal). *Le Mensuel des Professionnels du Tourisme*. 'Dans le Grand Sud'. Toulouse.

Witt, S.F. (1994). 'Opening of the Eastern Bloc Countries'. In: W. Theobald (ed.). *Global Tourism: The next Decade*. London: Butterworth Heinemann, pp.217-225.

World Tourism Organisation, (1994). *National and Regional Tourism Planning: Methodologies and Case Studies*. London: Routledge.

World Tourism Organisation, (1994). *Yearbook of Tourism Statistics*. Madrid: World Tourism Organisation.

# Chapter 14

# The Kodukant Programme and ecotourism in Estonia

**Aivar Ruukel**

*Kodukant* is a rural development programme in Estonia. It was started in 1992 through activities in one Estonian region, and has since spread to several other regions. It developed in part thanks to Swedish-Estonian cooperation, through which a number of Swedish institutions and individuals, together with various actors on the Estonian side, have worked to attain the objectives set out for the programme. An approximate translation of the word Kodukant might be a combination of 'home, environment, and heritage', a concept with no equivalent word in any other language, but its broad significance for Estonians is very clear.

The Kodukant Programme has three specific objectives:

1. The first objective is to stimulate local mobilisation and local democracy. The social and economic problems facing the Estonian countryside are great, and many of these problems need locally-developed solutions.

2. The second objective is to stimulate entrepreneurship. This objective is linked to the first, as starting small businesses is a way to solve problems locally.

3. The third aim is to develop supporting structures and promote cooperation at all levels: between villages, between the village and government and internationally.

The Kodukant concept centres around activities of various kinds. One sector identified as promising in the future for rural Estonia is the tourism sector in general, and ecotourism in particular. The Kodukant Programme seeks to find new livelihoods through tourism, which could present itself as one of several economic generators in the countryside. Tourism should find ways of contributing to the local communities and to the conservation of Estonian wildlands - so as to use resources in a sustainable, yet profitable way.

The way tourism was operated during the Soviet periods has drastically changed with Estonian independence and the consequent shift towards democracy and a market economy. The tourism industry in Estonia is still in its infancy. Large investments are being made in creating accommodation facilities and infrastructure, though mainly in larger cities. Although the potential of natural and cultural tourism in rural areas is high, this particular branch of the tourism industry is still lagging behind in Estonia.

Tourism is spreading world-wide and despite the poor image Estonia still suffers, we have reasons to believe that tourism will also arrive in the rural areas of Estonia and its many protected areas. According to World Tourism Organization data the turnover of tourism is increasing world-wide in general terms by 4% per year and what we can call 'ecotourism' by some 10-30% per annum. Hence, it is not a matter of whether tourists come or not, but rather on what conditions they can be best guided into Estonia's rural areas. And further, who will benefit from this development?

The academic capabilities of people in Estonia is high and there is labour available in abundance to be engaged in the tourism sector in rural areas. Young persons are highly receptive to the changes and once good business opportunities present themselves, they can be turned into results. Agriculture has been on the decline during the transformation of Estonia to a market economy and new opportunities will have to be created in rural Estonia. Tourism has been identified by the Kodukant project as one such opportunity.

## WHAT IS ECOTOURISM?

One of the most popular definitions of ecotourism has come from The Ecotourism Society, who define it as "Responsible travel to natural areas that promotes conservation and well-being of local people" (The Ecotourism Society, USA).

Ecotourism is also closely associated with other approaches to minimising the negative impacts of tourism and maximising the benefits. Other labels given to sell approaches include 'alternative tourism', 'sustainable tourism', 'green tourism' and many others.

A definition of sustainable tourism has been presented by the World Tourism Organization against the background of market demand for higher quality tourism products, ecological awareness, and the negative aspects of conventional mass tourism:

> Sustainable tourism meets the needs of present tourists and host regions while protecting and enhancing opportunity for the future. It is envisaged as leading to management of all resources in such a way that economic, social and aesthetic needs can be fulfilled while maintaining cultural integrity, essential ecological processes, biological diversity and life support systems (WTO; *Tourism to the Year 2000*).

Basically, all such definitions share four common denominators:

1. The first is that there are limits to the carrying capacity of an area, or resource, whether natural, cultural or social. Over-exploitation of a tourist resource reduces the value of the product for the tourist even if the resource as such is not 'consumed'. The concept of carrying capacity needs to be understood in all tourism planning and entails three different levels. These are:

> a) The level of tourism that causes the devaluation of a particular tourist attraction, which is dependent on the number of tourists in a particular area. 'Ecotourists' tend to be fairly sensitive to this level, and they are often willing to pay more for an exclusive experience.
>
> b) The second level of carrying capacity is the social level where the impacts of undesired tourism development provoke negative interaction and resentment among local people.
>
> c) The third is the ecological level - where the tourism impact on the environment is negative.

These different levels of carrying capacity exist together in a three dimensional way, are very dynamic and change over time. Tourism development that has not been planned, easily reaches saturation levels of carrying capacity. These impacts, however, can be monitored by keeping the initiative of tourism development at the local level, and by using price differentiation strategies to reach the desired levels of tourism.

2. The second common denominator is that local people should not be excluded from the opportunity to benefit from tourism. Nor should tourism development be imposed on them. Local people are persons living in or in the immediate surroundings of the tourist areas. There are two approaches to engage local people in the tourism industry:

> a) The 'hire the natives approach' which recommends tour operators hire the services of local people, buying their services and products as much as possible.
>
> b) The 'empowerment approach' which advocates that local people should be given the opportunity to be engaged commercially and directly in the operations.

Neither of the two is mutually exclusive, but we think the latter is the most desired, and in line with Kodukant rural development objectives.

3. The third common denominator is collaboration between various interest groups at the local and national level for sound use of open access resources such as cultural and natural landscapes, as well as protected areas. There is an urgent need to have a common understanding of the problems and opportunities of tourism dynamics between the government and private sector, as well as the various non-governmental organisations, before sensitive areas are promoted for tourism use.

4. The fourth common denominator is that ecotourism adds value to nature and culture. The tourism sector should offer its financial contribution for the sustainability of the very resources on which it depends. There are lots of examples in international tourism areas, where too low prices or a total lack of pricing have provoked over-exploitation of these resources.

More than 90% of the overall turnover in the tourism industry is accounted for by accommodation, transport, catering, and shopping. This means that tourists spend their money in hotels, airplanes, trains, buses, restaurants and shops, i.e. in establishments having a definite owner. This reveals one of the paradoxes in tourism: most tourists do not travel with the aim of just staying in hotels or travelling by bus, but rather to experience unique cultural and historical sights and nature.

Also, travel companies do not market hotels or buses but the nature and culture of the tourist destinations. These resources are the open access resources, that do not have a definite owner and are open to everyone.

It is important to understand that ecotourism is not a product. First and foremost, it is a philosophy relying on the common understanding by the various actors involved of the feasibility, opportunities and problems of the tourism industry.

The following section looks more specifically at ecotourism development in Estonia and the Kodukant initiative.

## KODUKANT ECOTOURISM PROJECT

The Kodukant ecotourism initiative was set up in September 1994 as a multidimensional project of the Kodukant Programme. The intent of this project is to visualise the opportunities tourism could offer people living in or near attractive areas, so that they become allies of sustainable development in their regions, rather than being subjected to excessive uncontrolled tourism developments. The Project also aims to expose the Estonian ecotourism life-support system, made up of various authorities, NGOs and the private sector, to the Ecotourism guidelines that could provide a framework for utilising natural and cultural resources in a sustainable way. The project also aims to create ownership in a common strategy expressed in a Reference Manual that is to be made available in the international marketplace.

## Implications of the project

To date, no active and licensed Estonian tourism companies have specialised in nature tourism, nor has it been actively marketed. Estonian tourism companies outside of Tallinn find it difficult to reach the marketplace and to adapt to the needs of international travel. The travel industry in Estonia is dominated by firms operating out of Tallinn or even foreign companies, who find it too complicated to work with the local communities and local tourism entrepreneurs.

The Kodukant Ecotourism Initiative will turn the natural and cultural resources of rural Estonia into a comprehensive travel product of high quality and will launch it through foreign and domestic travel agents into the international tourism market. It will provide the private sector with business opportunities at a local level, and with a new competitive product at the national and international levels.

Because of its stimulating effects on the economy, tourism is sometimes called ‘the engine of the economy’. Ecotourism will be a good change for the so-called ‘peripheral’ areas which frequently overlap with less inhabited, wild areas, which are often protected. The rural population living in these areas is characterised by very low incomes, with few viable economic options. Ecotourism can represent for these people a valid economic alternative, with the additional advantage that these inhabitants can be converted into the most efficient warders and conservationists of these natural areas, since their welfare depends on the preservation of the natural qualities of their environment. In partnership with the authorities the project will make every effort to make the potential of nature tourism serve the interests of society, and develop appropriate ecotourism strategies in different areas of Estonia.

Non-governmental organisations often play an important role in the conservation of cultural heritage and naturally unique areas. One aim of the project is to find, with the collaboration of the tour companies, means for the management and conservation of the cultural and natural resources.

A further target interest group is that of donors and development foundations, which have been established for promoting small business, nature conservation, biodiversity etc. The project will offer them opportunity to allocate their funds with a view to encouraging ecotourism in Estonia.

It is remarkable that everyone, including those not directly involved in ecotourism, will benefit from its developments. Being represented in the international market as a country offering high biodiversity and nature tourism services will contribute to the improvement of the image of Estonia in the West.

### REFERENCE MANUAL

One of the most important activities since the beginning of Kodukant Ecotourism Initiative has been the creation of a Reference Manual on the Estonian ecotourism 'product'. The manual expresses local desires of how ecotourism should be designed, and gives a description of the Estonian protected areas and its ecosystems and cultural heritage, along with ways to experience these in an ecotouristic way. This manual can work as a marketing tool for Estonian ecotourism rural operators and is also designed for the use of foreign tour operators with access to ecotourism markets worldwide.

The practical role of the Reference Manual is not only to make information available to the marketplace on how to make the best use of the Estonian wildlands, but is also a learning experience for the people directly involved in the project. International expertise and assistance has been provided by an ecotourism consultant, Jan Wigsten of Eco Tour Production AB of Sweden.

In order to produce a Reference Manual valid for the different areas of the country, Kodukant has tried to identify the human resources and attractions available for such use. In some areas tourism is desired, in others it is not.

A network of rural operators, mostly from protected areas, which cover about 10% of Estonia in total, have been connected with the Kodukant Ecotourism Initiative, and have during the process of elaborating the manual agreed a large number of issues. For example: what ecotourism means in the Estonian context, where it should take place, and where should it not? How should it benefit local people and nature conservation? How to reach the markets? How to develop a pricing strategy? Whether to use a common reservation centre or agents? And so on. All of the operators in the network have agreed to share profits with the local communities from the protected area in which they are operating, either by the purchase of local services or products, or through a direct financial contribution. The situation is not, however, homogeneous throughout Estonia. It is rather site-specific.

In western countries most nature tourism is independent and developed in terms of self-guided trails. This means that the tourist groups or individual visitors are provided with brochures or information on sign boards along trails. In Estonia practically no infrastructure whatsoever, in terms of marked trails, interpretation, proper guidebooks, lodging and nature guides are in place in the majority of the protected areas. This provides the potential for local people, who are often experts on local nature and culture, to be involved as guides.

Labour costs in Estonia are quite inexpensive, which is a great advantage in terms of competition. From this point of view it makes sense to begin with personnel-intensive full-service nature tourism. The fact is that this kind of tourism-product has a well-defined market segment, attracting mostly urbanised, highly-educated persons in western countries. The most interesting feature from the socio-economic point of view is that this kind of tourism is highly organised, easy to control and predictable. These kinds of tourists are also easy to instruct, and tolerant of local circumstances. It creates a good kind of tourism to begin with, which creates, in turn, a good business environment for potential rural entrepreneurs. In this way it is easier to develop sustainable tourism which is beneficial for local communities, than for tourism to develop by itself in an unplanned way.

## DIFFERENT INTEREST GROUPS

Ecotourism is a multidimensional activity that combines a large number of service elements, that together make up the total tourism product. It depends on the support of the private sector, the authorities and various NGOs. All key players need to have a common understanding of the problems, dynamics and opportunities that are made available to the local economy and the protected areas in the tourism sector. Individuals and organisations can choose to enter the sector according to their own perspectives and needs and it is hoped that any entry into the sector will facilitate more insight into the opportunities. One can then climb the ladder, develop more elaborate undertakings, and move up in the system. From the private sector the different interest groups can be divided into three levels of involvement.

The 'A' level offers the most complete tourist services. These are existing tour operators who have experience with foreign tourists. They are established businesses with an office, direct telecommunications available, that have foreign language capabilities, and which operate all year round. These operators are licensed under Estonian law and will act as reservation centers. A foreign tour operator can book a tour with any of the appointed local tour operators. Jan Wigsten's direct know-how transfer has been primarily given to this group, as well as to the 'B' level operators, provided they have English language capabilities.

The 'B' level consists of entrepreneurs with existing facilities or services who wish to enter the sector in a particular area. Their operations are primarily in the field. This level is likely to work full time during the main tourism season and probably revert to other activities during the off season. 'B' level operators can develop whole tour itineraries on their own and distribute these directly or via the 'A' level operators. The ecotourism concept and guidelines have reached this level through the Kodukant Ecotourism Initiative and the Estonian language material which it produces. The 'B' level operators are those with which people living within or near protected areas have the biggest potential to become new entrepreneurs.

The 'C' level consists mainly of individuals offering one particular tourist service. These may include private farmers offering accommodation and serving meals, handicraft workers, trailguides, storytellers, cooks that could be hired, etc. They would be hired by level 'A' and 'B' operators to make up a tour package. They are not working in tourism as professionals, but they receive benefits from tourism activities. One of the guidelines for ecotourism is to use and buy services and products as locally as possible.

The conservation groups are another important sector in the ecotourism picture. These are groups now working for the conservation of cultural landscapes and heritage, such as the community at Jalase village in northern Estonia. There are also nature conservation NGOs like the Estonian Fund for Nature, as well as administrations of the various protected areas. The ecotourism project also intends to create 'ownership' also with these groups, in such a way that they are being invited to endorse the itineraries and descriptions of the Estonian Ecotourism 'product' as being sustainable. One principle is that some portion of the income can be redirected into nature protection or management of the areas which are visited. Funding programmes for this group have to be worked out by the project. The tourism sector and the conservation sector will need to establish a division of roles beneficial to both and this is a very important exercise in the development of the Reference Manual.

Another interest group is the public authorities. Various authorities have an interest in tourism development, although it lies primarily within the mandate of the Estonian Tourist Board. They, however, feel they do not have sufficient funding for product development in the rural areas. The emergence of a Reference Manual for Estonia will enhance the Estonian general tour product and image.

The Kodukant Ecotourism Initiative is already working closely with the various Ministries and it is envisaged that an understanding of the dynamics of tourism will develop as the project continues. The private sector will learn how they can benefit in collaborating actively with the authorities.

An important 'milestone' in the process of ecotourism development was a national workshop on the potential of ecotourism in Estonia - in particular in its protected areas - that was undertaken on the initiative of the Biosphere Reserve of the West Estonian Archipelago, Hiiumaa Center, on May 30-31, 1995. Representatives from Estonian Ministry of Environment, the Estonian Tourist Board, different protected areas, county governments and Kodukant Ecotourism Initiative participated.

The results of the workshop included coming to an agreed understanding of Ecotourism in Estonia as: "Responsible travel to natural areas, that promotes conservation and the well-being of local people".

Ecotourism is generally understood as activities and impacts as a result of tourism taking place outside the very structures of the tourism industry, for example outside the bus, the hotel, the restaurants etc. It has been understood that in Estonia the most attractive areas for outdoor activities are without a doubt the many protected areas.

From the workshop, it also emerged that the concept of ecotourism is generally not understood in Estonia. In order for ecotourism to develop, the following criteria are vital:

- An Ecotourism Strategy for the use of the open access resources and the protected areas must be in place, so that policymakers, nature conservation organisations and authorities and tourism entrepreneurs have proper guidelines for their actions.

- Residents of the different regions should be active in a more pronounced way, as tourism entrepreneurs offering genuine experiences to tourists, and at the same time offering partnership to park managers. Nature and Culture Tourism need to be organised at the local level.

- The Ecotourism network should take the initiative in setting prices and directing its services to a more motivated and organised market, helping tourism to bear its own costs - to strike the balance of sustainability and profitability. The rural areas of Estonia are now attracting rather low yielding tourists from the nearby markets. Their willingness-to-pay is minimal, thus creating barriers for local entrepreneurs to enter the industry.

Also as a result of the workshop, the Kodukant Ecotourism Initiative was given further support for continuing activities now underway and in coordinating future activities.

The activities of Kodukant Ecotourism Initiative are:

- The dispersal of information on ecotourism development through its newsletter at national and international level.

- The creation of a Reference Manual for the international travel industry that will express local desires of how tourism should be implemented, describe the Estonian protected areas and its ecosystems and cultural heritage, and how to experience these in a sustainable way.

- Product development in conjunction with local people and local nature conservation authorities and NGOs in the various parts of Estonia. At the national level to identify areas where nature tourism should be promoted, and areas where it should be discouraged.

- To coordinate and facilitate the exchange of experiences in a network of local tourism entrepreneurs.

- On behalf of the Kodukant network seek the support of other stakeholders, such as the authorities, NGOs, and general tourism industry so that guidelines from these sectors are communicated back for implementation.

The Kodukant Ecotourism Initiative has facilitated a process, whereby a core group of people and organisations have been identified and connected to each other. Ecotourism values and guidelines have been transmitted to this group at the same time. They will make up the life-support system of the future ecotourism sector. It seems that the project may be so productive that the partners will see the benefit of formalising the collaboration in an Ecotourism Association of Estonia.

# Chapter 15

# Rural and agri-tourism in Central and Eastern Europe

**Frank McMahon**

## BACKGROUND

There are a number of factors on both the supply side and the demand side which are encouraging the development of rural tourism in Central and Eastern Europe and elsewhere.

On the supply side, the mechanisation of many farming activities and the increased productivity of land have reduced the need for agricultural labour. Thus, there are people available to provide rural tourism services. Secondly, there is a need for farmers to supplement their income through non-farming activities - one such activity is rural tourism. Finally, there is increased emphasis on the set-aside of land, i.e. its non-use for agricultural purposes. Such land is then available for rural tourism use.

On the demand side, there has been the phenomenal growth in tourism world-wide. The overall growth has been from 25 million tourist arrivals in 1950 to over 400 million arrivals per annum now. The growing awareness of the importance of environmental issues has led to an increased interest in holidays which are not damaging to the environment, and rural tourism holidays are seen as environmentally friendly. National governments, which have encouraged the growth of all inward tourism, now see particular benefits to encouraging rural tourism, partly because it is environmentally friendly, but also because it does not require such a large investment in infrastructure. Thirdly, it is attractive because it can lead to a good dispersal of income into regions which might otherwise be impoverished.

## TOURISM ACTIVITIES IN CENTRAL AND EASTERN EUROPE

The countries of Central and Eastern Europe are seeking to develop their tourism industries as are virtually all the countries of the world. Already, they are major participants in the world of tourism, and Poland, Hungary and the Czech Republic all figure high on the list of countries with the highest number of tourist arrivals.

Table 15.1 shows the number of arrivals in the top 20 countries in 1993.

**Table 15.1: International tourist arrivals 1993**

| Country | Tourist Arrivals (millions) |
|---|---|
| France | 60 |
| United States | 46 |
| Spain | 40 |
| Italy | 26 |
| Hungary | 23 |
| United Kingdom | 19 |
| China | 19 |
| Austria | 18 |
| Poland | 17 |
| Mexico | 17 |
| Canada | 15 |
| Germany | 14 |
| Switzerland | 12 |
| Czech Republic | 12 |
| Greece | 9 |
| Hong Kong | 9 |
| Portugal | 8 |
| Malaysia | 7 |
| Turkey | 6 |
| Singapore | 6 |

*Source*: World Tourism Organisation

Table 15.2 shows the average annual growth rate in the number of tourism arrivals in the period 1985-1993, showing that Poland and Hungary both grew at more than twice the world average.

**Table 15.2: Number of tourists**

Average Annual Growth Rate 1985 - 1993

| | % |
|---|---|
| France | 6.34 |
| USA | 7.65 |
| Spain | 4.83 |
| Hungary | 11.24 |
| China | 13.01 |
| Austria | 2.34 |
| Poland | 14.73 |
| Germany | 1.55 |
| Ireland | 6.95 |
| World | 5.77 |

The Czech Republic has not been included in Table 15.2 because of the complication of the split of the former Czechoslovakia during that period.

However, one area in which some Central European countries were not so successful was in regard to the average length of stay of tourists. Hungary, Poland, and the Czech Republic are well below France, Spain, Ireland or UK, as Table 15.3 shows.

**Table 15.3: Average length of stay in country, 1993**

| | nights |
|---|---|
| France | 7.2 |
| Ireland | 11.0 |
| Portugal | 17.0 |
| Spain | 9.0 |
| Poland | 4.6 |
| Hungary | 3.4 |
| Czech Republic | 2.8 |
| UK | 10.1 |

To encourage a longer stay, it is necessary to develop activities for tourists. Many such activities in Central Europe are likely to be in rural areas, hence the new emphasis on rural tourism. The fact that the vast majority of tourists arrive in Poland by car facilitates their dispersal to rural areas. Much of Central Europe is very well endowed with the natural amenities which appeal to tourists - the lakes, forests, mountains and attractive countryside. These features provide one, but only one, of the factors which assist the development of agri-tourism.

## FEATURES WHICH WORK FOR OR AGAINST TOURISM DEVELOPMENT IN POMERANIA

At a workshop held in Slupsk, Poland, in March 1995, a discussion was held on the positive and negative factors affecting tourism development in that part of the country. The delegates, all Polish, who had been selected to take part in a project to develop agri-tourism in Pomerania, considered a list of features which might work for or against tourism development.

They selected five features which they believed worked in favour of tourism development:

1. number of tourists who visit Poland;
2. attractiveness of countryside, lakes and forests;
3. large number of Polish and German people who have origins in the area;
4. highways from Germany through the area;

5. ferries from Finland and Sweden to Gdansk.

However, there were 12 features which they saw as negative in the tourism development process:

1. availability of investment capital;
2. training of tourism staff;
3. availability of overnight accommodation;
4. high cost of borrowing where capital is available;
5. sign-posting and public telephones;
6. trains and buses from all parts of Poland;
7. level of co-ordination between central, regional and local efforts in regard to tourism;
8. tourism marketing services available;
9. attitude of rural people to tourism;
10. foreign language ability;
11. crime levels, especially car thefts;
12. co-operative marketing.

Other factors from the original list were left in the undecided category or agreement could not be reached.

Most of the features, whether positive or negative, are self-explanatory. But there are some features which require some elaboration:

**Tourism marketing**

The perceived lack of co-ordination between central, regional and local efforts in regard to tourism and the poor view taken of the tourism marketing services may arise because of the way in which agri-tourism is being developed. The initiative to develop agri-tourism in Poland and in many other countries has come from the Ministry of Agriculture or other agricultural interests - it has not come from the Ministry of Tourism. Thus, agri-tourism is outside the responsibility of the Ministry of Tourism, the Tourist Board and other tourism bodies. There is sometimes a level of professional rivalry, of jealousy or of mutual suspicion between the tourism bodies and the agri-tourism bodies. To fully develop agri-tourism, it is necessary to move beyond this antipathy and to bring together the Tourism and Agricultural interests to co-operate in marketing and customer servicing.

**Overnight accommodation**

Tourists on their way to and from Rural or agri-tourism holidays often need a stop over place. Western European tourists, who are being attracted to Central and Eastern European countries in growing numbers, expect a good standard of accommodation with en suite facilities. This is often not available.

The registration and grading of agri-tourism accommodation is not
in Poland. Much of the accommodation is not registered and is of a p

### Taxation

An important amendment to the income tax code in Poland was enacted in December 1994. Income earned by letting guest rooms in houses located in country areas, at farms, and income earned by serving meals to them, is free from income tax provided the number of rooms being let is not greater than five.

## STEPS BEING TAKEN IN POLAND TO ENCOURAGE RURAL TOURISM

a. In October 1990 training courses in Alternative Enterprises were held under the auspices of the Agricultural Extension Services at Karniowice and Krakow, Poland.

b. In March 1995, an agri-tourism Workshop, funded by the EU PHARE programme was held in Pomerania, Poland. The workshop was one element of a development project to include marketing support, training of farmers, study tours and accommodation development. Twelve selected rural tourism leaders participated in the programme. This project was carried out by Tourism Development International, an Irish consultancy company, in conjunction with the ODR's (Agricultural Advisory Services) in Pomerania.

c. A major rural tourism project, funded by the EU PHARE programme will commence in Poland shortly. It has a budget of 3 million ECU, spread over three separate contracts. The major features of this project are:

1. Master Plan
- Preparation of a Master Plan for rural tourism for a ten year period.
- Plan and set up a rural tourism organisation for Poland and help to fit it into existing systems.
- Prepare a rural tourism Action Plan for a part of Poland.
- Prepare and begin implementation of a rural tourism Marketing Campaign.
- Identify and prepare business plans for the modernisation of one to three existing holiday centres.

2. Activity and Interest Tourism in Rural Poland
- Prepare action plans for five sectors (probably Equestrianism, Trails, Water-based Tourism, Rural Life Tourism and Nature-orientated Tourism).
- There is also a specific requirement to assist the planning and setting up a marketing stand at the Poznan World Equestrian Championships.
- Identifying and helping implement plans for three pilot schemes in each

sector.

- Plan and assist the implementation of about three pilot projects in each area, e.g. with local authorities, create a trail, develop the use of a lake to increase sustainable water-based tourism with the probate sector to upgrade an equestrian centre, etc.
- Help disseminate the knowledge gained.

3. Developing the Rural Accommodation Stock

- Review the existing categorisation, registration and inspection systems in Poland and overseas and make recommendations for a modern system for Poland.
- Help establish an organisation to undertake this activity.
- Provide training for trainers and operators of rural tourism accommodation.
- Recommend how to market the accommodation and help establish a marketing campaign.
- Recommend systems for business advice, funding, etc. for operators.
- Identify the improvements to legislative, regulatory and tax systems needed to allow progress, recommend improvements and help make the case for them to the authorities.
- Help disseminate the knowledge gained.

Expressions of interest were received in February 1995, and it is expected that the contracts will be awarded in the Autumn 1995.

**The Czech Republic**

In the Czech Republic the EU PHARE Labour Market Restructuring Programme provided 8.5 million ECU to support the transition to a market economy. This programme had many objectives, including re-training programmes, one of which was to support the starting up of own businesses in agri-tourism. The emphasis was on the design of a training programme of 8 days duration and the production of training materials (course manuals, videos, etc.).

The contract was awarded to a company called Inpro Institut; they relied heavily on the expertise of the Tourism Department, University of Economics, Prague, to design the course material and deliver the first course. Experts involved included Jarmila Indrova, Head of the Tourism Department and her colleague, Dana Slamova (marketing expert). Two foreign experts from Dublin Institute of Technology were appointed to evaluate the project and report on its effectiveness. The recipients of the training in the pilot phase were equal numbers of farmers (potential agri-tourism operators) and potential trainers. However, the mixture of backgrounds did not work well. Apart from the problems of two non-compatible groups, the project was successfully carried out in early 1995; modifications were made to the programme and it will now be offered throughout the Czech Republic.

**Hungary**

The Budapest College of Commerce, Hospitality and Tourism has taken a leading role in developing rural tourism in Hungary.

The emphasis has been on education and on the involvement of village and small town mayors in the development process.

An EU TEMPUS project, co-ordinated by the Budapest College, has been approved for funding for a three year period commencing September 1994. Partners include Colleges of Education in Hungary, Kempten (Germany), Huddersfield University (UK) and Dublin Institute of Technology, all of whom work under the co-ordinating influence of the Budapest College of Commerce, Hospitality and Tourism. Activities include long and short-term study visits by Hungarian students to EU Colleges (for example, two students are completing the one year Graduate Diploma in rural tourism at Dublin), short term visits by Hungarian Staff to the EU Colleges (typically two to four weeks), and the presentation of seminars in Hungary by experts from the West. A curriculum for rural tourism is being developed at the Teacher Training Colleges in Hungary; when finalised, the course will be offered widely throughout Hungary.

**Key steps to success**

Studies of the development of rural tourism in the EU have led to the following conclusion of the steps necessary to achieve success:

- Identification of an area with physical and human potential.
- Completion of a resource audit by the community themselves and prioritising areas with potential for development.
- Training in leadership, community development and marketing.
- Co-operation and creation of strong linkages with funding, support and marketing agencies and bodies that can help.
- Planning and objective setting.
- Training in products expansion and development.
- Setting up of legal structures.

It would be impossible to over-emphasise the importance of community involvement in achieving success in rural tourism initiatives. All studies to date indicate that it is crucial that all the resources of a village or small town be harnessed to overcome the difficulty that individual rural tourism operators are usually small scale. Thus, they need support from each other to be able to offer an enticing package to prospective clients.

The separate approaches being taken in Poland, Hungary and the Czech Republic all include elements of the steps necessary for success; a comprehensive approach has not yet emerged in any one country but seems closest in Poland with the implementation of the PHARE project.

Rural tourism was initially seen as a cheap form of tourism development because it did not involve a high level of investment - instead it utilised existing spare capacity in farm houses and small, unsophisticated restaurant facilities. However, today's tourists are increasingly seeking their creature comforts when on holidays - bedrooms must be of modern construction with en suite facilities, restaurants need to be well appointed, hygiene standards must be adequate, buildings must conform with fire and other safety requirements. All these attributes require substantial investment in facilities. In addition, effective marketing to a discerning international clientele requires a high level of expenditure. In the international market place, rural tourism is not such a cheap form of tourism as was earlier thought.

# Chapter 16

# Skills, understanding and knowledge for sustainable tourism

**Frank Howie**

## 1. SKILLS, UNDERSTANDING AND KNOWLEDGE

What skills, understanding and knowledge are required of today's tourism graduates? Is management the basic key to success in the new tourism? Can environmental, scientific, socio-cultural and other subject areas be 'bolted-on' to 'traditional' management skills as and when necessary 'on the job', or are they fundamental? Specifically, in a context of tourism quality and sustainability, are these new skills an essential component of the core curriculum or can they be relegated to the 'elective' category for those with special interests? If they are core, what existing subjects can be dropped from the core curriculum already packed with 'essentials'?

### 1.1. Sustainability - core or peripheral?

The answer depends on how sustainability is viewed, at the highest levels within government and industry and within individual institutions and businesses. If sustainable development generally, and sustainable tourism specifically, are viewed as add-ons for specialists then clearly their study - at least in any detail - can be optional. On the other hand, if sustainability is to be the touchstone of all policies within a state, an industry or a business, then a more fundamental integration of the topic into virtually all subjects is required as well as the opportunity for specialist study in depth.

### 1.2. Working definitions

*Sustainable development*
Working definitions of sustainability, sustainable development and, specifically sustainable tourism development are necessary. Interest in sustainability may be set within a consideration of contemporary social trends. Poon (1993) has listed these trends as:
- social values change;
- recession and consequent reassessment of individual and societal goals;
- increased awareness of environmental impacts;
- increased awareness of social/cultural impacts.

These have given rise to a period of reassessment of growth and development and other fundamental beliefs and expectations. Her perspective may be seen as providing a contemporary perspective on various writings of the late 1960s and 1970s such as those of Schumacher (1973) and Robertson (1978).

Some key publications in a brief history of sustainability are:

1972 *Limits to Growth.* Danella & Dennis Meadows
- drawing attention to finite resources; exponential population growth; the pace of development.

1974 *World Conservation Strategy.* I.U.C.N.
- defining sustainable development and proposing appropriate response strategies.

1987 *Our Common Future.* World Commission on Environment and Development.
- sustainable development as *the solution.*

1992 United Nations Conference on the Environment and Development (UNCED) *Rio Conference.* Rio de Janeiro.

The World Commission on Environment and Development (1987) proposed that the need for understanding of sustainable development has became widely recognised:"... development that meets the needs of the present without compromising the ability of future generations to meet their own needs".

The concept of sustainable development entered the contemporary public domain at the 'Earth Summit' (1992), the *United Nations Conference on the Environment and Development* (UNCED) held in Rio de Janeiro, which stressed the need for a global shift from an emphasis predominantly on economic growth to sustainable development.

While the basic concept of sustainable development has foundations in considerably earlier writings on conservation and stewardship of natural resources, such as those of Frank Fraser Darling (1969) and Aldo Leopold (1968), the contemporary perspective provides the essential additives of emphasis on a proactive stance, a commitment to continued economic growth rather than a 'steady-state' economy, alongside increased ecological and social equity considerations.

### 1.3. Tourism and sustainability

In her analysis of contemporary social trends Poon identifies key points for 'new tourism' which here may be taken as pointers for sustainable tourism:
- maintaining ecological diversity;
- increasing social equity;
- enabling more productivity in developing areas;

- increased community/local control;
- increased regional self-reliance;
- intervention by governments as necessary;
- partnerships between business and government;
- economic viability.

Clearly, sustainable development is more than a 'concern for the environment'; this raises the question as to how widely the ramifications of a commitment to sustainable development are understood.

Tourism 'sells' - and is fundamentally dependent on - the physical and human environments. The tourism industry, like any other major industry, must pass through two key stages of response to issues of sustainability: initially, becoming aware of its impacts; subsequently, developing a response to them. Perhaps it is surprising that an industry so dependent on environmental quality appears slower on the uptake than, say, the car industry which now wears a green mantle through its adoption of new norms such as lead-free petrol and catalytic converters. The fact that tourism has been regarded as a non-polluting, non-resource-extractive, people-friendly industry is at least part of the explanation. It should also be recognised that the technological 'solution' represented by catalytic converters in the car industry or the availability of 'green tours' in the tourism industry, while in themselves desirable, fall a long way short of true sustainable development, where a fundamental rethinking of the role of the industries in society is required.

The gulf between the awareness and the response stages for tourism businesses is generally large at the present time. Howatson (1990) considers that in Canada, which might be regarded as a country in the forefront of support for sustainable development, a minority of businesses are at the initial stage of reaction to evolving legislation (at this time largely environmental, rather than also socio-cultural legislation); a majority are at the stage of adapting business practices to compliance with legislation; while a minority are spearheading a proactive approach, characterised by the integration of an environmental dimension into corporate strategic planning. One mechanism for moving tourism businesses and agencies further up the scale of response to sustainability may be the growing interest in 'Total Quality Management' (TQM). Adams *et al.* (1991) have alluded to this in identifying corporate environmental policy as a desirable extension of TQM, approached through such mechanisms as company environmental and social audits.

It has been questioned whether the contemporary interest in sustainability is a passing fad. There are grounds for concern from previous experience of the environmental movement of the late 1960s/early 1970s. However, evidence of environmental change/deterioration is today clearer and increasingly substantiated, while there is also a wider audience of 'new consumers', rather than exclusively a protest movement. Governmental responses to date vary considerably. Canada has proposed setting parameters for sustainable development within which private businesses operate as advocated in the Canada Green Plan. The UK government does not currently favour such "intervention", placing reliance on the "voluntary principle" and the "best practical environmental option" (HMSO, 1994).

### 1.4. Sustainable tourism

Sustainable tourism development has been defined as: "....leading to management of all resources in such a way that we can fulfil economic, social and aesthetic needs while maintaining cultural integrity, essential ecological processes, biological diversity and life support systems" (Tourism Canada, 1990).

This implies consideration of resource management; the economic activity of tourism; social obligations of agencies, businesses and tourists; consideration of future generations' resource needs (intergenerational equity) and cultural diversity. This in turn implies consideration of intangible attributes essential to tourism quality such as the ambience and aesthetic appeal of destinations, the *genius loci* or spirit of place; as well as ecological parameters such as preservation of bio-diversity and carrying capacity.

Within this holistic perspective, both basic and higher level or discretionary needs of tourists and host communities must be considered. Quality considerations, underpinned by ecological principles, also infer limits of acceptable use and limits for development - not a traditional concept in business where increasing profitability has been the goal. Some leeway is possible where the objective of an absolute limit to development is replaced by the concept of levels of acceptable use or threshold levels. Here there is an acceptance of the inevitability of incremental change in any development context but, even here there are ultimately limitations on untrammelled growth (Stankey *et al.* 1985).

These issues are the subject of current research by the author and colleagues on the internationally renowned and consequently much visited Loch Lomond area, a proposed Scottish national park currently under-managed through inadequate legislation. Building on US and Canadian experience, the work may support a move from a traditional promotional and operational focus to a more proactive one of increasingly active management of visitor opportunities and improving visitor understanding of essential conservation requirements through interpretation. Research is also underway in the Parc National des Cevennes in France where case studies of examples of sustainable development may "...help to turn rhetoric into practice" (Murphy, 1989) and provide demonstration projects useful to proposed national parks for Scotland. In this context the 'motto' of the Regional Natural Volcanoes Park Auvergne of France is inspirational: "Development, Protection and Welcome," It seems to integrate necessary development and conservation in a context of active encouragement of appropriate tourism.

The Loch Lomond study recognises that a 'supply side' focus alone is inadequate; the tourist is also important, as is the viability of businesses dependent on tourism in the area. The complementarity of environment and tourist and the consequent need for a 'customer focus' is discussed by Murphy (1994). Demand issues can be addressed through marketing, (an established 'core curriculum' subject area) once marketing is recognised as a 'tool' for achieving sustainability. Modern marketing has moved on from an exclusive focus on promotion and selling to embrace long term management goals. 'De-marketing' to reduce consumption is already employed by utility companies and by certain tour operators who emphasise the 'exclusivity' of their holiday destinations. Creative interpretation is also used to explain the ecological and aesthetic reasons why certain areas are 'out of bounds'. In this context a further major goal must be the balancing of tourists' needs with the needs and aspirations of the host communities, creating economic opportunities as well as respect for community values.

The educational implications of a holistic interpretation of sustainable tourism development, are returned to later.

### 1.5. Forms of sustainable tourism

Sustainable tourism is far more complex than the assumed synonym 'green tourism' has been taken to imply. The latter term has served a useful purpose in drawing attention to increasingly popular alternatives to mass market 'sun-sand-sea' holidays. Sustainable tourism can be viewed as a version of green tourism, or it can be seen as an underlying philosophy for all tourism development. While the latter is the author's preference, this should realistically be seen as a future objective; inevitably the process of fundamental change of a major industry and of societal values will take time. In the shorter term, it is realistic to assume that variations on green/sustainable tourism will develop further as significant alternatives to '3S' tourism. Already it has been asserted that there is no such creature as 'the average tourist', the contemporary market being increasingly segmented.

*Alternative tourism*

Krippendorf (1987) described alternative tourism, where the tourist would: "try to establish more contact with the local population, try to do without the tourist infrastructure, and use the same accommodation and transport facilities as the natives".

*Eco-tourism*

In eco-tourism the tourist actively contributes to the well-being of the host ecology. Criteria include limits on levels of crowding by mutual agreement between tour operators, visitors and host communities, control of site visits by tour operators issued permits through government agreements and agreed, appropriate marketing images. There may also be purposeful strategy contribution to the broad tourism industry (Hall and Kinnaird, 1994). Poland's potential in this area is considerable, as discussed later (Nowicki, 1995).

*Special interest tourism*

This broad category can include both alternative and ecotourism as well as a wide range of other forms. It is broadly described by the World Tourism Organisation (1985) as "specialised tourism involving group or individual tours by people who wish to develop certain interests and visit sites and places connected with a specific subject. Generally speaking, the people concerned exercise the same profession or have a common hobby ... (the tourism experience can be enriched) ... by allowing greater integration with the place visited and fuller involvement in the social and cultural life of the holiday destination".

The above and various other 'new' categories of tourism ('soft tourism', 'responsible tourism'; 'tourism with insight', 'good tourism', 'rural tourism', 'agritourism' and others) have been criticised as failing to provide an alternative to 'mass tourism', as being elitist and relevant only to the wealthy and/or well educated tourist and offering no solution to the problems of scale associated with mass tourism. It has been pointed out that the desire for 'undisturbed areas' can initiate the destination lifecycle which on past experience has frequently destroyed the character of the area, while the desire for 'contact' can disrupt local cultural norms (Urry, 1992). Similar criticisms have been applied to sustainable tourism (Wheeler, 1990).

From today's perspective the critique is misplaced. Various forms of tourism which embody some or all of the principles of sustainability are appropriate to certain destinations and certain tourists. They do not themselves offer a total solution to the problems associated with mass tourism. It is essential to clarify the distinction between two alternative models for tourism development and the significance to each of sustainability.

*A. Addition*

The tourism industry will incorporate alternative and special interest tourism alongside the dominant form which will continue to be characterised by a desire for passivity, relaxation and service, largely dissociated from the actual environments and cultures of the regions visited, the choice of location being secondary to pricing of the packages offered.

*B. Transformation*

All tourism will be sustainable tourism, mass tourism as currently understood having been phased out as ecologically and culturally unacceptable.

It is likely that the future will see an industry located somewhere between these two models. All tourism development will incorporate certain principles of sustainability, notably increased environmental standards. Alternative or special interest forms of tourism will continue to grow, and should stabilise at levels of popularity somewhat higher than today's, characterised by varying degrees of sustainability: from 'highly sustainable' to 'barely sustainable', but with some form of 'tourist tax' imposed on the latter to counter ecological or cultural damage.

If the above position is accepted there is certainly a need for study of the nature and implications of sustainable tourism within tourism education. While some graduates will seek a deep involvement in forms of tourism requiring specialised environmental and/or sociocultural knowledge and skills, others will require as a minimum a sound understanding of the concepts and a clear awareness of when their own generalist skills are stretched to the point where a specialist consultant or adviser is required by their businesses, for the satisfaction of their customers, the continuing good will of host communities and their environments and, consequently, their profitability.

## 2. SUSTAINABILITY IN ONE COUNTRY, GUIDELINES FOR EDUCATION?

Within the UK 'sustainable development' appears to have been awarded central place. The Secretary of State for the Environment, John Gummer has stated:

> The United Kingdom is determined to make sustainable development the touchstone of its policies. We recognise that this means a change of attitudes throughout the nation. That change cannot be achieved overnight, but that gives no grounds for defeatism - it should act as a spur to action (HMSO 1994).

Significant clues to the nature of the disciplines essential to underpin this "change of attitudes" is given by the Prime Minister, John Major, writing in the same document:

> Sustainable development is difficult to define. But the goal of sustainable development can guide future policy. We need a hard-headed approach to sustainability based on good science and robust economics. We also need to be sensitive to the intangibles that cannot be reduced to scientific imperatives and the narrow language of economics.

There are key references made here: "good science", "robust economics" and "sensitivity to intangibles". While the question has been raised as to whether the signatories to the *Rio Declaration* - including the UK Prime Minister - were fully aware of the implications of the commitment so made, they are now enshrined in UK governmental policy. There appears to be a maturing of views from an easy allegiance to 'green is good'-environment as a god word - to a deeper commitment to sustainable development.

In the present context of education and training for higher education in sustainable development issues we have a valuable starting point for progress.

Further clarification of skill needs is available from a government agency in Scotland, Scottish Natural Heritage (HMSO 1993).

It should be noted that the applicability of this to the wider UK context requires some caution. As Paddison has noted (cited in Pearce, 1992), "Scotland's political status represents a transition from the federal state of the Federal Republic of Germany to the centralised examples of the Netherlands and the Republic of Ireland. The UK maybe classified as a 'compound unitary state' of the type ... whose federal-like practices stem from the establishment of regional governments, which are vested with legislative powers and/or functional responsibilities that in unitary states would normally be considered the prerogative of the central government." Currently this 'quasi-federal structure' is under considerable stress with all major opposition parties in the UK committed to setting up a Scottish parliament, given electoral success. Whether sustainability would retain the apparent prominence it is given by the Prime Minister is an important question.

The Scottish Natural Heritage agency, bases the theory and practice of sustainable development on fundamental premises and ethical principles, implemented through guidelines for sustainable development.

### 2.1. Fundamental premises

1. All human activity is ultimately dependent on environment - natural resources and processes.
2. The human population is growing rapidly.
3. Resource use per capita is high in developed countries and growing rapidly in developing countries.
4. The high level of human activity is likely to have serious consequences for quality of life and even survival.
5. Our interactions with environment and its natural processes are complex and it is often difficult to predict the consequences of our activities.

### 2.2. Ethical principles

1. Intergenerational equity - do nothing which puts at risk the natural environment's ability to meet the needs, material and non-material, of future generations.
2. International equity - countries should accept responsibility for the environmental impacts of their economic activities on other countries and should avoid 'exporting' their environmental problems.
3. Societal equity - one sector of society should not exploit natural resources nor damage the environment at the expense of another.

4. Inter-species equity - we should respect other life forms: we are rarely, if ever justified in driving them to extinction for our own purposes.

### 2.3. Guidelines for sustainable development

Scottish Natural Heritage emphasises that these are guidelines for action and advice, the agency having limited powers of direct control. In that context they will be interpreted and applied by individuals and organisations with values different from the agency's own and the achievement of greater sustainability will require changes in policy, regulatory and planning frameworks.

1. Non-renewable resources should be used wisely and sparingly, at a rate which does not restrict the options of future generations.
2. Renewable resources should be used within the limits of their capacity for regeneration.
3. The quality of the natural heritage as a whole should be maintained and improved.
4. In situations of great complexity or uncertainty we should act in a precautionary manner.
5. There should be an equitable distribution of the costs and benefits (material and non-material) of any development.

Scottish National Heritage agency offers a substantial, general basis for sustainable development. Specifically within the tourism industry a substantial contribution is offered by the International Institute for Sustainable Development (1993), noting that the "tourism manager" is: "typically faced with large quantities of data and information about social, economic and environmental conerns. Much of this is in a language or format which they little understand and infrequently have the time to examine in depth." The International Institute for Sustainable Development offers a pragmatic set of indicators for sustainable tourism development. In so doing, a positive indication is provided of what the 'typical tourism manager' requires to know - and therefore what his/her education should have provided, at least in part - and, an indication of at what point a specialist is required to assist the manager in his/her decision making. Since it is probable that some tourism degree students would wish themselves to become such specialists, further indication may be deduced of the specialist routes which should also be available within tourism degree courses.

## 3. TOO MUCH OF A GOOD THING: CAN EDUCATION COPE?

A challenging melange of science and ethics has been offered as essential for a sound consideration of sustainable development. The implication is that while science is impartial, neutral, objective, rational - it deals in 'facts' - the use and application of science depends on the users' values, the realm of ethics, which deals with rights, goodness, justice, respect and so on. And ultimately, the question of 'How much will it cost' is unavoidable. Can these three perspectives be integrated into the tourism education curriculum? Can educationally sound justice be done to the 3 E's of sustainable development- Ecology, Ethics and Economics?

### 3.1. Ethics

In a context of tourism development, where individual tourist expectations, business entrepreneurial demands and government responsibilities are present, the question as to 'Whose values?' takes on significance. Clearly a component of the tourism graduate's skills in sustainable development considerations is the ability to distinguish the winners from the losers in development decisions. A basic awareness of the principal ethical theories would be valuable within curricula- normative and philosophical ethics, utilitarianism, formalism, teleology and deontology. But is this an unreasonable expectation? Should ethical considerations not be part of general management or planning education?

There is a growing interest generally in business ethics. For example in the UK the Co-operative Bank notes a considerable increase in investors following a successful television marketing campaign emphasising the directions in which the company would NOT invest their investors' money - they have added a social as well as a financial dimension to the benchmark by which companies are judged. Other major companies - the Body Shop, Traidcraft and Allied Dunbar emphasise a policy towards development which integrates social and environmental considerations alongside the financial, a policy which clearly contributes to their success, and intend to publish social accounts detailing how they relate to all their suppliers, their employees, their customers and their shareholders. An American foundation, Redefining Progress, advocates the replacement of Gross Domestic Product as a measure of economic progress with an index called the Genuine Product Indicator which builds in external factors otherwise ignored such as environmental damage, national health and child care (Ivison, 1995).

Are there examples in tourism of such 'enlightened self interest'? Arguably there ought to be, in an industry which depends fundamentally on environmental quality and a welcoming attitude on the part of local residents to tourists.

Green Flag International and Green Globe are examples from the tourism industry of organisations seeking to influence businesses to adopt a more ethical stance in their business dealings, in other words incorporating environmental and socio-cultural considerations alongside the financial. The involvement of these commercially oriented organisations is an important step forward in the maturing 'green movement' from reactive protest to pro-active targeting of the developers themselves in the spirit of 'prevention is better than cure'.

If ethical considerations can be considered part of the 'intangibles' referred to by the UK Prime Minister as essential considerations for sustainable development, what of the "good science" and "robust economics"?

### 3.2. "Good science"

*The scientific perspective - basic ecological premises*

At the outset, a caution must be issued. 'Scientism' has unfortunately weakened the case for numerous environmental arguments - the application of scientific conclusions to inapplicable areas; covering up (unintentionally, or deliberately) social, economic and political implications of an issue. Ecology has too often been invoked as providing scientific 'evidence' for problems otherwise caused. There are well documented case studies from many industries. In the case of the tourism industry environmental awareness has come late. For most of its early phase of development the industry has regarded itself as a 'non-extractive' industry having no impact on the natural, cultural and social resources on which it depends. Today we know better. Tourism education must include the key elements of ecological/environmental science but students must be aware of its misapplication. As an example, famine in an area may be the result of a natural disaster such as a freak drought; or, as Malthus said, "plague, pestilence and war". However, it may be the result of social factors such as the disruption of traditional farming caused by loss of the workforce to jobs elsewhere in, for example, cattle ranching or tourism. Further, the migration may be encouraged or forced, rather than voluntary, for political reasons.

Scientific principles underpin environmental considerations in development, supplementing - not replacing - social, economic, political and other considerations. Ecological premises requiring understanding, with a view to their appropriate application, include the following:

- Connectivity: All organisms are part of a complex web of mutual interactions with energy as the 'currency'. This is relevant to understanding of, for example, 'biodiversity'.
- Balance: Animal and plant populations fluctuate but are in equilibrium with their environment. 'Technological man' has partly escaped from the restraints that maintain balance.
- Homeostasis: When an ecosystem is disturbed by external or internal events, equilibrium is restored through regeneration or succession.
- Scarcity: The potential geometric rate of increase of plant and animal populations is checked by these populations approaching the limit of available resources (space or food, usually).

These premises are illustrated within other concepts including biodiversity, carrying capacity and impacts of inappropriate/over-development, ecosystem management, natural communities, and the ultimate holistic perspective of Gaia - the Earth as a self-regulating 'organism'.

A major challenge to students (and practitioners) is the application of these principles and guidelines to their own professional areas, for example using the premises to explain the environmental 'impacts' of tourism and how to apply in them in practice to the attainment of sustainability in an actual tourism destination, attraction or facility, and to employ them in carrying out environmental audits of tourism businesses.

### 3.3. Ecology, ethics and economics - putting it all together

Environmental impact assessment has been available as a range of techniques and as a statutory requirement in some countries since the early 1970s, when the United States Federal Government introduced environmental impact assessment legislation. In the UK environmental impact assessment (E.I.A). has been mandatory for certain types and scales of development only and has been rarely applied to tourism related developments. While early EIAs focused largely on the bio-physical effects of development the approach is evolving to embrace the 'total environment', of the bio-physical and the socio economic contexts. As such it is increasingly addressing a complex of tangible and intangible values. In 'putting it all together' - clearly a desirable objective - there are difficulties in comparing like with like, notably in attempting 'evaluating environmental intangibles'. A common currency is sought. While in ecological terms energy flow may be used to represent values, and in ethical terms perhaps 'rightness', clearly in the mainstream of development economic values are dominant and the common currency is money. However, "economic analysis can measure the intensity with which we hold our beliefs; it cannot evaluate these beliefs on their merits" (Turner et al. 1994). Such evaluation is, however, essential to political decision making.

Within 'traditional' management education economics and related topics are core components. To what extent in tourism education should attention be given to contemporary developments in the economic field such as hedonic pricing, contingency valuation, true cost-benefit evaluation and so on?

This section has addressed a range of additional subjects - ethical, ecological and economic - considered essential within the tourism education curriculum for tomorrow's industry. There are other skills which might well be useful if not as core disciplines to certain tourism graduates. For example, evaluation and assessment of the qualities of a heritage landscape or townscape or a particular built environment may well be valuable in destination management. The "3-E's" thus widens to embrace not only ecological, ethical and economic considerations but also requires that these be integrated with aesthetic considerations, historical associations, literary connections and other connotations.

Hall (1994), referring specifically to eco-tourism, adds further requirements: "Staff training programme requirements reveal critical needs in such areas as ecology, social survey techniques, marketing, languages, computing, cartography, photogrammetry, geographical information systems, guiding and information centre staffing." He also notes: "Selective knowledge, and experience, rather than holistic perspectives, have been the norm. This partly results from the activities of professionals, who, whilst specialists in their own fields, have usually received training within relatively narrow disciplinary confines and have hitherto been unable to take a broader ecological view of any particular area".

It must also be recognised that at present, many of the above concepts and concerns continue to be viewed by many individuals in positions of power and within host communities as "... little more than fashionable buzz words and marketing babble" (Wickers, 1992). In certain areas, notably where traditional industry has recently collapsed or been closed down, or where hard-won political freedoms have recently been gained (as in Central and Eastern European countries), the generally inevitable 'constraints' on (over-) development required for sustainability are likely to be met with resistance or hostility.

Communication skills, the ability to work with - and persuade where necessary - officials, entrepreneurs and 'ordinary people' in the community, are a further requirement of the tourism professional, given the desirability of working in collaboration with local communities and local businesses.

All of these topic areas can be addressed within the core of, say, an undergraduate tourism programme. However, they cannot all be studied in adequate depth and retain the essential holistic perspective. Specialisation is almost certainly required within the course. What jobs are graduates expected to seek? What exactly is a 'tourism job'? Is it overly restrictive to aim at the production of 'tourism managers'? Should the educational basis be the generalist - though disciplined and structured - 'tourism studies' course? This approach could have the additional benefit of addressing the danger that, "even the experiential character of tourist interaction with the landscape is reduced to defining land as a 'tourism resource'. What has been washed out of this construction, by the privatising and domestication of affect, is the domain of culture" (Hughes, 1995).

Ryan (1995) also addresses this question. He writes in response to a contemporary argument that there are too many tourism graduates (in the UK) for the available posts (Evans, 1993). Evans' assertion had been made on the evidence of the Council for National Academic Awards. The Council had concluded that the educational establishment had responded well to the evidence of the previous decade of steady growth in the tourism industry and an assumed need for more and better trained employees. Recession had, however, ended that trend and a cut in university level tourism education was therefore necessary.

Ryan rejects this argument as taking too narrow a perspective. "It fails to recognise the wider changes within education and the changing pattern of the wider work-place." He concludes, therefore, "that in a post modernistic society there are good reasons for responding to student demands, subject to some caveats".

Ryan's article gives a challenging perspective. This paper has attempted to relate perceived needs of the evolving tourism industry to educational courses for future tourism professionals. Ryan is arguing that tourism studies - particularly now that it embraces a wide range of topics - is inherently attractive to students, only some of whom will work within it but who will be able to apply their skills within a wide range of work - and leisure - related contexts. The subjects' inherent attractiveness and its relevance to today's and tomorrow's world attracts to higher education future citizens as well as workers who otherwise might not have entered higher education but who, in so doing, will bring that beneficial experience to their own lives and wider society. So long as would-be students are given a realistic perspective on employment prospects then tourism education should be encouraged to respond to demand for it.

Ryan's argument is persuasive to this writer, whose experience is that questions of tourism sustainability are increasingly attractive to students. His enthusiasm for continuing growth in tourism studies is strong, though tempered by views such as those of the Confederation of British Industry (1995) that tourism education generally, though notably at the skills level rather than at management level, is considered by some of their members to be out of touch with industry requirements.

## 4. SUSTAINABILITY IN ONE COUNTRY - NEW COMMITMENT TO NEW TOURISM

New agendas for a new tourism with firm commitments to sustainable tourism have arisen in recent years, demonstrated in recent publications of the Scottish Tourist Board, the national tourist agency. The new agendas have arisen, perhaps, through the shock waves generated by realisation that, after years of more or less steady growth, in the early 1990s overseas tourism to Scotland (and the rest of the UK) was declining. Costs (overpricing?), new competitors, for example Poland and other Central and Eastern European countries which offer products similarly based on natural environment and cultural heritage (as opposed to a 'Sun-Sand-Sea' product); dissatisfaction with the traditional product ('tartanry') may be some of the reasons.

The new thinking was demonstrated with publication of *Tourism and the Scottish Environment: A Sustainable Partnership* in 1992 (Scottish Tourist Board, 1992).

Importantly, the report takes the word 'environment' to mean the natural and human environments and pays due regard to host communities, that is the residents of tourism destination areas, their needs and aspirations. For both rural and urban environments one of the practical ways forward advocated is local tourism management initiatives and pilot schemes are underway.

This positive identification of the above 'total environment', indicates the wide range of considerations essential to sustainable development. This contrasts with the early interpretations of 'green tourism' - tourism based exclusively on the natural environment - which have served a valuable purpose in highlighting the importance of 'green' or natural elements to tourism generally, but fall short of the considerations essential for understanding and management of the wider and deeper concept 'sustainable tourism'. Hughes (1995) addresses the recent changes in attitude towards tourism, relating them to wider dissatisfactions in society, but while acknowledging that these have arisen from an environmental movement barely two decades old, refers to the "infant pretensions of these strategies".

"Infant pretensions of the strategies" must be taken in context. Hughes is acknowledging the worth of the approach to sustainable tourism inherent in these strategies, but sees their limitations in a context of "post industrial tourism". Green tourism, sustainable tourism , post-industrial tourism: this progression was identified by Krippendorf in his seminal work, *The Holiday Makers*. He draws a contrast between the early phase of tourism where the industry's context was tourism as a response to the polarity of work and leisure to the evolving situation:

> the market is shifting from manipulated, uncritical 'old tourists' to mature, critical and emancipated 'new tourists'. While the 'old tourist' sought tourism as relief from work, the post-industrial tourist seeks self-fulfilment through (amongst other experiences) the tourism experience and thus makes a greater demand on the tourism product, though the demand is for quality of experience underpinned by concern for the conservation and or enhancement of the essential natural and cultural tourism resources that underpin the tourism experience.

### 4.1. How big is the market?

Krippendorf's critique and Hughes' application to the Scottish contemporary context are relevant to the present discussion. Krippendorf asserts that post-industrial tourism will be 30-45% of all tourism by the year 2000 with concomitant implications for tourism management and tourism resources. The assertions may be compared to Hall and Weiler's predictions for "Special Interest Tourism". Hall and Weiler (1992) compare their term with other contemporary forms: 'ethical travel' and 'social tourism' (Frommer, 1988), 'secondary tourism' (World Tourism Organisation, 1988), 'eco-tourism' (Boo, 1990) 'educational travel' (O'Rourke, 1990) and 'alternative', 'appropriate', 'environmental', 'nature-based', and 'sustainable' tourism (Gonsalves, 1987, 1989; Kutay, 1989). While there are differences between each, for the present purposes they may be seen as at least comparable and capable of collective description as "REAL" travel (Read, 1980):"REAL travel is travel with only four additives. That travel would be Rewarding; it would be Enriching; it would be Adventuresome; and it would be a Learning experience".

There is general agreement that special interest tourism is a growth industry. While special interest tourism is not synonymous with sustainable tourism there is common ground. While Krippendorf predicts, as noted above, that 'post-industrial tourism' will be 30-45% of all tourism by the year 2000, Hall and Weiller quote figures of 15% of all bookings as being for special interest tourism from a survey of US travel agents in 1989 and refer to a market as generally "booming". The World Tourism Organisation (1991) estimates that 'nature tourism' in 1989 generated approximately 7% of all international tourism expenditures while developing countries in particular represent untapped destinations featuring unique cultural and natural attractions. Moreover, 'eco' and 'nature' tourism are estimated to expand at a faster rate than the industry average. Mudge (quoted in Hawkins, 1994) estimates a 20-25% growth in the first half of the 90s, while related culture and adventure travel will grow from 10 to 15%. While these growth estimates make these specialist forms of tourism substantial minority interests it is noted that their 'greening' influence on the tourism industry in general is significant.

Comparison may be made to Poon's discussion of 'new tourism', replacing 'old tourism' -characterised by mass market products and resorts standardised and rigidly packaged - in response to changing times and 'signals from the world environment'. As previously noted, likely new characteristics of the tourism industry will be flexibility, segmentation and more authentic experiences.

This supports Ryan's plea that tourism education be seen in this dramatically changing context of environmental pressures, wider applications of new technology, changing leisure and work patterns and changing income distribution. A new set of factors characterised by a shift from mass services to 'high tech/high touch' individuality and greater care/conservation of natural environment.

Despite the limitations of the Scottish Tourist Board's approach to tourism and the environment as reviewed by Hughes, the future of Scottish tourism seems likely to be evolving along sustainable lines, tempered by a strong dose of 'economic realism' - not too dissimilar to the world view of Poon.

Other recent Scottish Tourist Board and related bodies' publications have continued the theme. The Chief Executive of the Board writes, in *A New Vision for Scotland*, "The good news is this. Worldwide, tourism is growing at four per cent per annum and may become the world's largest industry by the turn of the century. The bad news is that tourism in Scotland has been in decline and will continue to decline unless we do something about it." As a consequence, the

"Vision" for the Scottish Tourism Strategic Plan - the first ever strategic tourism plan for Scotland - is: "To enhance Scotland's established reputation as a high quality destination, by building on its history, culture, environment and the hospitality of its people".

The Mission of the Board, as expressed in the Corporate Plan 1995/1996 reads: "The mission of the Scottish Tourist Board is the generation of jobs and wealth for Scotland through the promotion and development of tourism". Given the stated "vision" of the strategic plan, these economic objectives would appear to be set within a context of sustainability. This writer does, however, foresee a certain problem relating to the emphasis on authenticity of experience demanded by the 'new tourist' which the Board would appear to seek.

### 4.2. Scotland and Poland: Ecological realities and the quest for authenticity

Scotland has frequently been described in tourist literature as "Europe's last Wilderness". As previously noted, 'new' tourists display a common desire for authenticity, immersion in the cultural and/or physical environment and the pursuit of environmental and experiential quality - "REAL tourism". There is much to be said in the climate of the 1990s in favour of Scotland opting for a tourism development model that builds on the country's existing reputation as a 'green' destination - high environmental quality, heritage, history, culture. However, the new tourist is well educated and aware and will not be deluded by a superficial "Europe's Green Lung" while in fact so many things are, to the experienced traveller, wrong. This 'New Tourist' is experienced: Scotland's "wilderness" in many parts is an ecological "wet desert" (Darling and Boyd, 1964). This is the result of centuries of mismanagement resulting in native forest cover reduced to several isolated (if poignantly beautiful) remnants and the widespread occurrence of blanket bog, the latter now representing a globally important 'carbon store'. Indeed, much of the 'wilderness' character is also partly the result of forced depopulation, a historical reality which the socio-culturally aware new tourist is also likely to find disturbing. The healthy and beautiful 'cultural landscape' that does indeed exists in places - farming and forestry in harmony with the upland environment - is in retreat in a changing world, where the removal of agricultural subsidies make upland farming unviable on its own. Traditional freedom of access to 'the people's land' is under threat in the absence of adequate laws. In tourism terms, many other countries now entering the international tourism market can, it has to be said, offer more authenticity as 'green' tourist destinations. Poland, for example, could offer tomorrow's tourist a natural and cultural heritage tourism 'product' which includes genuinely unspoiled landscapes and true wilderness, inhabited, unlike Scotland, by 'exotic' native wildlife such as the bear, the wild boar, the bison and the wolf, long ago exterminated in Scotland. Indeed, the Tatra Mountains on Poland's southern border, with their rich and striking vegetational diversity and zonation within a comparatively small area, offer a vision of how a regenerated Scottish mountain scene might once again appear, encouraged and partly financed by a dynamic tourism industry founded on sustainable tourism.

At the present time, however, the image of Poland - whether true or not - is more 'grey' than 'green'. (Howie, 1991; Howie and List, 1995). Nowicki (1995) writes:

> Poland's potential in this area (eco-tourism) is very large, estimated at about one thousand million dollars annual turnover, and this potential is almost completely unexploited. It is important to note that eco-tourism can flourish without any major investment in hotels, catering or infrastructure. Only market mechanisms, encouraged mainly through appropriate tax policies, are required to get private investors to develop eco-tourism. Ecotourists are usually satisfied with bed and breakfast accommodation. Most are content to stay in a small, neat boarding-house, to eat modest but healthy, tasty meals and to use well-organised public transport and use the services of a local guide who can highlight the special qualities of the place. A major advantage would be substantial increase in employment in tourism for the residents of villages and small towns located in protected areas. These areas currently have the highest unemployment rates in Poland. Thus the preconditions for (agricultural and) ecotourism in Poland are already met. Poland has a chance to lead Europe in these sectors in the twenty-first century.

Not all tourists will be 'eco-tourists' in the 21st century. Indeed, there are certain problems that advocates of eco-tourism must address before it can develop to its full potential (Mowforth, 1993; Blunt, 1995). More significant in this context is the 'New Tourist' (Poon, 1993). As previously discussed, the 'New Tourist' is in the ascendancy and will demand many of the values expressed in purest form in eco-tourism. The overall direction of tourism planning in the 1990s should be towards enlightened self-interest and the conservation - and reconstruction - of the quality and sustainability of both natural and human resources in tourism destinations. Authenticity will become increasingly a key concept. Today's tourists are second and third generation travellers - they have 'Been there, done that, bought the T-shirt'; they will not be satisfied with the second rate or the pastiche.

## 5. Historical backgrounds to tourism education: Barriers or opportunities for change in Scotland and Poland

The debate on educational needs to meet the challenges of sustainable tourism is made the more complex by the historical background to tourism education. In Britain, many courses in tourism have evolved from earlier established departments of 'hotels and catering' or 'hospitality studies' or from management or business studies departments where degree titles such as Business Studies with tourism are common. This is the case at Queen Margaret College, Edinburgh where the evolution is a classic example of vocational higher education responding to society's changing needs, though it is acknowledged that an alternative interpretation is possible - survival strategies in an uncertain world.

The college's origins are in late 19th century studies in domestic science. This led progressively to hotel and catering studies at Diploma level then to degree level hospitality management and currently to Honours level tourism management and postgraduate degree studies in sustainable tourism in 1994.

The most relevant aspect here is the evolution of subject content. 'Tourism' has attained a separate identity, while within the courses a modular structure has evolved offering a degree of specialisation, including sustainable tourism studies.

A Polish higher education establishment with which Queen Margaret College (QM) has a collaborative relationship is the Akademia Wychovania Fizycznego in Poznan (AWF, Academy of Physical Education). Staff from QM were able to collaborate with AWF through the support of an EU TEMPUS scheme running from 1993 to September 1995.

The evolution of tourism education at Akademia Wychovania Fizycznego in Poznan shows a similar rise in prominence of tourism.

Foundation of the Chair of Physical Education at the newly opened Poznan University in 1919; creation of the Higher School of Physical Education as a separate university level institution in 1950; granting of Academy status in 1973; creation of Department of Tourism and Recreation, the first of its kind in Poland, in 1974.

One route within the Academy's MA level courses in physical culture and tourism is the specialism for "managers of tourism and recreation". The Academy is also an important scientific institution doing research in fields related to its educational profile, "especially humanistic and nature bases of physical culture and tourism". This makes for an interesting comparison with the research focus of Queen Margaret College's equivalent department, the Department of Hospitality and Tourism Management, where the focus is on customers and products. The QM Mission Statement reads, "to create and maintain the highest quality provision for professions, vocations, and areas of application concerned with services to people".

Reflecting the historical origins of the two departments - or the different political contexts - there is clearly a contrast. Akademia Wychovania Fizycznego appears to have a focus on the resources for tourism and their scientific underpinning and on the societal significance of tourism/recreation. Queen Margaret College's Department of Hospitality and Tourism Management could be described as more 'product oriented'. Perhaps significantly, the TEMPUS scheme refers to the assistance from Queen Margaret College in "modernising tourism education in Poland".

This raises the question as to which department's research focus is the more relevant to its courses for "managers of tourism and recreation" and the courses "which have been designed to produce innovative and effective managers for the hospitality/tourism industries" (QM)? There is a related question, concerning the curriculum in Central and Eastern European tourism departments. Witt (1994) refers to "improved education for those working in the tourism industry is essential if Eastern Europe is to compete successfully with the West". He emphasises the need for management education, for a reorientation of economics education towards the market economy and for language education largely dropping the previous focus on Russian. Golemski (1991) similarly supports a westernisation "quickly and effectively", referring to market economics and marketing and proposing that "staff ... should be sent to corresponding institutions in the West in order to receive appropriate training which would enable them to carry out their new duties more effectively".

The writer's experience, and that of colleagues at Queen Margaret College Edinburgh, in working with colleagues at AWF, Poznan , supported by an EU TEMPUS scheme, has been founded on such a process of 'modernisation', or 'improvement' , though the writer prefers to think of the process as more of a two-way collaboration. Taking AWF, Poznan as an example, is there a risk that the 'scientific' content of courses - related to the Academy's status as "a scientific institution doing research in fields related to its educational profile ... especially the humanistic and nature bases of physical culture and tourism" - will be reduced to permit growth of modern management and business courses. Would this necessarily be 'progress' in a context of 'new tourism' or 'sustainable tourism' where understanding of the natural and cultural environments as a key to sustainable development and management is increasingly regarded as essential? Conversely, given the popularity of environmentally-oriented courses at QM could the business oriented courses - arguably essential in an increasingly market oriented economy - be allowed to decline?

Of course the reality of change will be less simplistic than suggested here. It does suggest to this author, however, that there is a strong case to be made for caution and for a broad perspective to be taken of the direction of change. Quoting from a report of the Polish Institute for Sustainable Development,

> If enterprises and state administration are not prepared in terms of organisation and equipped in appropriate legal instruments, then the programme of mass privatisation which Poland is looking forward to in the near future may not live up to expectations. The important problem which may be decisive to the success of the mass privatisation programme is the bad ecological situation of certain enterprises. (...) The promotion of

> ecology by persons who have direct influence on political and economic decisions will influence the development of ecological awareness of the society, which will result in setting up of pressure groups as powerful as political parties (Stodulski and Starczewska, 1993).

While these authors were not referring specifically to the tourism industry, their reference to the essential interconnections between the ecological, social, economic and political perspectives is relevant here.

Awareness of Central and Eastern European higher education traditions in the various 'parentages' of tourism education is an important contribution to the debate, currently undervalued in the simplistic language of 'modernising the curriculum' sometimes applied to Western assistance to elsewhere in the world. The 'East' has much to offer the 'West' in its contrasting and perhaps complimentary experience of tourism development and tourism education - it must not be a one-way flow. The 'East' also still has the opportunity to follow a path towards a redefined tourism industry which is founded on the individual spirit of place or *genius loci* of the individual, recently liberated countries and regions rather than uncritical adoption of a 'Western model' which has failed at least in part when measured against criteria for sustainable development. A defining slogan for improvement should be not "West is Best" but "Test the West".

## References


Adams, R., J. Carruthers and S. Hamil (1991). *Changing Corporate Values*. London: New Consumer.

Blunt, P. (1995). 'Cultural Relativism, 'Good' Governance and Sustainable Human Development'. *Public Administration and Development*, 15: pp.1-9.

Canada, Government of (1990). *Canada's Green Plan for a Healthy Environment*. Ottawa.

Council for National Academic Awards (1993). *Review of Tourism Studies Degree Courses*. London, CNNA.

Darling, F. (1969). *Wilderness and Plenty*. New York: Ballantine Books.

Darling, F. and J.M. Boyd (1964). 'The Highlands and Islands'. In: Collins, *New Naturalist*, pp.291-299, London.

Evans, J. (1993). 'Tourism graduates: a case of overproduction'. *Tourism Management*, August, 14: p.4.

Golemski, G. (1991). 'The needs of higher level education in tourism in post-communist countries of Middle-Eastern Europe'. *Tourist Review*, 46(1): pp.3-5.

Hall, D. and V. Kinnaird (1994). 'Ecotourism in Eastern Europe'. In: E. Cater and G. Lowman (eds.), *Ecotourism: A Sustainable Option*. John Wiley and sons: Chichester, pp.111-137.

Hawkins, D.E. (1994). 'Ecotourism: Opportunities for Developing Countries'. In: W.F. Theobold (ed.). *Global Tourism*. Oxford: Butterworth-Heinemann Ltd, pp.261-273.

HMSO (1994). Sustainable Development: the UK Strategy. Cm 2426.

Howie, F. (ed.) (1990). *Proceedings of the Sustainable Tourism Development Conference*. Queen Margaret College: Edinburgh.

Howie, F. (1991). *Scotland: Myths and Monsters; Tourism and Truth. Proceedings of the conference, Tourism och resande i teori och praktik.* Hogskolan Falun Borlange: Sweden.

Howie, F. and D. List, (Unpublished paper based on Honours Dissertation, Representations and images of Poland. (by D. List, 1995).

Howie, F. (Forthcoming). 'Sustainable Tourism in Challenging Circumstances: the Parc National des Cevennes, France'. *Tourism Management*.

Howatson, A.C. (1990). *Toward Proactive Environmental Management*. Ottawa: Conference Board of Canada.

Hughes, G. (1995). 'The Cultural Construction of Sustainable Tourism'. *Tourism Management* 16, 1: pp.49-59.

International Institute for Sustainable Development, (1993). 'Indicators for the Sustainable Management of Tourism'. In: World Tourism Organisation, *Report of the International Working Group on Indicators of Sustainable Tourism to the Environment Committee*. Winnipeg, Canada.

I.U.C.N. (1974). World Conservation Strategy.

Ivison, J. (1995). *Changing Tourism*. 1 September. Edinburgh: Scotsman Publications.

Krippendorf, J. (1987). *The Holiday Makers*. Oxford: Heinemann Professional Publishing Ltd.

Leopold, A. (1968). *Sand County Almanac.* University of Wisconsin Press.

Meadows, D. and D. Meadows D. (1972). *The Limits to Growth.* New York: Signet Books / New American Library

Mowforth, M. (1993). 'In Search of an Eco-tourist'. *Tourism in Focus Journal.* London: Tourism Concern.

Muir, J. (1984). *Summering in the Sierra.* Madison: University of Wisconsin Press.

Murphy, P.E. (1994). 'Tourism and Sustainable Development'. In: W. Theobold (ed.), *Global Tourism.* Oxford: Butterworth-Heinemann Ltd.

Parks Canada (1994). 'Case Study: Visitor Activity Monitoring Process (VAMP)'. In: W. Theobold, (ed.), *Global Tourism.* Oxford: Butterworth-Heinemann Ltd.

Pearce, D. (1992). *Tourist Organisations.* Longman: Harlow.

Poon, A. (1993). *Tourism, Technology and Competitive Strategies.* Wallingford: C.A.B. International.

Prentice, R., F. Howie, and S. Guerin (Forthcoming). *Wildland Management Requirements for Tourism Based on a Deep Understanding of Visitor Motivations - the Role of Substitutability.*

Read, S.E. (1980). 'Special Interest Tourism'. In: B. Weiler and C. Hall, (eds.). London: Belhaven Press, pp.4-5.

Robertson, J. (1978). *Signposts to a Self-fulfilling Future.* London: James Robertson Publications.

Royal Commission on Environmental Pollution, (1988). *Twelfth Report, Best Practicable Environmental Option.* London: Cm 310, HMSO.

Ryan, C. (1995). 'Tourism Courses: a New Concern for New Times?' *Tourism Management* 16, 2: pp.97-100.

Stodulski, W. and G. Starczewska. 'Ownership Transformations in Industry vs Environmental Protection'. *Report of the Institute for Sustainable Development* 3. Warsaw.

Scottish Natural Heritage, (1993). *Sustainable Development and the Natural Heritage: the SNH Approach.* SNH: Edinburgh.

Scottish Tourist Board (1992). *Tourism and the Scottish Environment: A Sustainable Partnership*. Edinburgh.

Scottish Tourism Co-ordinating Group (1994). *Scottish Tourism Strategic Plan*. Edinburgh.

Scottish Tourist Board (1995). *A New Vision for Scotland*. Edinburgh.

Scottish Tourist Board (1995). *Corporate Plan 1995/1996*. Edinburgh.

Schumacher, E.F. (1973). *Small is Beautiful: A study of economics as if people mattered*. London: Bloggs and Briggs.

Stankey, G.H., D.N. Cole, R.C. Lucas *et al.* (1985). *The limits of acceptable change (LAC) system for wilderness planning*. Washington DC: US Forest Service.

Tourism Action Group, (1995). *Filling the Gaps: Skills for Tourism*. London: Confederation of British Industry.

Turner, R.K., D. Pearce and I. Bateman (1994). *Environmental Economics*. London: Harvester-Wheatsheaf.

United Nations Conference on the Environment and Development (UNCED) Rio Conference, (1992). Rio de Janeiro.

Urry, J. (1992). *The Tourist Gaze*. London: Sage.

Weiler, B. and M.C. Hall (1992). *Special Interest Tourism*. London: Belhaven Press.

Wickers, D. (1992). 'Whither Green?'. *The Sunday Times*, 5 January.

World Commission on Environment and Development, (1987). *Our Common Future*. Oxford University Press.

World Tourism Organisation (1985) *The Role of Recreation Management in the Development of Active Holidays and Special Interest Tourism and Consequent Enrichment of the Holiday Experience*. Madrid.

# Chapter 17

# Developing sustainable tourism management education: a European project

**Bill Bramwell,**
**Ana Goytia and Ian Henry**

## 1. INTRODUCTION TO THE PROJECT

This paper describes a project to develop resources on sustainable tourism management for use by educators teaching on postgraduate and post-experience courses in Europe. The project, funded by the European Commission Directorate General XXIII, was developed in recognition of the importance of ensuring that tourism in Europe does not threaten the natural and human resources available for present and future generations, which includes maintaining a sustainable and competitive tourism industry. To achieve these ends, tourism managers are required to have new skills, which implies new approaches in management education and training. While there is a growing recognition that new management perspectives are required, so far this has not been matched by any significant provision in European Union (EU) countries of management education programmes specifically in sustainable tourism management. In addition, many tourism educators are unfamiliar with developments in the concepts and practical applications of sustainable tourism management and are unaware of, or do not have access to, materials on which courses can be based. These difficulties are limiting the incorporation of the issues of sustainability into tourism management courses more generally. Such gaps in management education will tend to perpetuate the current situation where many tourism professionals are either unaware of, or disinterested in, sustainable tourism concerns or else are finding it difficult to turn good intentions about sustainability into sound management practice.

In order to address this situation, this project provides an explanatory framework and materials on sustainable tourism management for those involved in tourism management education in EU countries in universities and other higher education establishments and in national and regional tourism related agencies. The project is intended to assist tourism management educators to inform their own courses with sustainable tourism management approaches and techniques. The language used and degree of conceptual and theoretical sophistication included is designed to be appropriate for application to postgraduate level study, although the issues and principles which have been identified are relevant at other levels. It was considered inappropriate to provide a single prescriptive curriculum, particularly given the wide range of courses and contexts in Europe, and it is intended that the materials should be used and adapted in many ways for differing needs and circumstances.

The main output of the project is a publication for tourism educators entitled *Sustainable Tourism Management: Principles and Practice* (Bramwell *et al.* 1996), which has been disseminated through ATLAS and other networks. It includes the resources for management educators which are outlined in this paper, and it is intended as a cost effective and influential means for the European Commission to assist in improving the quality of tourism management education across Europe. It was considered that the provision and promotion of such materials for use by tourism educators will mean that the maximum number of people in different European countries will benefit from the initiative.

There are several European transnational elements to this project. First, the educational resources produced draw upon sustainable tourism management practice in a range of EU Member States and they emphasise the need for sustainable tourism management to be applied sensitively to local environmental, economic and cultural conditions in different countries. Second, the development of the resources also draws upon a consultation exercise with practitioners and policy makers and with educators across Europe. Third, dissemination of the materials to educators throughout Europe using the ATLAS and other networks is also a central feature of the project. The project involves a project team from ATLAS member universities in three different countries: the University of Deusto, Spain (Ana Goytia); Loughborough University, UK (Ian Henry and Guy Jackson); Sheffield Hallam University, UK (Bill Bramwell); and Tilburg University, the Netherlands (Greg Richards and Jan van der Straaten). The European transnational character of the project is considered particularly important since many of the impacts of tourism cross national boundaries, there is now a wide range of EU policies affecting tourism, and increasing numbers of tourism managers are likely to work in more than one European country.

The present discussion will examine just two aspects of the project, both related to the content of the educational resources to be produced and then disseminated to tourism management educators. The first aspect is the content of the theoretical framework developed to assist understanding of sustainable tourism management. The second focus is on case studies of practical tourism management from a range of European Member States which were produced for this project and serve to illustrate the potential and the pitfalls of implementing sustainable tourism management in different types of context.

## 2. THE ELEMENTS OF THE PROJECT

The two aspects examined here in detail should be seen as integral elements of a project of five closely related parts. In brief, these are:

*1. A consultation process with relevant practitioners and policy makers in tourism and related cultural, environmental and economic fields in different European countries on the requirements of management education in sustainable tourism.*

This involved a postal questionnaire and also consultations and interviews with key individuals and experts from industry (including representatives from tourism industry associations, tourism enterprises, environmental organisations, and central government and other public sector bodies) and from management education. The postal questionnaire and consultations sought their reactions to the issues, approaches and techniques of sustainable tourism management identified by the project team as potentially important in management education. The consulters were also asked for their own views on the design of a sustainable tourism management education programme.

*2. The development of a summary of a broad range of principles and issues of sustainable tourism management for use by management educators.*

This is presented within a theoretical framework that serves to introduce and elaborate key ideas and to highlight approaches and issues considered particularly important. This theoretical framework was developed following a literature review and discussion among the project team, and it also drew on the findings of the consultation with industry and educators.

*3. The examination in eight detailed case studies of tourism developments involving a variety of commercial, public sector and partnership organisations, and in the fields of urban, rural and mass tourism.*

The case studies illustrate practical applications of ideas set out in the theoretical framework. They incorporate analysis of the environmental, economic and cultural impacts of tourism activity and of their planning and management in a variety of local contexts and in relation to different tourism markets. The principles and issues identified in the case studies focus on the approaches and skills in practical management which attempt to combine business practice with sensitivity to local culture and environment and which seek to sustain natural and human resources and diversity.

*4. The provision of guidelines for management educators on how these resources on sustainable tourism can assist them in devising their own curriculum suited to their specific needs and circumstances.*

These guidelines suggest ways in which the resources might be adapted by management educators to differing national contexts, educational systems and institutional settings, as well as to differing course lengths, modes of delivery, and so on.

5. *Dissemination of the project outputs to those responsible for tourism education and training in different national contexts, notably those who operate at the level of postgraduate education and post-experience education.*

Included in this is the production and distribution of the publication *Sustainable Tourism Management: Principles and Practice*, as well as a range of promotional activities.

When this process is complete a full set of materials, incorporating the theoretical framework, case studies and curriculum guidelines, will have been compiled and disseminated as a resource for tourism management educators to adapt to their specific contexts.

## 3. A FRAMEWORK FOR UNDERSTANDING SUSTAINABLE TOURISM MANAGEMENT

One important aspect of this project was the development of a framework to aid understanding and to review the principles and issues surrounding sustainable tourism management. This theoretical framework was developed for use by management educators alongside the eight case studies of sustainable tourism management practice. There has been considerable recent development of ideas on sustainable tourism management, as reflected in innumerable journal papers and many conferences all over the world. Despite this high level of interest, it is difficult to identify sources which reduce the work for management educators by systematically drawing together a wide range of the concerns of sustainable tourism management within a relatively concise review. This part of the project attempts to provide a theoretical framework to aid understanding of a range of important principles and issues of sustainable tourism management. The content was developed following discussion among the project team, and it incorporates the findings of the consultations with tourism industry representatives and tourism educators.

A key premise behind the theoretical framework is that the concept of sustainable tourism management is not value free. It is rare for this point to be made in the literature, which may suggest that sustainable tourism management is a single, unified perspective. However, it is argued here that it is what might be called a contestable concept, one that offers a variety of competing interpretations. These alternative interpretations are important as they will alter significantly our policy prescriptions and management practice. The analysis also develops in detail one approach to sustainable tourism management, as this was considered to give the analysis coherence and clarity and thus aid understanding, and the approach itself is regarded as particularly important and valuable. Notably, it broadens the field of concern by integrating social, cultural, economic, environmental and political issues, and it also advocates a multi-disciplinary approach to understanding sustainable tourism management, which removes the traditional boundaries between management, economic, political, cultural, sociological and environmental areas of study, boundaries that constrain a full understanding. The selected approach also focuses on policy and management as a means to work towards the desired ends of sustainable tourism. Its approach to this tourism policy and management emphasises adopting an holistic and a principled perspective, but it also suggests that in practice there is also a need for realism in policies and management given the existence of many constraints.

The overall framework used to examine sustainable tourism management provides a helpful sequence to introduce and elaborate on key ideas and it also serves to highlight the approaches and issues regarded as particularly important. Within the framework there are three elements: a discussion of the context for the field, an assessment of specific issues in sustainable tourism management, and a consideration of the practical means to implement sustainable tourism.

In explaining the context of the field, sustainable tourism is set within the wider concept of sustainable development, a concept which is evident in policy thinking at a variety of levels, not least in EU tourism policy debates. For instance, the recent *Green Paper on Tourism* from DGXXIII of the European Commission (1995) argues that it is vital for the future of the European tourism industry for it to operate according to the broad principles of sustainable development. Consideration then is given to why it is important to use the concepts of sustainable development and sustainable tourism development. This includes an appraisal of the potential environmental, social, cultural and political benefits and costs of tourism development, as well as of the reasons why the market economy may fail to allocate resources sustainably and why governmental and other interventions are necessary. Sustainable development provides an alternative starting point to the allocation of resources. This is the normative contention that there are ecological and other boundaries or limits to the use of resources. Consideration is then given to such terms as alternative tourism and ecotourism, which some regard as synonymous with sustainable tourism, but which are seen as more restricted terms that do not embrace the full richness of the philosophy of sustainable tourism.

The second element of the framework examines selected key issues in sustainable tourism management. Many respondents in the consultation with industry and with educators considered that a clear definition of sustainable tourism is a vital starting point for an educational programme, although some were concerned this may give the impression of simplicity in what is a complex field. Because of this, the framework pays a lot of attention to defining the potential characteristics of sustainable tourism and of sustainable tourism management. One specific approach to sustainable tourism management considered particularly valuable is examined in detail, including an assessment of its theoretical and conceptual foundations and its application in practice.

The third, and perhaps most important, concern of the framework is with the practical means to implement the principles of sustainable tourism. Both the project team and the respondents in the survey of tourism industry and tourism education professionals saw practical management and policy implementation as central to an effective education programme. Therefore, strategic and operational management interventions are outlined and assessed, and a series of case studies examine the potential and the pitfalls which may be involved in implementation within tourism organisations.

Some aspects of this framework will now be considered in a little more detail, starting with the important premise that sustainable tourism is a contestable concept, with many potential interpretations. It was considered important that an education programme in this field should touch on some of the issues involved in these alternative viewpoints as they will alter significantly the objectives and practice of tourism policy and management. These differing perspectives on sustainable tourism can helpfully be related to a distinction made by O'Riordan (1981) between two 'green' philosophies. This discussion elaborates and develops distinctions made by O'Riordan between the philosophies of 'ecocentricism' and 'technocentrism' (for a fuller discussion see Henry and Jackson, forthcoming).

Ecocentricism rejects market economy-based social relations as they are considered to provide the basis for a materialist and consumer-orientated society, promoting selfish values and short-term thinking and leading to the destruction of ecological resources. From the ecocentric approach, natural resources are seen to have an intrinsic or inherent value in themselves and so must be conserved whether or not they are likely to provide particular benefits to human society. From this perspective, emphasis may be placed on the importance of community participation in decision making, and this can lead to a rejection of modern technology as this requires 'elitist' technical and scientific expertise and thus reduces community involvement. New technologies and management techniques to provide technical fixes and provide resource substitutes may also be regarded as irrelevant as in the long term they are likely simply to reinforce our undesirable selfish and materialist values. From an ecocentric stance, there is likely to be a presumption that tourism should be reduced in scale in order to conserve resources and to strengthen local communities.

At the other end of the spectrum of 'green' philosophies for O'Riordan is technocentrism. This approach incorporates both an acceptance of market economy principles and of the centrality of scientific thinking in order to address the problems of resource misuse, with this scientific thinking represented by, for example, technology, planning and management. From this perspective, emphasis is usually placed on the instrumental value of resources to society, for the benefit of people in the present day and often also of future generations. Economic growth is likely to be supported, as it is considered to improve our ability to reduce the adverse impacts of economic activities such as tourism. Our increased ability to reduce these negative impacts is supposed to derive from greater investment in research, from new technologies and improved planning and management systems, and from the reduction in material poverty which enhances the ability of people to choose to behave more sustainably. Controls may be sought to reduce the adverse impacts of resource use, such as by taxing polluters, by imposing price mechanisms to ration resource use, and by setting legally enforced minimum environmental standards. In addition to regulation and control, more sustainable forms of tourism may also be developed and promoted. More generally, technocentricism may accept increased tourism, but only when it both promotes economic growth and is managed to conserve resources.

Hence, sustainable tourism is a contestable concept, which is important as the alternative interpretations will alter significantly our policies and management practices. The framework document then goes on to examine one approach in detail which was considered to have the important strengths of offering an holistic perspective, of emphasising putting ideas into practice and of identifying what may be feasible in practice. This approach to sustainable tourism management is based on a particular technocentric stance, and ten of the principles behind the approach are now briefly outlined.

*First, the approach sees policy, planning and management as appropriate and indeed essential responses to the problems of natural and human resource misuse in tourism.* From this perspective, sustainable tourism management is a positive approach intended to reduce the adverse consequences of, and to maximise the benefits resulting from, the complex interactions between the tourism industry, the visitors, the environment and the host communities (Bramwell and Lane, 1993). It is premised on the belief that all those involved in tourism have an ethical responsibility to seek to avoid the misuse of natural and human resources (Hultsman, 1995; Wight, 1993). This calls for not only an analysis of the impacts of tourism's operations but also the development and implementation of practical measures to secure more sustainable tourism practices.

*Second, the approach is generally not anti-growth, but it emphasises that there are limitations to growth and that tourism must be managed within these limits.* The emphasis is on preventing the over-exploitation of resources, which is seen as requiring the identification of limits considered to be sustainable and the management of growth within these standards (World Commission on Environment and Development, 1987; Butler, 1991).

*Third, long-term rather than short-term thinking is necessary.* The approach involves working for the long-term viability and quality of resources in nature and society. This means moving from short-term to long-term thinking and planning, so that it is no longer acceptable to exploit and exhaust scarce resources - natural, social or cultural - and then move on to new tourism products and destinations. A central proposition is that the stock of resources left to future generations should be no less than that inherited by the current generation.

*Fourth, the concerns of sustainable tourism management are not just environmental, but are also economic, social, cultural, political and managerial.* The consultation with tourism industry professionals showed a marked tendency for them to equate sustainability with environmental issues alone. This may well be because environmental problems have been more prominent in both the trade and popular press, and also because there are more government regulations in the area of the environment for industry to comply with. However, sustainability is also fundamentally about the viability and vibrancy of different ways of life, the conservation of heritage resources, and the diversity and strength of local economies and social structures (Craik, 1991; Pearce, 1994). These human resources are just as scarce and require just as much care and nurture as natural resources. Prominence is also given to politics, planning and management as crucial arenas to achieve the desired ends of sustainable tourism and sustainability more generally (Hall, 1994). Political decision-making and managerial practices appropriate for sustainable tourism need to be encouraged. This wider conception of sustainable tourism management - including environmental, economic, social, cultural, political, planning and managerial concerns - as well as the integration of these diverse elements are seen by the project team as key features of this present approach. This in turn requires multidisciplinary perspectives on issues and in policy and planning responses.

*Fifth, the approach emphasises the importance of satisfying human needs and aspirations, which entails a prominent concern for equity and fairness.* The World Commission on Environment and Development (1987) highlights our responsibility to ensure that development is directed towards meeting both the essential needs of the poor, including their need for sufficient food, clean water, shelter and clothing, and also their aspirations for an improved quality of life. The equitable distribution of wealth more generally is also closely related to sustainability. One reason why this is important is because poverty can often force people into unsustainable behaviour, while the wealthy can afford to ignore or escape the adverse environmental or social consequences of their actions. For the World Commission, meeting human needs and aspirations means equity or fairness in terms of access to resources and to their benefits and in the distribution of the costs and benefits of development. The overall point of sustainable development is to safeguard and improve the quality of life for present and future generations. Preserving the integrity of the global environment and its physical resources is a precondition of all other aspects of the quality of life, but people also value access to a diverse range of other types of resources, including material living standards, public health, and community and cultural resources.

*Sixth, all stakeholders need to be consulted and empowered in tourism decision making, and they also need to be informed about sustainable development issues.* Sustainable tourism means taking account of people's views and choices on their present and future needs and welfare and on environmental, economic, social and cultural issues. The processes of consultation are central to taking account of people's views and preferences, and this should involve exchanging information, opinion, evaluation and action as well as making the most of expertise, knowledge and resources (Drake, 1991; Ritchie, 1993; Simmons, 1994). Achieving a wider consultation and empowering all those with an interest in tourism and its consequences means giving full consideration to power, as power governs the interplay of individuals, organisations and other social groupings that influence, or try to influence the direction of strategic or operational decisions.

*Seventh, while sustainable development should be a goal for all policies and actions, putting the ideas of sustainable tourism into practice means recognising that in reality there are often limits to what will be achieved in the short- and medium-term.* It is important to recognise that in the real world there are many forces influencing the operation of the economy, the culture of business environments, the power of governments, and also affecting people's social relations, values and behaviour, which constrain the extent to which we will secure fully sustainable practices in the short- and medium-term. The consequence of such forces is that, whatever ambitions we have for sustainability as a goal for all policies and actions, there are likely to be limits to what will be achieved in practice. This certainly does not mean that one should not present policy alternatives or not have the ambitious objectives of sustainable development. It is simply an acknowledgement that the existence of a moral case for an action does not mean that the action will be taken. Hence, it is important to identify not just the ultimate goal or ideal outcome but also what may be feasible along the path to reach that goal. Of course, some tourism activities may produce irreversible or severe consequences over which there should not be compromises and they should be resisted.

*Eighth, an understanding of how market economies operate, of the cultures and management procedures of private sector businesses and of public and voluntary sector organisations, and of the values and attitudes of the public is necessary in order to turn good intentions into practical measures.*

*Ninth, there are frequently conflicts of interest over the use of resources, which means that in practice trade-offs and compromises may be necessary.*

*And, tenth, and last, the balancing of costs and benefits in decisions on different courses of action must extend to considering how much different individuals and groups will gain or lose.* While sustainable tourism should strive for equitable outcomes, in the real world it is likely that management decisions will still benefit some more than others and that some decisions will adversely affect some people. The distributional outcomes between individuals, groups and also generations are vital considerations when examining the relative costs and benefits of alternative courses of action. Social equity and fairness are seen as essential concerns of this present approach to sustainable tourism management.

After this examination of principles of sustainable tourism management, the framework document then considers practical and sustainable means of incorporating sustainable tourism objectives into strategic and operational management activities. For instance, it identifies such activities as the setting of key limits or targets for the use of resources, the formulation and implementation of formal strategic plans, the reduction of waste and use of recycling technology, the adoption of 'green' product purchasing policies and the use of eco-labelling to promote informed and more sustainable consumer choices. The framework also emphasises the importance of recognising the many different interest groups or stakeholders which are involved and also of appreciating their differing perspectives on the issues. These stakeholders include government, individual enterprises, 'green' and non-'green' consumers, lobbying and good practice groups and community based groups. Without an understanding of the views of such stakeholders, it will be difficult to consult successfully and to develop effective partnerships with all those involved. In practice stakeholders will also vary in their ability to influence decision-makers and they are also unlikely to gain or lose out equally from particular courses of action. These are all issues which need full consideration in approaches to sustainable tourism management.

## 4. Selecting and Developing the Case Studies in Sustainable Tourism Management

In this project a series of eight case studies provides the main means to examine the opportunities and difficulties which may be encountered in practice by managers involved in tourism-related organisations in Europe. These case studies were not selected on the basis of their exemplifying either good or bad practice in sustainable tourism management. Instead, they were chosen to illustrate some of the issues and problems facing managers in a variety of tourism contexts in Europe in relation to the expanded approach to sustainable tourism management discussed in the framework document. The eight case studies are of:

- Alpine resort tourism in Switzerland.
- Environmental policies of Eurodisney in France.
- The development of the National Forest in the UK.
- Event-led tourism in Sheffield in the UK.
- The LEADER project in the La Rioja region in Spain.
- Environmental policies on the Costa Brava in Spain.
- Airline and holiday operations of British Airways.
- The Sumava National Park on the Czech Republic's border with Austria and Germany.

Several criteria were involved in their selection by the project team, including intentions that they reflect: a geographical spread with cases from Northern, Southern, Eastern and Western Europe; a mix of rural and urban contexts; both mass tourism and special interest tourism; large- and also small-scale provision; different sectors of the tourism industry (such as a tourist carrier and a commercial tourist attraction in the private sector, and regional and city-level tourism planning involving the public and sometimes also the private sectors); strategic and also operational levels of policy and management; and tourist products at varying product life cycle stages. In addition, the selection incorporates three case studies of particular significance in relation to European Union policies both for regional development and more generally. The La Rioja region in Spain represents one of the less developed, rural regions identified by the EU for regional aid under Objective 5b of the European Regional Development Fund. This case study examines the EU-funded LEADER project which involves rural tourism development. Sheffield is a city with declining manufacturing employment and which has benefited from EU European Regional Development Funds as it lies within an Objective 2 region. The Sumava National Park case study is of particular interest in respect of the area being funded by the EU as a trans-border initiative to ease problems resulting from the existence of a shared border between two Member States and another country. Although the Park is based in the Czech Republic, it shares borders with both Austria and Bavaria (see Figure 1), and it is this case study which will now be examined in a little more detail (for a fuller account of the Sumava case see Evans and Henry, 1996).

## 5. THE SUMAVA NATIONAL PARK CASE STUDY

The discussion of this case study is limited to aspects which exemplify the wider notion of sustainable tourism management adopted by the project team, which embraces not just environmental, but also economic, social, cultural, political and managerial concerns. The choice of this case study is particularly appropriate given the location and subject matter of this conference. However, there is a second reason to focus here on a case study from Central and Eastern Europe. The approach which has been proposed here for sustainable tourism management poses fundamental questions about political policies and practices, the balance between market forces and government intervention, and about the consequences of tourism for social equality and social stratification. It may be the case that these issues are sometimes easier to discuss and debate in the context of the transformation of Central and Eastern Europe where, in the post-communist era, few ways of working are accepted unquestioningly.

The Sumava National Park incorporates an area of significance for a wide variety of flora and fauna and a range of habitats, most notably meadow pasture, peat bogs and forest. During the communist era the area was protected by legislation and an 8 km zone adjoining the border was depopulated by the authorities in order to secure the border. The area lost most of its ethnic German population after the Second World War, with many being replaced by Slovaks and Eastern Czechs brought in to work in agriculture. Much of the Park is undeveloped and mainly accommodates such small-scale activities as camping, cycling and hiking. Although the development of a new through traffic route threatens a corridor within the Park, other infrastructural proposals are limited so far to outline proposals to allow some development on the left bank of Lake Ligno. As yet, the tourism sector in the Park has not grown significantly since the advent of the liberal democratic era in 1989, although there has been some modest tourism-related development with the building of an information centre and information signage provided by commercial operators.

Five sets of sustainable tourism management issues in the Park will be examined here very briefly. These identify the sustainable ends which may be sought, and also consider the sustainable political and managerial means which might be employed to achieve those ends. The case study does not seek to offer easy solutions to the problems in the Park, but rather it identifies issues that have to be addressed, sustainable ends that may be sought, and sustainable means of addressing these issues.

### 5.1. Environmental sustainability

The economic system of the communist era had fostered small-scale tourism, and this has since persisted and been further developed through a commitment to public transport, enforced restrictions on access which is limited to key routes and sites, support for cyclists and walkers and for walking and hiking trails, and provision of some good quality camping sites. However, managers now consider that they must not become over-dependent on this inherited pattern of tourism use, and much of the EU and Austrian grant aid for the Park area is targeted at diversifying the existing economic base. There is now a danger that infrastructural proposals, such as for roads and petrol stations, will have deleterious effects on the environment as a result of increases in visitor numbers and changes in the nature of tourist activities.

The Czech cultural view of tourism is relatively conservative, which may mean that the promotion of sustainable tourism may be different between the domestic Czech market and foreign markets. The foreign markets are still at an early stage of development despite the border location of the Park, and they have not grown as rapidly as expected since 1989, especially for long stay visits. Managers are developing programmes to widen the base of products and to move away from an over-reliance on the day visitor market. In particular, they need to overcome the tendency in the Austrian market to regard the Southern Czech Republic predominantly as a day recreation destination.

### 5.2. Cultural sustainability

The historical and cultural legacy of the area together with the landscape in its widest sense, currently represent the strongest tourism products. While indigenous craft markets have been targeted for development, there would appear to be other aspects of local craft production which could be further promoted, such as the use of local minerals for decorative products.

Farm tourism in the area is in its infancy, but before its potential is realised the hurdle of the cultural identity of the region will have to be crossed. Cultural identity is a problem issue for the country as a whole because of the imprint of its political subordination within the Soviet block, but it is even more marked as a problem in this region as it has endured the clearance of the ethnic German population and its replacement by people from the East, particularly from Slovakia, so that there is a multicultural legacy here. However, the new Czech Republic seems likely to promote the notion of Czech national and regional identity. If this region is to promote its indigenous culture as a tourism resource, this implies reflecting the German and Slovak histories, but these are viewed by some Czech people as negative cultural features.

### 5.3. Economic and managerial sustainability

Few sources of data exist on the tourism industry in the area, but there are clear indications that tourism investment represents largely small-scale, local capital. Share option capital plays little role in tourism infrastructural investment, this being limited to relatively large, former state controlled organisations, such as state owned breweries. Hence most of the tourism operators in the area - such as in craft production, accommodation provision, cycle and boat hire, camping grounds and catering - are likely to be relatively local, and this militates against the 'leakage' of tourism revenues from the regional economy. However, one exception to this may be smaller hotel chains operating under Czech names but with Austrian and German investment. The tourism industry in the area is also likely to include numbers of relatively new operators (established since 1989), and thus it is difficult to judge the medium- and long-term viability and volatility of this economic sector.

## 5.4. Political sustainability

The development of community involvement in decision making affecting tourism will clearly be influenced by the recent general pressures for economic liberalisation and the development of democratic systems. In the new Czech system there are legislative requirements to consult local communities about planning proposals, but in many instances Non Government Organisations (NGO's) have taken over *de facto* some of the decision-making functions which might be associated with local government.

The prevalence of pressure group activity in the period before the 'Velvet Revolution' has largely been replaced by a localisation of political parties, with a mobilisation of national political parties at local level around local issues. Consequently, there is potential for local participation and political involvement. However, with planning legislation only being phased in on a piecemeal basis and with pressures to reduce government intervention in markets, there is considerable potential for a laissez faire philosophy to dominate tourism development in the region. Despite this danger, the combination of pressure for community involvement and for the liberalisation of market opportunities, seems to be encouraging the advocacy of what might be called a socially responsible laissez faire system. Such an approach is exemplified in one proposed project to redevelop a deserted border village in this region. The village was to be purchased by one of Prague's major department stores and then converted to house a project for disabled children. The cost of running the project was to be met by the sale of a line of 'environmentally friendly' products in the department store. Part of the proposal also involved developing a game park on the site, which also had commercial implications. Although the project did not proceed beyond the proposal stage, it illustrates both the character of what is seen as good practice and also the difficulties of putting these ideas into practice. One important challenge for the political system will be for it to sustain such benign free market practices, and this challenge directly affects all areas of public and private sector activity, including those in the National Park.

## 5.5. The development of tourism management skills in a market economy

The establishment of a five year management education qualification for tourism managers in the region represents a significant local initiative, and this may facilitate the development of new management practices to counter some of the difficulties which have been identified by local tourism managers. One difficulty they have highlighted is that sustainable policies for tourism marketing and also visitor interpretation and information provision have developed more slowly than they have for tourism product development. In addition, the view of the landscape of the region is still dominated by interpretation of historic sites which was inherited from the former political regime and reflects an unproblematised perspective. Managers are aware of this issue and are seeking a wider range of initiatives and a more integrated approach to marketing and interpretation.

### 5.6. Trans-border issues

One issue being addressed only by the larger independent NGOs is that there are few tourism policies concerned with sustainability in either Upper Austria or Bavaria to complement those being considered in the Czech Republic. It is unclear whether this reflects a belief among Austrian authorities that some parts of Austria are too developed to be worthy of a sustainable tourism policy. The main area of trans-border co-operation has been in trails for hiking and walking, but there is clearly a need for much broader co-ordination of trans-border policies, notably in respect of environmental and transport policy. The absence of such policy co-ordination between Austria, Bavaria and the Czech Republic must be a threat to the economic and environmental sustainability of the region, and hence its ability to sustain its current social structure.

## 6. CONCLUSIONS

The issues arising from the Sumava National Park case study illustrate the multidimensional concerns which are associated with the approach to sustainable tourism management adopted by the project team. Taken together, the eight case studies raise a wide range of such issues and they show the potential and the problems of sustainable tourism management encountered in practice in a range of contexts.

The discussion has explained the approach taken in this European Commission funded project to develop resources on sustainable tourism management for use by educators teaching on postgraduate and post-experience courses in Europe. Most attention has been directed at the content of the theoretical framework on sustainable tourism management and on one of the eight case studies developed to illustrate the potential and the difficulties of implementing sustainable tourism. As well as developing an explanatory framework and case study materials on sustainable tourism management, the project will also disseminate these educational resources to tourism management educators in EU countries using the ATLAS network and through other promotional activities in 1996.

The project is intended as a cost effective and influential means for the European Commission to assist in improving the quality of tourism management education across Europe. There are a number of European transnational elements to this project, and these were explained briefly as they may assist others to develop transnational tourism education projects.

**References**

Bramwell, B., I. Henry, G. Jackson, A. Goytia, G. Richards and J. van der Straaten (1996). *Sustainable Tourism Management: Principles and Practice.* Tilburg: Tilburg University Press.

Bramwell, B. and B. Lane (1993). 'Sustainable Tourism: An Evolving Global Approach'. *Journal of Sustainable Tourism* 1,1: pp.1-5.

Butler, R.W. (1991). 'Tourism, Environment, and Sustainable Development'. *Environmental Conservation* 18,3: pp.201-209.

Craik, J. (1991). *Resorting to Tourism: Cultural Policies for Tourist Development in Australia.* Sydney: Allen and Unwin.

Drake, S.P. (1991). 'Local Participation in Ecotourism Projects'. In: T. Whelan (ed.), *Nature Tourism: Managing for the Environment.* Washington D.C.: Island Press, pp.132-163.

DGXXIII (1995). *Green Paper on Tourism.* Brussels: DGXXIII, European Commission.

Evans, D. and I. Henry (1996). In: B. Bramwell, I. Henry, G. Jackson, A. Goytia, G. Richards and J. van der Straaten (eds.). *Sustainable Tourism Management: Principles and Practice.* Tilburg: Tilburg University Press, pp. 201-216.

Hall, C.M. (1995). *Tourism Politics: Policy, Power and Place.* Chichester: Wiley.

Henry, I. and G. Jackson (1996 forthcoming). 'Sustainability of Management Processes and Tourism Products and Contexts'. *Journal of Sustainable Tourism.*

Hultsman, J. (1995). 'Just Tourism: An Ethical Framework'. *Annals of Tourism Research* 22,3: pp.553-567.

O'Riordan, T. (1981). *Environmentalism.* London: Pion.

Pearce, P. (1994). 'Tourist-Resident Impacts: Examples, Explanations and Emerging Solutions'. In: W. F. Theobald (ed.), *Global Tourism: The Next Decade.* Oxford: Butterworth-Heinemann, pp.103-123.

Ritchie, J.R.B. (1993). 'Crafting a Destination Vision: Putting the Concept of Resident-Responsive Tourism into Practice'. *Tourism Management* October 1993: pp.379-389.

Simmons, D.G. (1994). 'Community Participation in Tourism Planning'. *Tourism Management* 15,2: pp.98-108.

Wight, P. (1993). 'Ecotourism: Ethics or Eco-Sell?'. *Journal of Travel Research* 31,3: pp.3-9.

World Commission on Environment and Development, (1987). *Our Common Future*. Oxford: Oxford University Press.

# Chapter 18

# Developing quality in tourism services: A brief overview

**Henryk Handszuh**

## DEFINING QUALITY

What makes a tourist choose one holiday destination over another? One of the most important factors is the price-quality ratio. Subjectively, quality in tourism can be defined as the relation between expectation and reality, which is assessed by consumer satisfaction. Quality is attained when pre-sale expectation of the client coincides with after-sale perception, or the latter slightly exceeds the former. There must be 'no negative surprises' on the part of the client, and the terms of the contract must be honoured. There may be various notions of quality, each corresponding to the kind and level of expectation of the various consumer segments. Nevertheless, all such segments will require common technical quality values which can be measured or compared to other products.

At the enterprise level, both management and staff intervene considerably in the perception of quality by the client. All in all, various discrepancies or gaps may be responsible for missing quality:

- the level of service expected by the client does not coincide with the company management perception of the client's expectations;
- the client's expectations are not efficiently communicated to all members of the company's staff;
- not all members of the staff can provide, or do provide, the service the way the client would expect;
- communication of the company to its clients about its service is inadequate, thus preventing the clients from identifying themselves with the service rendered;
- basic factors and conditions for quality in the establishment are not met and its environment (location) is inadequate to provide quality service.

Quality does not mean luxury, quality can and should be achieved at every, even the most modest, product category. Should the resulting product positively exceed the client's expectations, one may talk of excellence. However, if the service rendered considerably exceeds such expectations, it may mean excessive allocation of the company's resources which do not receive adequate remuneration.

One should also talk about the price paid for quality. Attaining quality does not mean that the client's requirements should be met at any cost. Considering this aspect, quality in fact can be defined as 'satisfying all the legitimate requirements and expectations of the client at an acceptable price' (Moullin, 1994).

There is an intrinsic link between quality and category, but both concepts are different, although they may refer to the same functional use of given facilities such as hotels, restaurants, rented cars, etc. Category denotes the level of luxury, the variety and sophistication of service designed for a given market segment, while quality means attaining expected standards at a given category.

Finally, quality in tourism services is a dynamic, not static, concept due to the ever changing demand and environment. Commitment to quality signifies that 'you do it all the time, or you undo it immediately'.

## TOURISM SERVICES

There is a distinction between 'a tourism service' and 'service', the latter normally meaning a single procedure, a person-to-person contact, between tourism staff and the client (there may also be automated services not requiring personal intervention or physical presence of staff). A tourism service means a tourism experience as a result of a whole process.

From another approach, in a narrow sense, tourism services are meant to denote services supplied by individuals, or juridical persons (companies), to travellers, i.e. the direct tourism consumers.

The popular approach considers also quality in tourism services as relating only to the delivery and consumption of a service. Nevertheless it should be accepted that this is but a part, although a culminating one, of the entire process intervening in the total quality of tourism services.

In a broader sense, tourism services will mean services supplied or traded to tourism companies and individual service suppliers directly servicing travellers or visitors (final consumers). *The General Agreement on Trade in Services (GATS)* defines 'supply of a service' as including 'the production, distribution, marketing, sale and delivery of a service' (GATS, 1994).

This supplier's approach coincides in considerable part with service perception by the client who relates quality to all the constituent elements of the total product (product, price, distribution, communication), or to the total service integrating all individual services and the process of their creation.

In conclusion, in identifying quality-related factors, a tourism company must pay due and equal attention to its both external and internal clients. The approach integrating both the quality of services and the processes leading to their supply brings about Total Quality Management (Abierta, 1994).

The company may also attempt to achieve the 'zero defects' result by eliminating the factors responsible for incompliance with quality, and resolving the problems derived from incompliance.

## TOURISM

A popular approach is to think of quality only in terms of international tourism, particularly leisure tourism, to be satisfied from the destination's own resources.

From the demand side, tourism is defined by WTO/United Nations as comprising 'the activities of persons travelling to and staying in places outside their usual environment for not more than one consecutive year for leisure, business and other purposes'.

What stems from this definition is that we should talk in broad terms about quality as applying to *all activities of visitors*, and *all travel purposes* (including, in particular, business-induced trips).

This suggests a more comprehensive approach to quality in tourism. But there are more elements to be considered:

- tourism brings to the destination new consumer demand, from the same country (*domestic tourism*), or from abroad (*inbound tourism*), and the conclusion is that the same quality must be available to both groups of visitors;
- second, products and services generated by tourism establishments at the destinations are consumed by both the resident population and visitors, unless there is an imposed or natural, socio-economic or physical segregation of each consumer group due to inequality or market segmentation (eg. holiday villages). In other words, there must not be different 'qualities' of service for foreigners and locals;
- third, in addition to services provided by tourism establishments, visitors normally also make use of public amenities and service establishments (security, communications, water supply, banking, shopping, etc.). Accordingly, their quality impacts upon the total tourism product;
- fourth, visitor demand must be satisfied not only from *local*, but also from *imported* resources, and the conclusion is that the quality of both inputs, including imported resources (material, human, transborder) must be evaluated in respect of tourist requirements;

- finally, any site can be considered as a tourist destination or having a tourism vocation. Some destinations, for example, will be good only for business tourism, health services or the purpose of study. Such travel motivations should not be disregarded from the focus on total quality.

This comprehensive approach to understanding tourism and its quality is recommended, as it finally leads to the sustainability of tourism as an economic and cultural activity, since it will:
- benefit all kinds of travellers, and both visitors and residents;
- enhance local resources and imported goods and services for tourist use, and also resident use;
- create harmony between these resources and the interests of consumers, whether local or external.

The result of an all-inclusive quality approach to tourism is that, as tourism develops and consolidates, it will bring quality of life to everyone.

## BASIC FACTORS FOR QUALITY IN TOURISM SERVICES

An integrated or total approach to tourism services: in travel, in tourist sites, at destinations, suggests that work in favour of their quality must necessarily take into consideration its infrastructure and basic quality factors such as safety and security, hygiene, sanitation and salubrity, the condition of the natural environment, consumer protection and accessibility. These are predominantly technical factors, equally important to everyone, although some of these, for example, security, may be perceived differently by different clients. Not having such basic factors in place, seriously affects any work on quality at the company or establishment level.

The World Tourism Organisation, so far, has focused on these basic factors for quality. It adopted the *Tourism Bill of Rights and Tourist Code* (Sofia, 1985) concentrating on the social and cultural environment of tourism, it published a manual on *Quality Control of Tourism Products and Services* (Madrid, 1988), and as of 1990 it began a whole series of activities aimed at the environmental issues in tourism. It later adopted *Recommended Measures for Tourism Safety* (Buenos Aires, 1991) which urge states to undertake measures aimed at prevention, assistance and international cooperation, in respect of:
- risk identification;
- safety standards (fire prevention, food safety and other health requirements, environmental safeguards);
- public safety information;
- non-exposure of clients to security risks in the establishment;
- prevention of unlawful interference;
- prevention of illicit drugs;

- staff safety training;
- tourist health polices and medical assistance;
- facilities for insurance and travel assistance;
- definition of liability rules;
- consumer protection;
- legal protection and assistance.

Destinations plagued with delinquency, fraud, litter and drug problems; lacking safe water and support facilities for visitors and presenting uncertainty about the observance of tourist rights, are not good for individual work on quality in tourism services, and certainly will not attract new, and generate repeat, visitors, unless there are strong travel motivations disregarding basic factors for quality.

Some of these factors (risk identification and information, health services) are especially important to international visitors due to their orientation and communication problems. Their problems are evident especially in the field of consumer protection.

The United Nations *Guidelines for Consumer Protection* (New York, 1985) set out the following 'legitimate needs' of consumers:

"(a) The protection of consumers from hazards to their health and safety;
(b) The promotion and protection of the economic interests of consumers;
(c) Access of consumers to adequate information to enable them to make informed choices according to individual wishes and needs;
(d) Consumer education;
(e) Availability of effective consumer redress;
(f) Freedom to form consumer groups (...)".

A similar preliminary programme of consumer rights was already adopted by the Council of Ministers of the European Community in 1975.

The WTO *Safety Measures* distinguish the consumer situation of independent travellers and those buying packages of services through a travel organiser so that there exist: "clear-cut procedures for the expeditious, and possibly non-judicial, settlement of consumer disputes", particularly in favour of independent travellers.

The short time available to visitors for settling consumer differences, particularly international ones, justifies such speedy procedures. These should also be clearly determined liabilities of organisers, retailers and direct suppliers of tourism services and products for contract failures.

In the event of all-inclusive trips the *EC Directive on Package Travel, Package Holiday and Package Tours* (1990) establishes the travel organiser's responsibility for individual services contracted from within the countries of the European Union, i.e. the *Directive* affects all tourist destinations and products sold in this area. I believe this obligation corresponds to the natural consumer reaction to seek redress from the company to which the client is actually paying. Although the Directive has been slow in being implemented at national levels, it is already exerting strong pressure on tour operators and destination services alike to guarantee tourists sufficient consumer safety.

This instrument, together with other European Union legislation, such as on unfair terms in consumer contracts, general product safety, fraudulent publicity, the quality of bathing water and compensation rights of the passengers of air companies has instituted a uniform level of consumer protection from which tourism consumers seeking quality can benefit.

According to the *White Book on the Internal Market* published by the Commission of the European Community, the definition of detailed technical standards should be within the competence of the experts of European organisations on standardisation.

## HEALTH

In WTO's *Recommended Measures* regarding prevention, assistance and international cooperation for tourism safety, tourist health features as a vital issue for quality. It is recommended that the following standards should be available:

- food safety and water safety;
- hygiene, sanitation and salubrity;
- effective tourist health information on: vaccination requirements, sanitary and climatic characteristics of the destination, and health advice;
- availability and choice of health insurance and travel assistance (without, however, health insurance being a required frontier formality in international travel).

WTO addressed these issues in more detail in a set of policy guidelines on *Health Protection: Health Information and Formalities in International Travel* (Bali, 1993).

WTO believes that providing health-oriented information, including warnings about health hazards, by tourist information offices, tour operators and travel agents, tourist carriers and global distribution systems, does not frighten off travel, but is actually is a service to quality which will be appreciated by a mature, quality-conscious traveller and holiday maker.

**ACCESSIBILITY**

The perception of quality depends on the various modes of accessibility or barriers:

- administrative barriers in international tourism (so-called frontier formalities: visas, foreign exchange facilities, border controls, etc.);
- physical and communications, e.g. access by road, telephone (unless difficult physical access is appreciated by adventure travellers!);
- discriminating between consumers without or with disabilities;
- competitive barriers.

The contemporary tourist is increasingly sensitive to administrative barriers which affect the quality of a tourism experience more than that of a single tourism service. Therefore, the entrepreneur supplying the service usually does not feel concerned with such barriers. Nevertheless, in an open, democratic society the entrepreneur may be interested in demanding that the State dismantle barriers impeding freer access of external consumers to the country concerned, although such barriers may be the result of important political and economic considerations. At least efforts should be made to reduce, if not eliminate, all bureaucratic red tape.

Quality in tourism services is fully attained if such services are accessed by all willing consumers, including people with minor or more important, temporary or permanent, disabilities, which may be due to accidents, special care needs, medical condition or old age due to increased life expectancy. In other words, quality tourism must be accessible to all potential consumers representing the varied composition of society.

The following points are made:

- quality service, in addition to accessibility, is especially important for people with disabilities;
- clients with disabilities are especially vulnerable to risks due to the lack of quality;
- such clients must not be discriminated against, but rather provisions must be made to facilitate their tourist consumption.

WTO's position on this issue is given in the policy document *Creating Tourism Opportunities for Handicapped People in the Nineties (Buenos Aires, 1991)* in respect of:

- tourist information policy;
- preparation of staff;
- common requirements for tourist facilities;
- requirements concerning specific facilities.

Following these recommendations, a number of standards and practices are possible, such as:

- adequate design and tangible architectural standards;
- technical equipment to facilitate tourist visits and stays;
- availability of signs, symbols and other means of communication.

In the main tourist generating areas, namely Europe, North America and Japan, there is increasing pressure exerted by organisations for the disabled seeking indiscriminate access to tourism by consumers with disabilities. At the other end, such access is seen as a viable commercial opportunity to increase sales of tourism services.

### COMPETITIVE BARRIERS

It is important for the consumer to have the freedom of choice to select a quality service. A monopolistic situation in the marketplace, the lack of effective access to the market, or discrimination by the administration of tourism services suppliers on the grounds of their foreign or national origin, reduce pressure on quality.

Competition is healthy because it fosters quality. Various kinds of competition are at stake: with other national tourism companies, with foreign tourism companies, and with non-tourism national and international companies. The authorities are responsible for creating a fair competitive environment in the procedures of establishment, fiscal measures and investment incentives.

Market economies, and economic integration as is taking place in the European Union, naturally lead to free competition in the tourism marketplace. However, such competition, so far, is more strongly felt thanks to international hotel chains, European- and non-European-based, fast food chains, car rentals and CRS's. Tour operations and travel agency businesses are less effectively liberalised.

In a wider perspective, *the General Agreement on Trade in Services (GATS)* of the World Trade Organisation poses another long-term opportunity to introduce competition in the tourism sector from third countries, particularly the developing ones. Such countries will be interested in receiving facilities to increase their participation in the distribution channels and to allow market access to their individual service suppliers.

## ENVIRONMENT

People do not travel to live in comfortable hotels and eat in nice restaurants, although both are essential for the quality of their travel experience. They travel to live this experience in an appropriate, genuine environment. The situation is changing quickly. Although the majority of holiday makers and other travellers do not choose their destinations to enjoy 'green' tourism specifically, and may still not openly show environmental concerns, the environment, both natural and cultural, is becoming an increasing priority to tourists and, accordingly, the key asset of the tourism industry.

Disregarding this factor at present, even by a single enterprise, runs against its commercial interests - even in the short-term. More so, if this lack of concern for the environment takes place at a community or destination level. The environment is the source of uniqueness, which is considered a resource for quality in the situation where an increasing number of destinations seem to offer similar, standard products. There are already ample initiatives, guidelines and literature suggesting this approach to tourism development and quality. The following rules illustrate pretty well the message (Plog, 1991):

- **P**rotect the natural and beautiful;
- **R**educe density;
- **E**nhance seclusion and privacy;
- **S**eek quality;
- **E**mphasise diversity;
- **R**estore the natural, historical;
- **V**alue local culture, traditions;
- **I**nstitute building height limits;
- **N**egotiate open spaces;
- **G**ain community acceptance;

(while forming an attractive acronym PRESERVING).

## ROLE OF GOVERNMENTS

*'The constituents of the State Tourism System are obliged to:*
*1. Strictly comply with the conditions of efficiency and quality in the provision of tourism and leisure services.'*
From: Art. 18, Tourism Law of the State of Bolivar (Venezuela), June 1994.

This legal provision from Venezuela is quite meaningful. Although the law in point does not explain how this obligation is going to be enforced and the quality controlled, it is a testimony to government awareness of the importance of quality for successful tourism.

The question arises, to what extent the government can actually intervene in this matter. Several instruments and ways of intervention are possible, some of which have already been mentioned:

- reducing administrative barriers to travel;
- providing frameworks for fair competition;
- adopting and executing tourism master plans, including tourism zoning;
- responsibility for tourism's infrastructure (including public utilities);
- enforcing all kinds of safety requirements, particularly by means of licensing and inspection;
- providing public safety facilities, which are of equal interest to the population at large;
- instituting consumer protection laws and facilities, providing for standard setting frameworks;
- providing fiscal/grant assistance to quality-driven programmes;
- taking the lead in some outstanding services.

The adoption of appropriate government measures to promote quality may be the responsibility of national authorities and can be coordinated internationally, as seen in the example of the EC Directive and other European Union instruments.

In Europe, there are many examples of state aid to quality-oriented programmes. In France, for example, there is a beautification campaign to plant flowers in all towns and villages and, in the United Kingdom and Ireland incentives are available to restore and preserve old farms, manors and castles. In Spain the state has taken the initiative of establishing hotels in historical buildings thus setting an example of quality and authenticity, which has been followed by the private sector.

It is, however, unnecessary, not feasible, hardly practicable, costly and totally ineffective for the state to intervene in the stage of services provision in an attempt to enforce quality standards. In an open tourism economic system it is the tourist who chooses the services, establishment or destination.

## EDUCATION AND TRAINING

To design, observe and maintain technical quality standards, and to provide service, is the job of people. When introducing Total Quality the Japanese found that staff preparation represented a differentiating factor in competition. Hence two famous slogans: "Total quality begins and ends with training" (Kaoru Ishikawa), and "Before making goods we must produce people" (Konosuke Matsushita).

Disregarding semantic differences, when talking about staff preparation for quality, we must distinguish between the meaning and function of training and education.

The possibilities of training, meaning the development of personal skill, are limited. In contrast, the function of education is to enable staff to make full use of their own intellectual capacity, and therefore education has no limits. Total Quality 'discovers' the brain and its limitless capacity (Bray and Marin, 1994). Accordingly, training for specific functions comes after or during education.

When selecting personnel for jobs, all companies check candidates for knowledge, experience, aptitude and attitude. When selecting personnel for quality work in a tourism job, the attitude matters most, while experience, particularly outdated and poor experience, can be considered an aggravating factor.

We can analyse the psychological profiles of candidates, and try to select the 'right' people for the job. However, they may still not be able to function properly, unless we can ensure staff compatibility with the company, its functional modes, values and objectives. Once this is achieved, there is room to develop confidence and staff autonomy (Fernández López, 1995).

In his visionary *Global Paradox* John Naisbitt finds that "The bigger the world economy, the more powerful its smallest players". This statement fits the tourism industry very well because it is fragmented at the service level, and it consists of both large and small units. More powerful smaller units is the result of sharing and delegating, not diluting but sharply defining responsibilities by means of 'contracts with the staff'.

In large units the relationship between managers and staff is crucial for quality. The management must be trusted by the staff. Trust must be won by the management's own quality approach to work, its coherence between ideas and actions; giving an example by its conduct; showing loyalty to the company, superiors, and team members; never renouncing the leadership role and assuming corresponding responsibility; admonishing without hurting, etc.

There is a Spanish *refrán* (saying): *las palabras conmueven, el ejemplo arrastra* (action speaks louder than words). Popular wisdom tells us, indeed, that there is really nothing new when we talk about the modern, renewed approach to quality.

Internal, open and sincere communication, an open mentality and exchange of ideas in the company, all contribute to confidence, security and loyalty between staff members (Moller, 1995). In a big hotel, for example, any member of the staff must be able to handle the client's urgent business without referring the client to fellow staff members.

There is a growing need for quality education and training in the tourism sector. The World Tourism Organisation aims at this goal by acting as a catalyst in bringing out harmonised tourism curricula, each corresponding to well-defined needs.

The specific objectives are:
- To define quality standards for tourism education and training applicable on a global scale and in tourism regions of the world;
- To define human capital requirements of employers in the tourism industry in the member states;
- To strengthen National Tourism Administrations in terms of their human capital requirements and those of the tourism in industries they administer;
- To define tourism training programmes that meet the needs of the future professionals, of the employers in the tourism industry and of the member states.

## Costs of quality in tourism

Quality can be measured in a variety of ways. The company's growth, increasing its market or the net economic effect from its operations can be considered indirect indicators of quality.

Another way would be to evaluate the company's economic sustainability, not necessarily meaning continual growth and generating fresh profits, but rather maintaining healthy profit margins by continuously adapting to the changing demand, keeping costs under control, developing imaginative marketing, and preventing all kinds of losses.

A way to ensure sustainability may consist in keeping repeat clients, gaining new clients, and making all the clients open to accept innovative products. Gaining clients and keeping them is fundamental: there is a measurement to the effect that in order to gain a new client, we must invest 5 times more than to keep the old one. Investing in having repeat clients means continuously investing in quality.

Quality cannot be obtained without costs. But should increased costs lead to higher prices? They should not. Investing in quality means streamlining the processes and eliminating all dead wood in the enterprise, all these increasing operating costs and diminishing quality. Let us then look at the quality-related costs.

*Planning costs*
Quality cannot be improvised. Before undertaking measures to improve quality, the level of satisfaction of the clients must be determined, the strong and weak points must be identified, as well as the time and resources necessary to make improvements. An external audit is preferable.

*Education costs*
Education should be continuous to maintain staff sensitivity to quality. The management often lacks the capacity and the credibility to do so.

*Prevention costs*
Work aimed at the prevention of errors should be on-going or recurrent.

*Control costs*
The human and material costs of control need to be checked and kept under control.

*The costs of checking consumer satisfaction*
To analyse the results of business activity, clients' suggestions and complaints need to be monitored, open and closed clients' surveys need to be carried out, and the ratios of repeat and recommended customers need to be researched.

*Permanent maintenance costs*
Technical defects need to be attended to on a permanent basis.

*Working order and architectural costs*
To maintain consumer well-being, comfort and safety.

*Regaining unsatisfied clients' costs*
Reconciliation with unsatisfied clients must be swift.

*Labour sanitation costs*
To maintain a healthy, quality-oriented programme, the enterprise must be prepared to assume staff sanitation and reform costs, and to motivate and reward staff.

*Company image costs*
To offset adverse publicity originating, in particular, as a result of competition

*Quality Management costs*
Effective quality management staff should be remunerated accordingly (Vidal, 1994).

From this review it can be seen that disregarding quality-driven measures (which imply corresponding costs), leads the company to increase other expenditure (additional workforce, publicity, expensive thorough external audits, etc.) normally exceeding overall quality-maintenance costs, while the results for quality may still remain uncertain.

## TOOLS AND METHODOLOGIES AIMED AT QUALITY IN TOURISM SERVICES

In 1949 quality 'guru' Edward Deming gave his first course in Tokyo on measuring quality statistically. Deming's and other quality classics' (Juran, Crosby, Shingo) teaching has proliferated in the industrial sector and then in the services sector, including tourism.

A number of techniques to promote and audit quality have been developed at the tourism enterprise and destination levels.

### ISO Standard 9000

This standard is used to certify companies in the industrial and services sectors for quality by analysing the production processes. There are now over 30 countries, mainly European ones, which have adopted this and related standards. For the European Union countries it constitutes the basis for their policies concerning free circulation of goods and services.

The use of ISO standards is not obligatory, but is regulated by industry demand to deal with companies which have been certified for quality in accordance with this standard by recognised auditors. So far, however, there has hardly been any direct use of this methodology among tourism companies. In the meantime, related systems are developing. Examples include:

### ITQ 2000 (International Tourist Quality)

The method consists of three phases:
(a) Appraisal (qualitative evaluation of facilities and products/services, analysis of critical points).
(b) Consulting (education programmes, improvement plans to comply with ITQ Model).
(c) Audit (checking quality levels against the parametric model to confer a respective quality label to be entered in the ITQ 2000 register).

### HACCP

After its initial application in industrial processes in the sixties, the Hazard Analysis Critical Control Points (HACCP) system has today found new uses in food processing, catering, and specifically, food safety in the tourism industry. The system is broken down by the following phases:

- conduct of hazard analysis, identification of hazards and specification of preventive measures;
- identification of Critical Control Points;
- establishment of critical limits at each point;
- establishment of corrective action procedures;
- establishment of verification procedures;
- establishment of documentation procedures as appropriate.

WTO has begun food safety courses for tourism establishments with the use of this system which can be also considered appropriate in other tourism operations.

**Holonic - Virtual Organisation**

This can be applied to tourism destinations or large tourism systems, and can be defined as:

> A set of companies that acts integratedly and organically; it is constantly re-configured to manage each business opportunity a customer presents. Each company in the network provides a different process capability and is called a holon.
>
> Each configuration of process capabilities within the holonic network is called a virtual company. By combining the core competencies of many individual companies within the network, each virtual company is more powerful and flexible than the participating members alone could be. Each company in a virtual company is chosen because of its process excellence.
>
> Virtual companies are time based, value driven, and proconsumer oriented, but they are not a system of individual companies, an alliance of companies of the same sector, a purely informatic network, a system of companies open one to each other, long-term supply contracts in a value chain, a consortium of companies, or a partnership and/or a joint venture (Merli, 1995).

## WHY QUALITY HAS SUDDENLY BECOME SO IMPORTANT?

Quality has been always on people's minds, and the concept of quality has never been alien to tourism. However, the massification of travel and fierce competition have added a new impetus to the concept and application of this quality. This is due, in particular, to a number of factors:

- in the traditional tourist generating countries tourist demand is mature and saturated;

- leisure and business travellers are more demanding in terms in the price/quality ratio;
- new tourist destinations offer attractions similar to those in traditional destinations;
- new demand is originating in regions sensitive to quality;
- repeat demand is increasingly coming not only from experienced, but also aging travellers sensitive to quality.

As a result, destinations and tourism companies are forced to use all their reserves to compete successfully and survive. Work on quality in tourism services promotes quality standards but does not lead to uniformity, because it includes a large set of variables which must be contrasted with heterogeneous groups of customers. Since there are no limits to quality in tourism, work in this sector may be considered not only challenging, but also very attractive.

## REFERENCES

Abierta, A. (1994). 'Algunos criterios erróneos sobre la calidad'. *Turismo & Gestión de la calidad.*

Bray, L. and A. Marín (1994). In: Coopers & Lybrand Gálgano (ed.). *Manual de calidad en Turismo*. Barcelona: EDITUR.

Fernández López, J. (1995). *La nueva selección de personas.*

GATS article XXVIII (b).

Merli, G. (1995). 'The enhancement of business capacities in tourism'. *Cooperation between public and private sectors for quality in tourism.* Lisbon: Portugal.

Moller, C. (1995). *Aspectos del employeeship para directivos.*

Moullin, M. (1994). *Redefinir la calidad.* Sheffield: Centre for Quality, Sheffield Hallam University.

Plog, S.C. (1991). *Leisure Travel. Making it a Growth Market... Again!.* Chichester: John Wiley.

Vidal D.B. (1994). 'Los 12 costos de la calidad'. *Turismo & Gestión de la calidad.*

# Chapter 19

# The importance of customer expectations in measuring service quality

**Marco Antonio Robledo**

Service quality has been shown to be a strategy that results in competitive advantage for the tourism companies that apply it successfully. Companies like Ritz Carlton, British Airways, SAS, Singapore Airlines and Club Med provide some classic examples of service excellence that creates market leadership.

Therefore, it is not surprising that the issue of service quality is becoming crucial for tourism companies and that this issue receives considerable attention from researchers and academics.

However, an examination of the quality literature reveals some surprising paradoxes and misconceptions about the notion of quality. These include:

- Service Quality and customer satisfaction, being different constructs, are often used as synonyms.
- The relationships between service quality, customer satisfaction, and purchase intention remain to be identified.
- The conceptualisation and measurement of service quality is still controversial.
- The term 'expectations', which is of primary importance for the understanding of how customer satisfaction operates, has not been successfully defined and examined.
- The sources of expectations are largely unexplored.
- The management of expectations is an area of study yet to be created.

This paper tries to address some of these points and shed some light on them. The analysis focuses on expectations since these are in my opinion the most controversial and unexplored area of service quality.

## 1. SERVICE QUALITY AND CUSTOMER SATISFACTION

Quality is about giving satisfaction to the customer. This relationship between quality and satisfaction is recognised by all experts in the field. Probably, this is also the cause of the confusion between the two terms. Customer satisfaction and service quality have in common that both result from the customers' comparison of their expectations with their perceptions of the service delivered. However, these concepts are not equivalent. Service quality experts point out that the main difference between the two is that perceived service quality is a long-run overall evaluation, whereas satisfaction is a transaction specific measure (Bitner, 1990; Bolton and Drew, 1991a; Parasuraman, Zeithaml and Berry, 1988).

On the other hand, there are important discrepancies when researchers try to determine what comes first, service quality or customer satisfaction. Parasuraman, Zeithaml and Berry (1985, 1988), first suggested that service quality was an antecedent of customer satisfaction. This view is supported by further research carried out by Cronin and Taylor (1992). Other researchers (Bitner, 1990; Bolton and Drew, 1991a,b) argue that on the contrary, perception of the quality of a service is a result of several satisfying experiences for the customer.

## 2. SERVICE QUALITY, CUSTOMER SATISFACTION AND PURCHASE INTENTION

All quality manuals preach that total customer satisfaction has to be the main objective of the organisation, on the basis that if we achieve total satisfaction we will automatically maximise our profits. The rationale is that a satisfied customer:

- Makes a repeat purchase.
- Speaks well of the company.
- Is less receptive to the competitor's products and promotion.
- Buys other products from the same organisation.

A satisfied customer communicates his experience to an average of three people. A dissatisfied one tells it to 11. Therefore one dissatisfied customer creates up to 12 lost customers.

Research by Cronin and Taylor (cf. 1992) demonstrates that in four sectors of service companies (banking, pest control, dry cleaning and fast food) satisfaction has a stronger influence on purchase intentions than does service quality. Assuming this is true, the main implication is that consumers do not buy the best quality service, rather the basis for their purchases is what they receive for the price they pay.

## 3. MEASURING SERVICE QUALITY

Basically there are two different approaches to measuring service quality:

The first is based on the disconfirmation paradigm; according to this approach customers evaluate a service by comparing their perceptions of the service received with their expectations. From this comparison, three outcomes can result:

1- EXPECTATIONS = PERCEPTION: Customer satisfied
2- EXPECTATIONS > PERCEPTION: Customer dissatisfied.
3- EXPECTATIONS < PERCEPTION: Customer satisfied.

To sum up, customer satisfaction will occur only when the service provided meets or exceeds his expectations. The most important model developed on the basis of this theory is SERVQUAL (Parasuraman, Zeithaml and Berry, 1985). The research carried out by Parasuraman *et al.*, which has had among other outcomes the development of the SERVQUAL instrument for measuring service quality, is probably the most comprehensive and important investigation about service quality to date.

A second model, mainly resulting from examinations and assessments of the disconfirmation paradigm, is based only in performance (or rather, perceptions of performance). Frameworks for service quality measurement following this approach are for example SERVPERF (Cronin and Taylor, 1992), and EP (Teas, 1993). In practice, performance-based scales are more widely used for reasons of simplification but this is not a criterion of superiority.

We do not have enough space for a thorough evaluation of the two approaches, but the author's view is that the reason for rejecting the perception-minus-expectations gap could be partially due to misconceptions about the nature of expectations. This view is supported by the small body of research published about this issue. As Hesket, Sasser and Hart (1990) argue: "absolute measurements of service quality that do not include customer expectations miss the point".

## 4. CUSTOMER EXPECTATIONS

There is consensus about defining perceptions as consumer's beliefs concerning the service received or experienced (Parasuraman *et al.*; 1988; Brown and Swartz, 1989). Parasuraman *et al.* define expectations as follows: "Expectations are desires or wants of consumers, i.e. what they feel a service provider should offer rather than would offer". According to this definition, expectations represent *ideal standards* of performance based on past experience. This view is shared by authors such as Brown and Swartz (1989) and Carman (1990). Parasuraman *et al.* make clear that this definition is only valid when it comes to talking about service quality. If we are talking about customer satisfaction the appropriate comparison is what a consumer *would* expect.

An interpretation of this definition suggests that in the context of service quality, the most important determinant of expectations is past experience. But, are there any others? And, what are the sources of expectations for measuring customer satisfaction?

Parasuraman *et al.* only mention three sources of expectations: word of mouth communications, personal needs and past experience. However, in this author's opinion there are many others (Robledo, forthcoming). The main sources of expectations that a tourist can have are:

- Past experience, not only with the service provider, but with competitors and companies in other sectors.
- Informal recommendations, i.e. word-of-mouth communication. According to Zeithaml (1981) this is one of the most influential sources of expectations.
- Formal recommendations, i.e. recommendations of travel agents or quality assessments found in guides such as Michelin or AA.
- Price. The price paid for a service determines in the customer's mind the level of quality to be demanded.
- Promotion. All the promotional mix conveys a message to the customer that influences expectations.
- Location. The location of a hotel, for example, tells us something about its category.
- Personal needs. Personal needs determine what is important for the customer and what is not.
- Brand and corporate image. If we think about the Ritz Hotel in Paris we think automatically about quality, sophistication and exclusivity. For many companies the name is the most important asset because it shapes positively the expectations of the customers.

In service quality measures it is clear that the most important source of expectation should be past experience, but all the others may also have a certain effect on the customer's expectations. If the company manages properly all the controllable sources of expectations, it could even compensate negative past experiences of the customer, who could decide to give another chance to the company. In cases where there is no past experience whatsoever with the service provider, all the other sources above described play a more important role.

The company, knowing about the sources of expectations of its customers, must try to manage those expectations so it can match them with its performance (cf. Horovitz, 1990). For this purpose, the company has a number of tools it can use, such as:

- Positioning statements.
- Promotional campaigns.
- Mission statements.
- Corporate communication campaigns.
- Communications audits.
- Service guarantees.
- Educating the consumer.

## 5. Conclusion

I hope that this paper at least will have given some food for thought and will contribute to fostering further research in the area of service quality. The objective has been to raise some important questions rather than providing answers.

Issues addressed such as the distinction between service quality and customer satisfaction are of primary importance for tourism companies. These companies need to know whether their objective has to be satisfying customers or reaching the highest possible service quality.

The current approach to measuring service quality needs to be refined urgently. Further work is needed on the measurement of expectations, the sources of expectations, the relative importance of each one and the management of expectations.

## References

Bitner, M.J. (1990). 'Evaluating Service Encounters: The Effects of Physical Surroundings and Employee Responses'. *Journal of Marketing* 54 (April): pp.69-82.

Bolton, R.N. and J.H. Drew (1991a). 'A Longitudinal Analysis of the Impact of Service Changes on Customer Attitudes'. *Journal of Marketing* 55 (January): pp.1-9.

Bolton, R.N. and J.H. Drew (1991b). 'A Multistage Model of Customers' Assessments of Service Quality and Value'. *Journal of Consumer Research* 17 (March): pp.375-384.

Brown, S.W. and T.H. Swartz (1989). 'A Gap Analysis of Professional Service Quality', *Journal of Marketing* 53 (April): pp.92-98.

Carman, J.M. (1990). 'Consumer Perceptions of Service Quality: An Assessment of the SERVQUAL Dimensions'. *Journal of Retailing*, 66 (1) (Spring): pp.33-55.

Cronin, J. and S.A. Taylor (1992). 'Measuring Service Quality: A Reexamination and Extension'. *Journal of Marketing* 56 (July): pp.55-68.

Heskett, J.L., W.E. Sasser Jr. and C.W.L. Hart (1990). *Service Breakthroughs: Changing the Rules of the Game.* New York: The Free Press.

Horovitz, J. (1990). *La Qualité de Service.* Paris: McGraw-Hill.

Parasuraman, A., V. Zeithaml and L. Berry (1985). 'A Conceptual Model of Service Quality and Its Implications for Future Research.' *Journal of Marketing* 49 (Fall): pp.41-50.

Parasuraman, A., V. Zeithaml and L. Berry (1988). 'SERVQUAL: A Multiple-Item Scale for Measuring Consumer Perceptions of Quality.' *Journal of Retailing* 64 (Spring): pp.12-40.

Robledo, M.A. (forthcoming). 'Fuentes de Expectativas del Turista'. *Turismo y Calidad.*

Teas, R.K. (1993). 'Expectations, Performance, Evaluation, and Consumers' Perceptions of Quality'. *Journal of Marketing* 57 (October): pp.18-34.

Zeithaml, V. (1981). 'How Consumer Evaluation Processes Differ Between Goods and Services'. In: James H. Donnelly and William R. George (eds.) *Marketing of Services*. American Marketing Association: Chicago, pp.186-189.

# Chapter 20

# Studying and improving the quality of visitor services - a blueprinting approach to understanding service delivery systems

**Eric Laws**

## INTRODUCTION

A great deal of managerial effort is directed towards achieving improvements in the efficiency and effectiveness of organisations, and a common focus of interest is to improve reliability in the performance and delivery of products or services. Amongst the distinguishing characteristics of services is their dependence on direct contact between staff and clients in the delivery of the service. In contrast, the manufacturing of most products occurs 'offstage', remote from the view of customers. Although managers may wish to specify precise standards for their services, just as a production manager in a factory setting would be expect to, in reality each service transaction is itself a variable, and the quality of the service is dependant on the interaction between staff and client in the context of the physical setting and the technical features of the service delivery system designed by its managers.

From this point of view, two primary functions can be identified for service sector managers. One is fundamentally concerned with designing and resourcing an appropriate delivery system which also defines the parameters for service encounters between staff and customers. The second function is concerned with staff selection and training, and beyond that, the development of an organisational culture which empowers staff to solve problems on behalf of customers, within the company's cost or profit policies, and rewards them for contributing to customer satisfaction. The first management function, service design, underpins successful service delivery, it minimises dysfunction, and maximises effective service transactions, providing satisfying experiences for customers.

This chapter presents a brief review of relevant theory from the evolving field of service management, demonstrates how to draw up a service blueprint, and discusses the way this technique can be applied by tourism, leisure and hospitality managers and educators.

## SERVICE SYSTEM CONCEPTS

Any service, such as the example of a restaurant meal examined later in this chapter, can be understood as being a system in which selected inputs are combined in a series of processes to produce specified outputs. Efficiency in the system's operation can be evaluated by measuring outputs against the inputs required to produce them, by examining the quality of the outputs, and by considering the way each process contributes to the overall service. Kirk (1995) has pointed out that systems theory has traditionally been applied to 'hard' engineering situations, with clear and unique outcomes, but notes that the socio-technical features of services also benefit from systems insights when these are expanded to include human 'soft' issues where there is less certainty (Jones, 1993).

Blueprinting also has its origins in hard applications, where the symbols in an ordered technical drawing represent instructions to technicians which they use as a template in constructing buildings, or in wiring circuitry. Shostack (1988) demonstrated how the concept can be applied in the analysis of service delivery systems. "The purpose of blueprinting (is) to make sure that all elements are there, and to find out their cost and contribution to revenue in the composition of the service." The service blueprint presented later in this chapter illustrates how the technique enables attention to be focused on three key factors in the quality of a service: its design, the roles of staff, and the interaction between staff and customers.

## DELIVERING QUALITY TOURISM SERVICES

In contrast with manufactured products, it is less clear that criteria for tourism service standards can be achieved consistently. The difficulty revolves around the two bases to services, termed Type A and Type B by Laws (1986). Type A factors are the technical aspects of running a restaurant, hotel, transport operation, or tourist attraction, and are similar to the 'hard' systems elements discussed earlier. Type B factors are the interactions between staff and clients which characterise the delivery of tourism services, and have much in common with the 'soft' features of systems.

Differing, though connected implications flow from a recognition of the two factors in tourism management. Type A factors are the technical factors which often form the main basis for the service which managers design, but while type A factors are generally under the direct control of managers, the type B factors are more complex. They include the skills and motivations of staff, their ability to interact effectively with clients, and the highly variable expectations and behaviour which different clients bring to the service episode and its constituent elements. Both type A and type B factors must be considered in designing an effective service delivery system, or in diagnosing difficulties and evaluating improvements to existing services.

## INTERACTION BETWEEN STAFF AND CUSTOMERS

A feature distinguishing services, including tourism, from the production of manufactured goods is that managerial decisions about the characteristics of the services offered are dependant to a greater extent on the way individual employees interpret service design and performance criteria, and in the presence of the customer. Furthermore, service delivery entails interaction with the customer, and its quality therefore depends partly on gaining their cooperation. A familiar example is the difficulty and dissatisfaction which all other passengers experience when one client on a coach tour is consistently late in returning to the vehicle after a sightseeing stop. The view that service quality is produced in the interaction between a customer and elements in the service organisation has been referred to as 'interactive quality.' This means that quality derives from "the interaction of personnel with customers as well as that between customers and other customers".

A related problem is that customers' behaviour and perceived attitudes can please or distress staff. Supportive customer behaviour has been shown to correlate positively with job satisfaction and performance, whereas instrumental behaviour by passengers has negative outcomes for staff. Lovelock (1992) has cited Bony's definition of service as "a deed, a performance, an effort". The performance is experiential, and it involves the customer during a period of time, and the way that the customer participates helps or hinders the process. Normann (1991) referred to the points of interaction in a service episode as "moments of truth" a phrase which Carlzon adopted in his perceptive book (1987) in which he argues that the each of the many occurrences is used by customers to judge the quality of the service. Gronross (1980) has distinguished between technical and functional quality, the latter being how it is delivered, and the customers' attitudes to 'each element in the bundle of service attributes.' Two approaches for analysing the quality of services have been suggested by Gummesson (1988):

1. Technology driven and product oriented definitions, similar to the consumerist gap type A technical management concerns.
2. Fitness for use definitions, market driven and customer oriented, focusing on customer utility and satisfaction. This is similar to consumerist gap type B service management.

## TECHNICAL APPROACHES TO TOURISM SERVICE QUALITY

One strategy which service managers often adopt in their search for consistent service is to eliminate employee discretion and judgement whenever possible. (Saaser, Olsen and Wyckoff, 1978). This approach relies on the specification of tasks to a standard of performance expected by management, and then provides them with a basis for measuring the effectiveness of staff performing services.

Increased standardisation implies a reduction in the discretion allowed to individual employees, although this contradicts clients' expectations of being treated as individuals, with needs which may vary during the many events of which a service is composed. Efficiency goals may clarify performance targets for staff, but can conflict with the customers' expectation of warm and friendly service. Underlying this approach are the twin assumptions that consumers see a service as a series of events, while managers see the service as a set of elements which require skilled coordination, and an understanding of the customers' perspectives.

The technical approach to quality is found in the performance criteria which are often specified for service delivery systems. Thus, transport companies including railways and airlines publicise the proportion of their 'on-time' arrivals, airlines aim to open the plane's doors within two minutes of 'engines-off' (although they rarely make claims about the length of time taken for their passengers to clear immigration and customs). Commenting on technical performance goals, Locke and his co-author (Locke and Schweiger, 1981) identified seven important characteristics of effective programmes. They suggested that the goals set must be specific, accepted, cover important job dimensions, be reviewed, with appropriate feedback, be measurable and challenging, but attainable. The design stage is the first opportunity to influence customer satisfaction.

## CUSTOMER ORIENTED TOURISM QUALITY

The second quality approach discussed by Gummesson (1988) is fitness for use. In the case of tourism services this can best be understood in terms of customers' expectations of satisfaction, against which they match their subsequent individual experiences during the service. Marketing theory argues that customers' experiences with any purchase give rise to outcomes for them varying from satisfaction to dissatisfaction. This reflects a divergence from the standards of service which clients had anticipated, as the following abbreviated quotations indicate:

"The seeds of consumer satisfaction are planted during the prepurchase phase of the consumer decision process" (Wilkie, 1986). It is against this individual benchmark that tourists measure the quality of their service experiences. "Satisfaction is defined as a postconsumption evaluation that the chosen alternative is consistent with prior beliefs and expectations (with respect to it). Dissatisfaction, of course, is the outcome when this confirmation does not take place" (Engel, Blackwell and Miniard, 1986).

Dissatisfaction has also been defined as a state of cognitive or affective discomfort. The consumer has allocated some of his resources, spending money and time, and building up an anticipation of satisfaction, but if his judgement of the service he received is that it was not up to his standard, he will experience cognitive dissonance (Festinger, 1957). The response to any dissonant experience is an effort to correct the situation, or a determination to avoid it in the future, and it causes varying degrees of dissatisfaction. A study by Zemke and Shaaf, (1989) of 101 successful service firms in America concluded that they had several features in common:

- Listen, understand and respond to customers.

- Define superior service and establish a service strategy.

- Set standards and measure performance.

- Select, train, and empower employees to work for the customer.

- Recognise and reward accomplishment.

## CUSTOMER PERSPECTIVES ON SERVICE

Drawing on the earlier discussion of service as a process, it can be suggested that the customer experiences the service as a number of phases. Even before it begins, he or she decides to become a client, and therefore develops an anticipation of the benefits to be gained, during the actual delivery of the service, while after it, the customer evaluates the service received against what had been anticipated. A more formal definition of each of these phases is given below.

## ANTICIPATING SATISFACTION WITH TOURISM SERVICES

A key factor in managing tourism for quality is therefore to understand the satisfaction which clients anticipate from the purchase of a service. Consumer decision taking represents a choice between alternative allocations of time and funds and such choices can cause anxiety about the correctness of the decision taken. One method by which consumers can reduce the potential risk of making an unsatisfactory purchase is to seek information beforehand, from friends or formal marketing communication sources such as advertising, tourism brochures or travel agency staff.

### ATTACHMENT

The period before the customer arrives at the service location. During this phase he decides to purchase the service and selects a supplier. The technical aspects of the service also begin to operate, and all must be in place before the customer arrives.

### CORE

The consumption phase in which the client experiences the tangible and intangible service, and judges his/her experiences against expectations. Service gaps may occur, representing either satisfaction or dissatisfaction.

### DETACHMENT

After completing consumption of the core service, the customer returns home in a state of indifference, satisfaction or dissatisfaction. Additional processes are also undertaken such as cleaning, which have no direct significance for the original client, but affect the enjoyment of subsequent customers.

### POST PURCHASE EVALUATION

Purchase and subsequent use of goods or services can have two outcomes: satisfaction, or dissatisfaction and post decision dissonance. The consumer evaluates whether (or not) the pre-purchase expectations of satisfaction which they held were met. The vendor's hope is that a client will conclude from the experience of a service that the decision was correct, and consequently that the purchase will be repeated. However, dissatisfaction with a service may trigger further action, perhaps in the form of complaints to the company. Its response may reassure the client that their choice had been correct. But if any continuing dissatisfaction is not dealt with effectively, the customer is likely to switch to alternative suppliers' brands for future purchases.

The ultimate risk reduction strategy for customers is to avoid situations which in the past have been seen as an incorrect choice, with the result that the industry, rather than one supplier, loses customers.

> The outcome of the evaluation process through which the consumer automatically goes may be viewed as an operational definition of service quality...Thus, quality is not inherent in the properties of the product or service itself, but is a function of the consumer's CS/PS (consumption specific/ product specific) values which govern expectations and perceptions (Klien, Lewis and Scott, 1989).

## SERVICE BLUEPRINTING

The concept of a service blueprint has been described as "... the process of defining the range of resources required for the performance of services, and of co-ordinating the various components" (Laws, 1991). Gummesson (1990) stated that "service blueprinting is a systematic way of describing a service.... The purpose of blueprinting (is) to make sure that all elements are there, and to find out their cost and contribution to revenue in the composition of the service". Shostack (1981) herself considered that a service blueprint should have three main features. Firstly, it must incorporate within the design a time dimension, enabling the researcher to follow the progression of the service delivery system which the customer experiences. Secondly, it should show the main functions which together comprise the service, and show their interconnectedness. A third feature of the blueprint is that it should incorporate performance standards and the deviance levels which are acceptable at each stage of the process. The various elements in a service blueprint are arranged with reference to a line of visibility. Above this, the customer is aware of and often involved in, the service processes. Below the line of visibility, a range of resources and skills are deployed, which, although the customer is not directly involved in them, are fundamental to the customer's satisfaction. This introduces a further feature of service blueprints, they can be used to identify failpoints, "the parts of a service which are most sensitive to errors" (Gummesson, 1990). George and Gibson (1988) defined failpoints as "the parts of a service blueprint which identify those processes of the service which are most likely to go wrong, and to function other than intended".

Any service blueprint is best regarded as a 'plan', and it may not be an accurate nor a full representation of the service provision because the method relies on the interpretation of data provided by a sample of the firm's customers, and it therefore includes their perceptions and feelings. However, the blueprinting technique entails several steps, and these limitations can be largely overcome in the ensuing, analytical phase of the service blueprinting methodology: it takes on some of the characteristics of iterative or action research, in which managers are interrogated about the operational meaning (and validity) of their clients' commentary on the existing service delivery system. A subsequent phase explores the setting of managerial priorities and the remedial action to be taken in redressing the failpoints identified earlier.

## AN INTRODUCTION TO SERVICE BLUEPRINTING METHODOLOGY

A service blueprint is a diagram which shows all the elements that go to make up the service being studied, its purpose is to enable the service to be analysed as objectively as possible. Table 20.1 shows the sequence of steps in blueprinting a service, while Table 20.2 indicates the range of methodologies which underpin the procedures (although these are not discussed further in this chapter).

The blueprint is divided horizontally by a line of visibility. Above this, what the client 'sees' is shown in the form of a flowchart beginning when the customer decides to purchase the service and following their contact with the various elements of the core phase that constitute the service they expect to experience. Below the line of visibility, the blueprint shows the elements, and the processes connecting them, which are required to make the service available. Thus, the blueprint traces all the components of the service, and identifies how they culminate in the various encounter points during which the customer interacts with the service, thereby providing a framework for service design analysis.

The starting point for analysis of the blueprint is to identify the points where an existing service delivery system may cause problems for clients or staff. Fail points can be identified while drawing up the blueprint, by adding specific questions to the instruments used to explore customers' and managers' experiences of a service delivery system, but additional methods are required to investigate their relative significance (primarily to customers, but also to staff and the firm) or to examine the methods and costs of remedying them. However, the blueprinting method provides managers with valuable insights into where their customers believe that service is failing.

### Table 20.1: Steps drawing up a service blueprint

1. Study the sequence of service elements experienced by a range of clients.
2. Present the clients' experience as a simplified flowchart.
3. Study the features of the service delivery system(s).
4. Flowchart the elements in the service delivery system.
5. Analyse customers' experience of the service delivery system to identify critical points.
6. Analyse the rationales for the crisis points in the existing service delivery system.
7. Assess the costs of service delivery system weaknesses.
8. Evaluate the opportunities for improvements, and assess the costs of implementation.

**Table 20.2: Methodologies in studying service delivery systems**

1. Observation
2. Participant observation
3. Interviews
4. Focus groups
5. Analysis of customer correspondence
6. Study of company documents

## SERVICE BLUEPRINTING AS A MANAGEMENT TOOL

An organisation incurs costs from any service failure, but implementing a quality control system also incurs costs. These costs result from actions taken to get a service right from the start, auditing that it is correctly delivered and the expenses of responding to any failure (Lockyer and Oakland, 1981).

From a managerial perspective, the technique of service blueprinting can assist in auding an existing service to locate problems with the service delivery system (Leppard and Molyneux, 1994), and it can also be helpful in evaluating the benefits of alternative remedial actions. Apart from the physical or psychological consequences for customers and staff of unsatisfactory services, the costs include disturbance in the running of departments, and a reduction in future sales levels, resulting from dissatisfaction. Further costs are incurred in implementing preventative measures to reduce future dissatisfaction, including the redesign of service delivery systems or training and motivational programmes for staff.

## SERVICE BLUEPRINTING AS AN EDUCATIONAL TOOL

In addition to its original diagnostic function as a managerial tool, blueprinting can be used to enable students (whether on management development courses, or reading for a degree) to investigate the features and effectiveness of service delivery systems.

By providing a structured way to investigate the nature of service design and service interactions, students can better understand them, and the operational distinctions between different types of services (for example, restaurant, hotel and travel services) can be investigated academically in terms of general management and service management theories.

The blueprint presented in Figure 20.1 shows the features of a meal in a combined pub / restaurant. It is based on work prepared by a Final Year Honours Degree student, the original identified some forty elements in the service delivery system, and discussed a dozen fail points. This simplified version is presented here for brevity, and to highlight the method.

Students were asked to present a detailed report which described the service they had chosen to analyse, explained the way they had developed the blueprint, and critically evaluated the key issues they had identified. This example is based on a pub housed in a late medieval building within a small historic city in England. The new owners had decided to diversify their service by converting one of the public rooms into one of the most expensive restaurants in the city, offering high quality catering, relaxed service and a pleasant ambience within the setting of a successful public house.

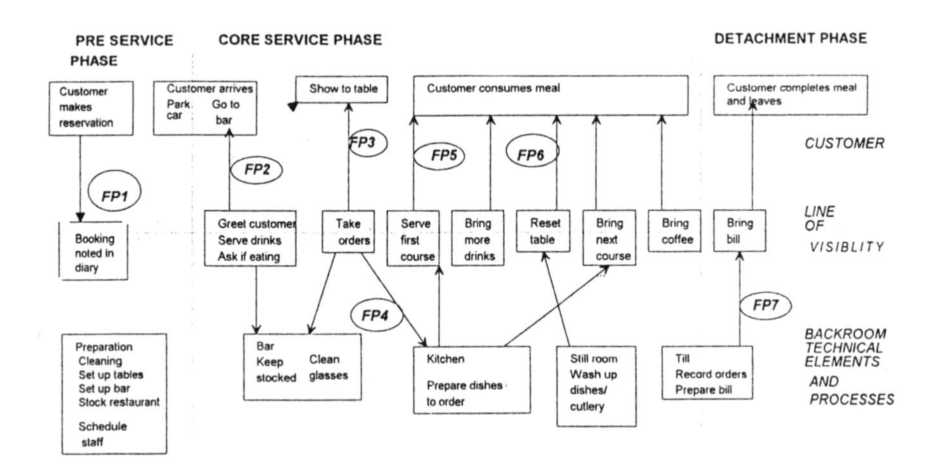


**Figure 20.1: Schematic service blueprint for pub / restaurant**

Following the conventions outlined earlier in this Chapter, the blueprint is divided into sections. The vertical dotted lines separate the three service phases, attachment (when the customer telephones to make a booking), the core service (during which the meal is consumed), and the detachment phase (when the bill is settled, the customer leaves, and subsequently reflects on his experience, evaluating it as satisfactory or not). The horizontal dotted line separates the features of the service. The top section can be understood as the customer's conceptual flow chart of the sequence of events he or she is likely to experience during the service episode. The bottom section is below the line of the customer's visibility, and consists of the range of activities and events which are required to create the service. These areas of the blueprint are linked by service staff who span the line of visibility.

Any of these elements has the potential to cause problems, but difficulties are more likely to occur with certain aspects of a given service operation. The seven potential fail points discussed below were identified by observation and interviews with customers, and were further clarified through discussion with the manager.

*FP1*

This service fail point arises from the delay often experienced before the call is answered by one of the few staff on duty before the restaurant opens to customers. This may have the effect of losing business, as frustrated potential customers transfer their reservation to an alternative restaurant. Another difficulty results from customers who book a table, but fail to arrive, come at a different time from that booked, or bring fewer or more guests than anticipated. This occurrence can delay or inconvenience other customers, and is indicated on the blueprint by a dotted line connecting the bookings diary to the event where the customer is shown to his or her table.

*FP2*

During business hours the pub itself is usually crowded and noisy. Restaurant clients are in the minority, and usually go to the single bar in the pub on arrival. The staff member who first serves any client with drinks is expected by the manager to find out whether they are also going to have a meal, and if so, whether they have booked. A number of problems are associated with this fail point. Some customers are asked about their dining intentions by different staff members on several occasions, resulting in irritation, and a feeling that they are being pressurised to take a meal. Others are not asked whether they intend to eat, and become frustrated when other clients are escorted to the tables which are visible in another room.

*FP3*

A member of staff escorts clients to the table, and takes their orders, both for more drinks and for the main courses of their meal. The problems associated with this phase of the service are typical of many restaurants. The clients may prefer an alternative table, their order may be recorded incorrectly, items may no longer be available, or the order may be recorded incorrectly in the till, leading to difficulties later, during the detachment phase.

*FP4, 5, 6*

These are related problems, when kitchen staff may misread the order, or, when it is brought to the table, a particular dish may not prove satisfying to the client. An additional problem arises if the cutlery and plates brought to reset the table between courses have been washed up properly

*FP7*
The person running the till has to keep track of each table's orders, including drinks, sweets and coffee. Bills are written on a standard triplicate form by the waiter, who is expected to identify each table by its number. (This is not displayed on the table, both because the restaurant is reconfigured as needed during the day by bringing together or separating tables according to the size of the parties currently eating, and in order to make the ambience more personal to the customers. However, this sometimes causes mistakes to occur in attributing items to the correct client). During their meal, customers may alter their original order, or sometimes refuse a dish when it is brought. The manager's policy is to accept any reasonable alteration, but the factors noted above sometimes result in inaccurate bills being presented to clients at the end of their meal.

## FURTHER DISCUSSION

The preceding commentary on failpoints is drawn directly from the student's report, but has been abbreviated for this chapter. Many other issues were discussed in the student's original paper. For example, it was noted that this pub has a small car park which can only accommodate ten vehicles, and the nearest public parking is several minutes walk away. It is known that, in bad weather, some clients, unable to park nearby and unwilling to get wet, have driven away to an alternative restaurant. In this blueprint, this has not been identified as a fail point but other students have recognised that the environment has detracted from the feeling of anticipation usually associated with going out for a fairly expensive meal.

## CONCLUSION

The technique of blueprinting service delivery systems offers an effective way of focusing students' attention on the reality of managing existing services. In drawing up the blueprint diagram, they are required to investigate customers' perceptions, and to discuss these with managers in order to present a highly structured diagram. They are required to synthesise their knowledge of a specific service delivery system with the theoretical literature on management, particularly in the fields of marketing and services in order to reach the level of understanding expected of advanced students.

Over a hundred studies of this type have now been completed, and almost without exception, the students report that they have both benefited from, and enjoyed the exercise. Services studied have ranged from restaurants (where many of the students have part time jobs) to historic houses, ferry companies, tour operators and travel agencies, and other types of retail outlets. Furthermore, many of the managers who have acted as hosts to these studies have commented favourably on the exercise, and have remarked on the insights which they have gained into their customers' perspectives on the services which they provide.

## References


Carlzon, J. (1987). *Moments of Truth.* New York: Harper and Row.

Engel, J.F., R.D. Blackwell and P.W. Miniard (1986). *Consumer Behaviour.* New York: Dryden Press.

Festinger, L.A. (1957). *A Theory of Cognitive Dissonance.* Stanford: Stanford University Press.

George, W.R. and B.E. Gibson (1988). *Blueprinting: A Tool for Managing Quality in Organisations.* QUIS Symposium at the University of Karlstad, Sweden, August 1988.

Gronross, C. (1980). *An Applied Service Marketing Theory*, Working Paper 57. Helsinki: Swedish School of Economics.

Gummesson, E. (1990). Service Quality and Product Quality Combined. *Review of Business*, 9(3), pp.14-19.

Gummesson, E. (1990). Service Design. *The Total Quality Magazine*, 2(2), pp.97-101.

Jones, P. (1993). *Managing Foodservice Operations.* London: Cassell.

Kirk, D. (1995). Hard and Soft Systems: A Common Paradigm For Operations Management? *International Journal Of Contemporary Hospitality Management,* 7(5).

Laws, E. (1986). *Identifying and Managing the Consumerist Gap.* Service Industries Journal, 6(2), pp.131-143.

Laws, E. (1991). *Tourism Marketing, Service and Quality Management Perspectives.* Cheltenham: Stanley Thornes.

Leppard J. and L. Molyneux (1994). *Auditing your Customer Service.* Routledge, London.

Locke, E.A. and D.M. Schweiger (1979). Participating in Decision Making, One More Look. In: B.M. Staw *Research in Organisational Behaviour*, vol.1, Connecticut: JAI Press.

Lockyer, K.G. and J.S. Oakland (1981). *How to sample success*. Management Today, July, pp.75-81.

Lovelock, C.H. (1992). *Managing Services Marketing Operations and Human Resources*. London: Prentice Hall.

Normann, R. (1991). *Service Management: Strategy and Leadership In Service Businesses*. Chichester: Wiley.

Saaser W.E., P. Olsen, D.D. Wyckoff (1978). *Management of service operations: Test and cases.* Boston: Allyn and Bacon.

Shostack, L. (1981). How to Design a Service. In: J.H. Donnelly and W.R. George (eds.). *The Marketing Of Services*. Chicago, Illinois: American Marketing Association.

Wilkie, W. L. (1986). *Consumer Behaviour*. New York: Wiley.

Zemke R. and P. Schaaf (1989) *The Service Edge, 101 Companies that Profit from Customer Care*. New York: NAL Penguin Inc.

# Chapter 21

## Marketing tourism regions: effectiveness through cooperation

**Marcjanna Augustyn**

The increasing competition in the world tourism market and the changing needs, attitudes and preferences of consumers have given marketing prominence in tourism. It is generally assumed that marketing should be the domain of individual enterprises directly involved in production and distribution of goods and services. However, marketing in tourism is different from traditional product marketing, due to the peculiar characteristics of tourism supply and demand.

There are several factors making tourism distinct. One of them is the multi-sectoral and complex nature of a tourism product which is actually a mixture of various components such as destination attractions, facilities and accessibility. Rigidity of the main components of the tourism product often make the product not responsive to rapid changes of tastes and needs of tourists. Many tourism producers are relatively small, which makes tourism supply highly fragmented, scattered over many economic sectors. In fact, the producers have little control over the development and delivery of the product. Moreover, due to the fact that tourism is a people business, the visitors' satisfaction depends highly on the staff providing their personal services.

Other factors making tourism different from other industries relate to demand which is highly elastic, flexible and seasonal in its nature. Finally, the many impacts of tourism on economy, host community and environment also make tourism distinct.

These peculiarities of tourism supply and tourism demand require special approach to marketing in tourism. According to Krippendorf, marketing in tourism means "[...] the systematic and co-ordinated adaptation of the policy of tourist enterprises as well as the tourist policy of the state on local, regional, national and international levels, to achieve an optimal satisfaction of the needs of certain determined groups of consumers and to reach an appropriate profit" (Wahab *et al.*, 1976). This definition underlines that marketing in tourism is not just a policy of an individual tourism organisation but involves co-ordination of policies of several organisations at several levels within a particular tourism destination region. The complex nature of the tourism product and tourists themselves, as well as the many impacts of tourism development, should make both public and private sector involvement in marketing tourism regions essential.

Speaking of marketing tourism regions, it is worth explaining what is meant by this term. A destination region in broad terms means a tourist-receiving region within the administrative boundaries of a city, a village, a county or a country. Those regions vary in many aspects, such as size or market segments they serve. However, some administrative regions have common features, since many natural attractions and other components of tourism products extend beyond those administrative boundaries. This calls for the creation of coherent structures to enable effective development and marketing of such regions. This concept is known as a Tourism Destination Area concept and is regarded to be a tool for subregional product development and marketing. In other words, a Tourism Destination Area is "[...] a coherent area of potential for tourism destination development based upon significant tourism factors - past, present and possible future" (Travis, 1993). Such an approach means that a tourism region is not merely one city, county or country but that two or more administrative units (for example two counties or two countries) may create a common tourism region.

## COOPERATIVE MARKETING AND FACTORS INFLUENCING ITS EFFECTIVENESS

A logical extension of the peculiar characteristics of tourism supply and demand is the need for co-operation within a tourism region. The diversity of firms, products and services in the tourism industry increases the opportunities for co-operation.

Cooperative marketing may be exercised through an agreement between different groups designed to help facilitate the performance of the marketing function while sharing the costs of the marketing task (Okoroafo, 1989). It may involve either horizontal or vertical co-operation.

According to the tourism region, cooperative marketing may assume different forms. If a tourism region is composed of two or more administrative units at local (or regional) level then an inter-communal (or inter-regional) cooperative agreement may be concluded. However, links also should be established with the next higher administrative level so that marketing efforts of a tourism region are consistent with those of the whole country. Thus, both horizontal and vertical co-operation is required in marketing a tourism region. To ensure the effectiveness of cooperative marketing endeavours, both private and public sectors should be involved in such an agreement with their respective responsibilities and tasks.

Horizontal co-operation on marketing may also be established at international level. A tourism region may then be composed of two or more countries (inter-governmental or inter-organisational co-operation at central level) or of two or more regions belonging administratively to different countries (for example transborder co-operation). Whatever the form of cooperative marketing, it should be based on formally established links.

It may seem that cooperative marketing is contradictory to the general idea and purpose of the marketing activities of competing companies in the regional tourism market. However, cooperative marketing may be complementary rather than contradictory, if certain rules of effective cooperative marketing are taken into account while deciding on such an agreement.

First, the relationship should be reciprocal. The partners should possess specific strengths that they are willing to share.

Second, partners entering a cooperative agreement within a tourism region should develop a common long-term strategy aimed at building competitive advantage. The strategy should be formulated only after determining the present and future needs of potential visitors and their attitudes to the attributes of the destination. It thus requires extensive marketing research and comprehensive forecasting prior to marketing strategy formulation. Such research allows the target market segments and their individual characteristics to be identified.

Third, the formulation of a tourism marketing strategy at regional level requires consideration of the peculiarities of tourism at national and global levels. Regional marketing objectives should be integrated with national ones.

Fourth, the marketing strategy should focus on the satisfaction of tourists' needs and wants while taking into account the long-term negative impacts of tourism development on the host community and the environment. Those effects should be considered before any action is taken to ensure sustainable tourism development across the region.

Fifth, the marketing strategy of a tourism region should be effectively implemented. Proper organisation and co-ordination of activities as well as staff training and monitoring may help this process. Effective organisation requires allocation of responsibilities for tourism marketing. Both public and private sectors should perform their own tasks in the process. Co-ordination is critical, since it prevents duplication of effort and contributes to maximising the benefits while minimising the costs. It also promotes harmonious tourism development. Effective co-ordination requires, however, establishment of an efficient information system and consultation network.

Another important aspect of effective marketing strategy implementation is staff training. Any marketing initiatives within a tourism region require securing well qualified staff. Investing in hospitality and other kinds of service training may be a decisive factor of destination success.

To implement a marketing strategy effectively it is also essential to monitor tourism processes at each implementation level. Changes appearing in the external and internal environment of a tourism region should be reflected in changes in marketing strategy.

The organisation and co-ordination of tourism marketing efforts within a tourism region is very important. Since the tourism product is so highly fragmented, the success or failure of one component of a tourism product impacts on the others. To be effective, marketing requires the cooperative efforts of everyone within a tourism region, if it is to bring benefits to all interested parties.

The concept of cooperative marketing may be applied at international level as well, with two or more countries forming a tourism region. In this case, there are additional factors influencing the effectiveness of such efforts (Hill, 1992).

It is of utmost importance that the countries establishing a cooperative relationship possess compatible attributes that may attract tourists, such as proximity and convenient accessibility, similar or complementary tourism attractions (social, cultural and physical) as well as similar standards of tourism products, including trained personnel. Another important factor is the existence of multinational tourism enterprises in the co-operating countries which may enable co-ordination of resources across the two counties. Establishing co-operative relationships at the international level should respect, however, the participating countries' national and ideological identities while competing in those markets which are excluded from the partnership.

The above mentioned factors influencing cooperative marketing effectiveness should be considered in any process of establishing cooperative relations. In practice, cooperative marketing may assume various forms depending on the specific situation.

## EXAMPLES OF HORIZONTAL AND VERTICAL CO-OPERATION IN TOURISM MARKETING

As a part of a broader research project on "The Role of the State in Development of Tourism Industry" carried out in Denmark, Italy, Norway, Spain and Poland in 1994-1995, the issue of tourism marketing in those countries was studied. A comprehensive questionnaire as well as further inquiries were addressed to the respective National Tourism Administrations in those countries. In Poland, a number of interviews with the representatives of National Tourism Administration as well as regional authorities and regional branches of Polish Tourism Chamber were conducted.

The results of the comparative study on tourism marketing show some examples of cooperative marketing initiatives in those countries. They also allow us to distinguish the responsibilities and tasks of various partners in a cooperative marketing system, i.e. the government, the National Tourism Organisation, regional and local authorities as well as the travel trade. Although it is impossible to analyse all the different kinds of cooperative marketing initiatives taken in those countries, some of the examples are worth mentioning.

The concept of cooperative marketing in Denmark was initiated by the government in 1987. The aim of adopting the policy of close co-operation with the tourism trade was to promote tourism through marketing but only in those markets where the tourism enterprises were interested in joint funding of such activities. The Danish Tourism Board was entrusted with the responsibility of implementing this programme.

As a result, Denmark was divided into nine regional marketing groups (four in Jutland, one on Fynn, one on Bornholm and three in Zeeland) which got their funding from local authorities. In each marketing group, a private industry steering group was appointed. The structure of each steering group depends on which companies are active in a given market.

The Danish Tourism Board co-operates only with those regions which are willing to co-finance joint marketing initiatives. Co-operation is effected mainly via common marketing campaigns launched in foreign markets. However, according to the latest government statement of national tourism policy (1994), less government funds for cooperative marketing are to be provided in the future. The idea is to decrease the government share of cooperative marketing so that the tourism enterprises should assume a steadily growing share of expenses. The government funds will instead be spent on the development of new markets (Ministry for Communication and Tourism, 1994).

In contrast to Denmark, the initiative in cooperative marketing in Norway has been taken by a number of Norwegian counties. They have drawn up tourism programmes specifying geographical areas to be developed. Cooperative relationships among tourism enterprises, local and county authorities have been established at county level. Thus the counties themselves are responsible for developing and marketing these areas with the aid of government funding. So far, efforts have mainly been focused on promoting a geographical concentration of regional holiday facilities in rural districts (Royal Ministry of Industry, 1989).

Another interesting example of regional co-operation on marketing in Norway is the establishment of a commercial organisation for marketing tourism services in Northern Norway in 1990. It resulted from the criticism of the previous ineffective organisation model with several regional tourism boards. The commercial marketing organisation was the first company in Norway with formalised co-operation across regional boundaries. This organisation markets the tourism products of Nordland, Troms and Finnmark.

Marketing efforts in Italy have been highly fragmented, reflecting Italy's administrative borders - national, regional and local. As a response to this fragmentation as well as to ineffective work of public tourism promotion entities at all levels, the idea of establishing tourism promotion consortia has emerged. The consortia differ both in forms and purposes of co-operation. Figure 21.1 presents three different examples of such consortia.

The Portofino Coast Consortium, set up in 1987, is the oldest. It is different from the others in involving local authorities. Moreover, it has established an operational company to co-ordinate the provision of services, manage incoming tourism, promote and market the tourism product, guarantee quality in member businesses, promote training and optimise resources to increase market penetration. Members of the other two consortia are exclusively either tourism businesses or tourism associations with the participation of the Chamber of Commerce. The latter is solely a promotional consortium having no product marketing or consultancy role. The activity of tourism promotion consortia is subsidised by the government but the subsidies can be obtained only for the administrative costs of promotion and promotional expenses such as travel, trade fair participation costs, market research, advertising, interpretation and training.

The cooperative movement is becoming very strong in Italy. Horizontal co-operation is being encouraged by the government and more recently service co-operation on tourism marketing has emerged including, for instance, travel agencies, beach facilities, transport and tour guides (Dipartimento Turismo Presidenza del Consiglio dei Ministri, 1994).

Co-operation on marketing in Spain is effected mainly along vertical lines: among central, regional and local governments. There are few travel trade initiatives in the field of horizontal co-operation on tourism marketing. However, the government encourages horizontal co-operation and envisages greater contribution from the private sector.

There are many examples of tourism marketing co-operation initiatives both at local and regional levels in Poland. At regional level seven tourism regions have been formed and altogether there are to be eight of them across almost the whole territory of Poland. The initiator of these tourism regions was the National Tourism Administration which encourages regional public officers to conclude cooperative agreements with other regional administrative units. The main fields of activity of those tourism regions include development of a tourism product, staff training, promotion of the region and tourism market monitoring. The regions co-operate also with the central government to co-ordinate their efforts with the main goals of national marketing strategy.

These examples clearly show the present trend towards horizontal co-operation in tourism marketing with the increasing role of the private sector in those agreements. Active involvement of the tourism trade seems to be essential, if the concept of cooperative marketing is to be effective.

| | RIVERA DEL SOLE (CALABRIA) | POTOFINO COAST | VERONA ALL YEAR |
|---|---|---|---|
| BACKERS | 12 local businesses (Hotel, restaurants, Service Providers) | Local authorities of: PORTOFINO, SAN MARGHERITA, RAPALLO<br><br>14 Hotels<br>2 travel agents | Hotel, Restaurant, Travel agency associations +<br><br>Chamber of Commerce |
| COST OF MEMBERSHIP | L 50,000 | L 1 million | L 10 million |
| OBJECTIVES | Assist in maximising management expenditures<br><br>Joint purchasing of food and other goods<br><br>Improve management techniques<br><br>Harmonised domestic and foreign image promotion/combined marketing | Maximise tourism potential of region<br><br>Joint promotion | Develop and increase tourism to Verona<br><br>Domestic and foreign promotion |

**Figure 21.1: Tourism promotion consortia: three examples**
*Source:* Fifth Report on Italian Tourism, Dipartimento Turismo Prezidenca del Consiglio dei Ministri, Roma, 1994, p.111.

**HORIZONTAL CO-OPERATION IN TOURISM MARKETING AT INTERNATIONAL LEVEL - AN EXAMPLE OF NORDIC CO-OPERATION**

The Nordic region comprises five sovereign states (Denmark, Finland, Iceland, Norway, Sweden) and three autonomous territories (The Faroe Islands, Greenland - both Danish, and The Aland Islands - Finnish). Both the government administrations and the tourist trades of Nordic countries co-operate on tourism marketing.

Inter-Nordic co-operation at governmental level is effected via two official inter-governmental organisations: the Nordic Council of Ministers and the Nordic Council. Among other fields, Nordic countries have been co-operating on tourism since the establishment of the Nordic Tourist Traffic Committee (Nordiska Turisttrafikkomitten - NTTK) in 1923. In 1978, the Tourist Committee was set up by the Nordic Council of Ministers.

There are two factors which stimulate Nordic co-operation on matters related to tourism and in particular to tourism marketing: the negative image of those countries due to their unfavourable climate and high prices and, on the other hand, compatible tourism products.

Based upon research conducted jointly by the partners, a common programme for Nordic co-operation on tourism was developed and adopted by the Nordic Council of Ministers in 1978. The main aims of the programme were the following: 1) to promote inter-Nordic travel, 2) to attract foreign tourists to the Nordic region, and 3) to support the development of tourism products (Nordisk Ministerraad, 1989: 40). The general aims for 1978 are still valid. The programme is periodically revised and adapted to changes occurring in the tourism market.

Inter-Nordic co-operation on tourism is based on those goals which are common to all countries according to the tourism policies adopted by the individual countries. The common goals are: 1) to improve the balance of payments, 2) to increase employment, 3) to increase the Nordic countries' share of the international tourism market, and 4) to improve conditions for the tourism enterprises, especially in less developed parts of these countries. Thus the co-operation of Nordic countries focuses on those matters which can be more easily dealt with at Nordic level rather than at national level. Such co-operation ensures gains to all interested parties.

To achieve these goals, common strategies - applicable in each of the five countries - were adopted. One of them is a common marketing strategy. The raising of the level of competence through providing various training schemes for staff employed in specific branches of the trade is also underlined.

Cooperative promotion of the Nordic region is effected mainly by the private Norwegian Tourism Board: Nortravel Marketing (NORTRA). This task was allocated to NORTRA by the Nordic Council of Ministers.

NORTRA - acting as a Nordic Tourist Board for common issues - is responsible for research as well as for planning, organisation and implementation of joint promotional campaigns in foreign markets and in particular in overseas markets. By common effort, tourism offices were opened in the U.S.A. and Japan to handle inter-Nordic marketing in those markets. As a result, a promotional campaign "Focus on Scandinavia" was launched there in the early 1990s (OECD, 1992).

It is worth mentioning that at the same time NORTRA conducts its marketing activities focused only on Norway in European markets where the Nordic countries are actually competitors.

The Nordic countries also co-operate on product development to tackle the problem of surplus accommodation capacity. Tourist offers, which lead to improved utilisation of resources, are developed. The main focus here is the extension of the tourist season. However, the development of the tourist trade is undertaken at national level and initiated by the tourist trade itself. The role of the Inter-Nordic Tourism Committee is to serve as a forum for the exchange of ideas and discussion of the results obtained.

The effectiveness of Nordic co-operation on tourism is an important issue for the Tourism Committee. To this end, co-ordination and co-operation with other organs of the Nordic Council of Ministers, dealing with regional policy, cultural affairs, the environment, trade and industry and agriculture and transport, is being improved. Nordic co-operation on tourism concentrates also on establishing contacts with sports and music bodies to promote youth travel in the Nordic region. For the same reasons, school camp programmes, summer camp schemes and field exploration trip programmes have been developed.

Moreover, the Tourist Committee focuses on close co-operation with other interested parties who are involved in the work, especially the decision-makers from the tourism trade. The tourism trade's primary task is to develop and market its products, while the primary task of the Tourism Committee is to take the initiative on co-operation and co-ordination issues.

The co-operation programme is financed via joint Nordic founding, national allocations and contributions from tourist councils, the tourist trade and other sources (Nordisk Ministerraad, 1989: 43-49).

Inter-Nordic co-operation is of great importance to each of the co-operating countries. It serves as an important tool to overcome difficulties in the increasingly competitive tourism market.

## RESPONSIBILITIES AND TASKS OF PARTNERS IN COOPERATIVE MARKETING

The responsibilities and tasks of partners in cooperative marketing differ greatly according to the form of cooperative agreement, the level of country's tourism development and the economic and political system of a country. It has been recognised, however, that if the concept of cooperative marketing applied by a tourism region is to be advantageous to all interested parties within a tourism system, both private and public sectors should be involved in this co-operation with their respective roles. Some general responsibilities of different players in a marketing system can be thus distinguished irrespective of the specific situation of a country, a tourism region or the form of cooperative agreement.

The major function of the government at central level is to advise and co-ordinate marketing actions within the marketing system of a country. The government responsibility is to set up guidelines to ensure that marketing activities at all levels are consistent with the national tourism policy and marketing strategy goals. The government should then encourage the establishment of co-ordination and co-operation networks and ensure effective information flow among all actors in the tourism system.

The scope of government involvement in tourism marketing varies from country to country. In well developed countries with a strong private sector, government actions in the field of tourism are limited to indicating only the desired direction of tourism marketing activities. In less developed countries, the government is more actively involved also in formulating marketing strategy or even marketing plans for different tourism regions. Despite the fact that the scope of governmental involvement in tourism marketing depends to a high degree on the political and economic system of a given country, the engagement of government in this field should decline as the tourism market matures.

There are also some responsibilities of the National Tourism Organisation (NTO) in the marketing system of a country. By its nature, an NTO is responsible for marketing and especially promotion of the whole country - or some parts of it - as a destination region. Its task is to run national tourism offices abroad. Research and information as well as development of tourism markets and tourism products are other important functions of NTOs. They should also play an advisory role vis-a-vis various trades and industries which relate to tourism.

The scope of the NTOs involvement in the marketing system of a country depends on the scope of government responsibility in the country. The wider the scope of responsibilities and tasks of the government, the narrower those of the NTO. It has been recognised that an NTO should perform its tasks on a commercial basis in close co-operation with the tourism trade to ensure effectiveness of its activities.

In cooperative marketing at regional or local levels there are also separate roles to be played by the public and the private sectors. The major role of regional or local authorities is to ensure that the marketing strategies of a tourism region are consistent with the goals of national tourism policy and marketing strategy. The public sector should also ensure that the negative environmental and social impacts of tourism development are considered while developing the tourism region. Regional (local) authorities should care of the interests of the resident community. Moreover, they are responsible for many of the public services needed for the proper functioning of the tourism destination including police, fire service, social services, education, roads, public transport and consumer protection.

As far as tourism businesses are concerned, they should be responsible for the proper tourism product development and the provision of high quality services at reasonable prices. Other aspects of regional marketing should be the shared responsibility of public and private sectors.

Cooperative marketing within a tourism region can be either a private or a public sector initiative. However, if the tourism destination area is to develop properly, the partners of cooperative agreement should represent both public and private sectors and should be willing to share the costs of cooperative efforts.

## ADVANTAGES OF APPLYING THE CONCEPT OF COOPERATIVE MARKETING

In the face of increasing competition in the international tourism market and the peculiar characteristics of tourism supply and demand, adoption of cooperative regional marketing approaches may bring various advantages to all players in the tourism system. In most cases, those benefits depend on the nature and objectives of a cooperative agreement. Nonetheless, some general advantages can be distinguished.

Cooperative marketing efforts within a tourism region help first and foremost to increase the competitiveness of the destination. Joint efforts place a regional tourism market in a better position to compete with third parties. Co-operation reduces marketing costs (especially the costs of research, product development and promotion) which becomes very important where budgets are insufficient to carry out the job separately. Developing large projects by common effort is usually more profitable than several small projects. Common marketing campaigns may be less expensive and more effective than a campaign initiated by a single enterprise. Thus shared costs improve the cost efficiency of marketing efforts and joint efforts may produce benefits from scale economies.

Cooperative regional marketing ensures, moreover, the development of an integrated product. Co-operation is particularly beneficial for new product development. At the same time, it reduces the negative effects of the fragmented and diversified nature of tourism and thus ensures better control over the entire tourism product. Co-operation may also give visitors the feeling that firms endorse one another's products.

Important advantages of cooperative marketing result from formulation of a common marketing strategy. Such a strategy co-ordinates marketing efforts of all partners contributing to better utilisation of limited resources, more effective use of facilities and reduced negative environmental and social impacts of tourism development within the tourism region. Co-operation is all the more important, since limited information often makes it difficult for a single enterprise to plan its activities properly.

Cooperative marketing also creates opportunities to gain experience and increases marketing knowledge through contact with a wider range of tourism businesses. Cooperation increases training opportunities, reducing training costs.

Finally, co-operation is important, since it provides political influence upon the decision-makers at higher administrative levels.

It is worth underlining again that the benefits of cooperative marketing within a tourism region depend greatly on the active involvement of both public and private sectors and on good planning and co-ordination of each partner's efforts to achieving a successful, integrated marketing programme.

A challenge in tourism marketing is to satisfy visitors' needs, raise the standard of living and quality of life in the host region and generate profits for the industry. Thus cooperative regional marketing seems to be the best tool to achieve those three goals simultaneously.

## DIRECTIONS OF FUTURE TOURISM MARKETING DEVELOPMENT IN CENTRAL AND EASTERN EUROPE AND EDUCATIONAL NEEDS

The prevailing trend towards horizontal cooperation within tourism destination areas and the many advantages of cooperative regional marketing should become important factors influencing future tourism marketing development in Central and Eastern Europe. Efforts to create such a co-operation network may be initiated by the government at any administrative level or by the tourism trade itself. However, irrespective of who the initiator is, cooperative marketing agreements should involve both private and public sectors to produce benefits to all interested parties, namely the local communities, the visitors and the tourism businesses. Any initiatives towards establishing cooperative relationships should take into consideration factors influencing effectiveness of such arrangements. In particular, the actions of the partners should be co-ordinated via a common marketing strategy. The strategy should be based upon the goals and objectives of a marketing strategy formulated at a higher level.

The marketing efforts of individual countries of Central and Eastern Europe might also be combined at international level. The proximity of these countries, as well as their compatible tourism products constitute basic factors for such co-operation, make this idea worth considering. It does not necessarily have to be inter-governmental co-operation as is the case in Nordic countries; it may well be co-operation of two or more neighbouring regions in different countries.

There have already been some transnational initiatives, such as the Carpathians Euroregion or the Nysa Euroregion, but these initiatives do not directly concern tourism marketing. Nonetheless, they show the potential for establishing co-operation on tourism marketing on a similar basis but including active involvement of the tourism trade.

Any initiatives promoting the concept of co-operative regional marketing should be based upon availability of adequate numbers of educated and trained personnel. Since marketing thinking is not common amid tourism entrepreneurs and local authority personnel in Central and Eastern Europe, there is a need to develop training programmes on marketing based upon both marketing theory and - what is even more important - practice.

Another field of education and training to ensure effectiveness of marketing efforts is hospitality training of service providers. At the same time community awareness programmes should be developed.

Cooperative marketing at international level calls for co-operation on education with the possibility of getting experience in the international environment. To implement international education programmes however, the first thing to be done is to develop the foreign language skills of both teachers and students.

The task of improving regional marketing effectiveness seems to be a medium- or even a long-term one. However, with the increasing importance of tourism in the world and growing competition in the world tourism market, the measures contributing towards improving regional tourism marketing effectiveness in Central and Eastern Europe should not be postponed.

## REFERENCES

Dipartimento Turismo Presidenza del Consiglio dei Ministri (1994). *Fifth Report on Italian Tourism.* Roma.

Hill, T. (1992). 'Partnerships in International Tourism Marketing'. In: TTRA Conference Proceedings, *Tourism Partnerships and Strategies.* USA.

Ministry for Communication and Tourism (1994). *Review of Tourism Policy in Denmark.* Copenhagen.

Nordiskt Ministerraad (1989). *Nordisk Turistprogram.* Copenhagen.

OECD (1992). *Tourism Policy and International Tourism in OECD Member Countries.* Paris.

Okoroafo S. (1989). 'Cooperative Marketing'. In: S.F. Witt and L. Moutinho (eds.). *Marketing and Management Handbook.* London.

The Royal Ministry of Industry (1989). *Tourism Policy Objectives and Priorities. Plans and Programmes and Institutional Framework.* Oslo.

Travis A.S. (1993). 'Tourism Destination Area Development'. In: S.F. Witt and L. Moutinho (eds.). *Tourism Marketing and Management Handbook.* London: Prentice Hall, pp.487-498.

Wahab, S., L. Crampon and L. Rothfield, (1976). *Tourism Marketing.* London: Tourism International Press.

# Chapter 22

# The relationship between tourism products and demand: the example of equestrian tourism

**Barbara Marciszewska and**
**Anita Wyznikiewicz-Nawracala**

## INTRODUCTION

This paper attempts to identify some of the features of tourism products which influence tourism demand in Poland. Changes in leisure consumption are linked to both economic transformation and social change. Therefore, the tourism product and, consequently, the product offer should highlight its specific benefits, which meet the needs and expectations of leisure consumers, often from the small segments of a market. Such a focus is important, because tourism demand is shaped not only by the individual's way of life, but also by the structure of the product and the way in which it is promoted.

The characteristics of tourism as a specialised service product need to be fully understood if consumers are to be satisfied and tourism organisations are to be successful. The management of tourism should not only focus on market research, analysis, price policy, product formulation and finally, sale. Competition in the tourism market also leads to the differentiation of functions of similarly formulated products.

In this paper we stress that the main factors which managers of tourism have to understand are the service management aspects related to the purchase of the tourism product: the product structure, the functions of the product, the way the product is presented and the form of the offer.

## THE TOURISM PRODUCT FORMULATION

Leisure products (tourism, recreation, sport products) have specific characteristics in common with other service products. Some textbooks related to services marketing give a number of different approaches to explaining what services are. Cowell (1990) identifies a number of approaches, including: definitions of services, characteristics of services, functional differences and classifications of services.

In this paper we focus on the definitions of services and functional differences, which, in our opinion, play an important role in tourism product formulation.

The American Marketing Association definition of services was refined by many authors including Gronroos (1978), Stanton (1981) and Kotler (1982). Kotler defines a service as: "...any activity or benefits that one party can offer to another that is essentially intangible and does not result in the ownership of anything. Its production may or may not be tied to a physical product". Many of the current definitions stress, directly or indirectly, the essentially intangible nature of a service. It is often not possible to test, feel, see, hear or smell services before they are purchased. Therefore, the service product formulation and promotion is more difficult than in case of goods and requires more attention to prepare an optimal offer. This applies to the tourism product, too.

Many authors stress the importance of tourism as a service product (Holloway and Plant, 1988; Buttle, 1986), which is usually described in terms of the characteristics of intangibility, perishability and inseparability. In accordance with this approach it is necessary to stress that a tourism product is a kind of leisure product (Figure 22.1), based mainly on services but also consisting of tangible components, too (Altkorn, 1994).

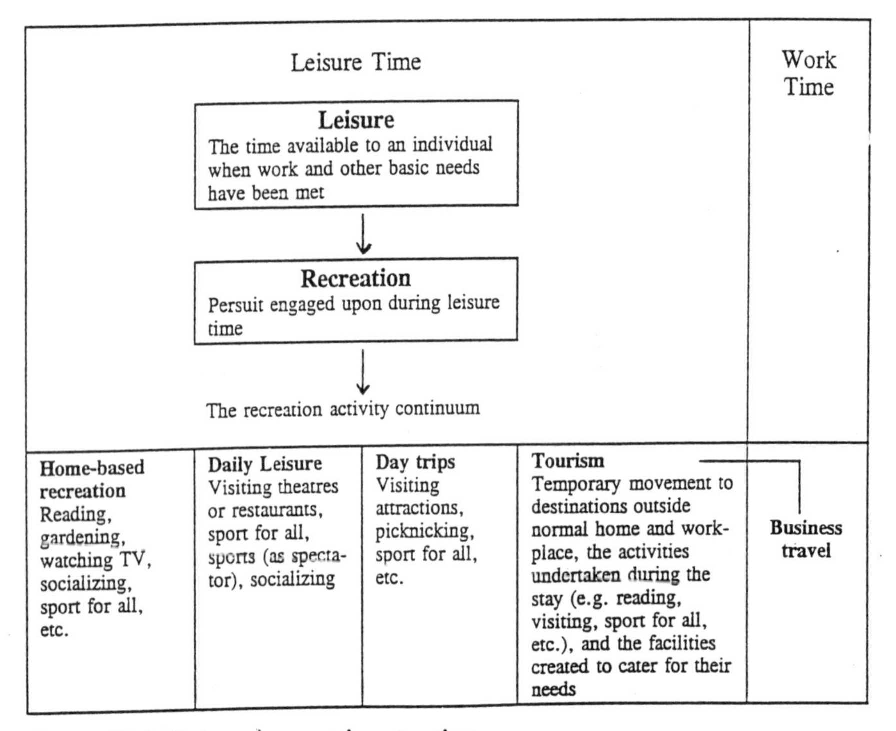


**Figure 22.1: Leisure, recreation, tourism**
*Source*: based on Cooper (1993)

Figure 22.1 shows that tourism has a close relationship with other activities, and that the tourism product can consist of various combinations of different recreation activities (e.g. watching TV, visiting theatres, sport for all, visiting attractions). A tourism product structure depends on consumers' needs and expectations, that the producer of a product attempts to satisfy (Klisinski, 1994). In each particular case tourism organisations should select among the elements of potential tourism supply exclusively those components that will give an optimal combination of product functions for separate groups of consumers.

The process of re-establishing the macro-economic balance and conducting structural reforms entailed high social costs in Poland. The difficult financial situation of a significant part of Polish society has differentiated the consumer needs hierarchy, and, consequently, the tourism demand for several kinds of tourism product. The structure of demand should depend on consumer's needs, defined in the market research process, but real demand is strongly connected with the form of the product offer. For example, at the present time the tourism offer should include recreation activities, because people not only want to rest during their holidays, but also improve their health. Thus our market research carried out among participants of recreational slimming holidays confirms that people prefer this form of rest because of the recreational profile of the proposed services (Figure 22.2). Gilbert (1994) has identified a growing trend towards active recreation in European countries. Thus a tourism product including some elements of recreation activities could provide personal fitness benefits for people of all ages. These expectations have led to a greater demand for participative sports, specialist activity holidays and more active than passive pastimes. Gilbert (1994) says: "Among those who are interested in activity pursuits can be found the small core of enthusiasts who are committed to their chosen form of recreation and require specialist serving". This also applies to equestrian tourism.

In a situation where the scope of the tourism product has been expanding in response to consumers' expectations and includes more recreation activities than before, we should attempt to formulate a tourist recreation product. This term is used in the literature (Dietvorst, 1994), but our interpretation is a little wider. We base our approach not only upon the common aspects of supply and demand in recreation and tourism, but also on the necessity to improve the health of consumers during their leisure time. The increasing number of paid services in the health sector in Poland makes them inaccessible for many groups in our society. Therefore, the optimal tourism supply in Poland should be based upon common market research in the field of the tourism and recreation demand. Yet in Polish texts, the demand for tourist recreation products is given little attention. Investigation of the tourism market should be continued in cooperation with specialists from several disciplines, e.g. sciences of physical culture, medicine, sociology and economics, to identify the changing expectations of consumers now and in the near future. Integrated research in fields related to tourism could make it possible to define the optimal recreation tourism supply, and, on the other hand, to influence tourism demand by stimulating supply and adequate forms of recreation tourism product promotion.

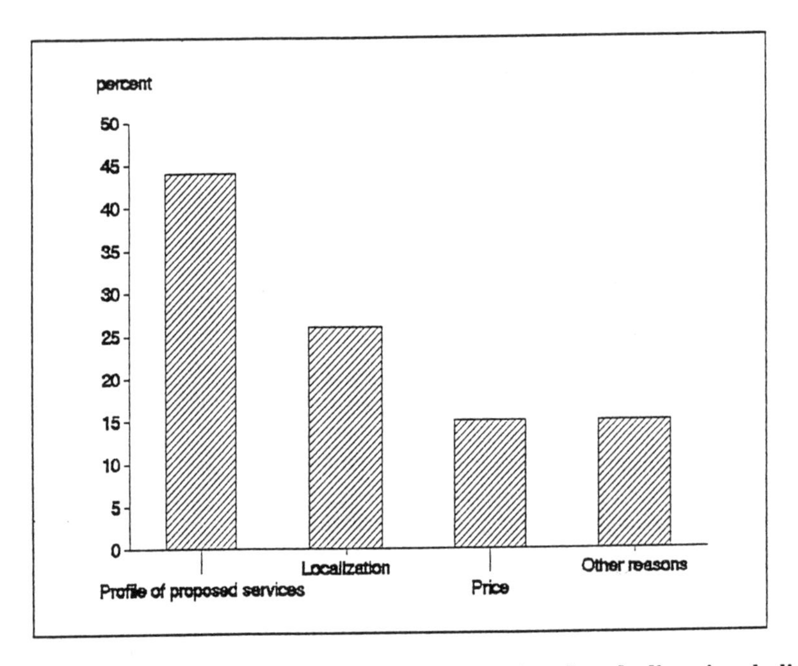


**Figure 22.2: Motives for choosing recreational and slimming holidays by consumers**

## WHAT IS THE ROLE OF THE PRODUCT OFFER FOR TOURIST RECREATION PROMOTION?

Our attempt to define the role of the product offer for tourist recreation product promotion, and, finally, demand for this product, is based upon Cowells' (1990) approach to functional differences of services:

- services cannot be stocked;
- services cannot be patented;
- services channels are usually short;
- services cannot be sampled;
- service standards cannot be precise.

The difficulty with this approach is the problem of defining the dependence between tourism recreation facilities and tourism recreation standards, because this relationship can determine the nature of the recreation tourism product. In this connection tourism recreation standards can be precise with reference to tangible elements of the product but cannot be accurate with regard to its intangible components. The relative dominance of intangible attributes in the make up of the tourist recreation product makes it necessary to develop strong principles for its promotion, the ways the product is bought and motives for its purchase. It is easier for non-profit motivated tourism organisations to resolve this problem. Profit-oriented tourism enterprises have to consider not only consumers' interests but also the efficiency of their activity. Being limited by tourism recreation facilities on one side and their own criteria of efficiency on the other, they create products on the basis of their resources and consumers' needs, but their products are not always competitive in the marketplace. In this situation, the form of presentation of the tourist recreation product has great influence on the motivation for the purchase of the product.

The touristic offer presented below takes into consideration many conditions which make it attractive for consumers as well as for producers of the product.

## Riding route Sopot - Ostrzyce - Sopot

The riding route from Sopot to Ostrzyce is the main attraction of the offer of a six day tourist stay on the Gdansk Coast and in the Kaszuby Region in Northern Poland. The route runs through the following towns: Owczarnia, Osowa, Tuchomek, Tokary, Smoldzino, Borowo, Mezowo, Kielpino and Goreczyno. The route is divided into three stages and includes two breaks: one hour and two hours long. It takes 9 hours to cover the distance from Sopot to Ostrzyce. The main forms of riding are the walk and the trot with the principle that there should be as much walk as trot. In the individual rides the duration of trot does not exceed 15 minutes.

Along the route there are many interesting tourist sights, e.g. nature reserves such as Starodrzew (an old tree reserve) on Zajecze Wzgórze, springs and sources in Ewa Valley, the Radunia River Gorge, the Wiezyca Peak as well as landmarks of regional culture, such as 16th and 17th century church in Goreczyno and the old mill in Mlynek.

The tourist offer comprises:

- a field ride preceding the outset so that riders and horses become acquainted;
- the ride proper;
- two days rest is indispensable for the horses after the ride, walks in hand, bare-back riding, watering the horses; for riders walks on horseback, trips on foot, canoeing and bicycle trips in the picturesque Kaszuby 'Switzerland' area, also a barbecue and a disco.

The details of the offer concerning the ride itself can be modified and adapted to the financial means of the participants, their riding skills, the size of the group, time of the year and free time available to the participants. The possibility to introduce changes in the proposed tourist offer favours recreation through movement with sightseeing in focus.

The riding route Sopot - Ostrzyce creates an opportunity for an interesting and attractive way of spending free time among trees in still relatively unpolluted fresh air. For those who ride it is a magnificent opportunity to spend a few days with their favourite horse in the picturesque surroundings of the Kaszuby 'Switzerland' area.

## CHARACTERISTICS OF TOURISM ON HORSEBACK

The main characteristics of tourism on horseback is that it is a very attractive and enjoyable form of spending free time for those who ride. Yet it requires horsemanship skills as well as geographical and ecological knowledge of regulations concerning environmental protection and first aid for people and horses. It is also necessary to have knowledge of marketing.

Tourism on horseback can be an individual or group activity. The individual tourist can choose the time, the route and what interests him or her most. Riding in a group requires discipline from all the participants. It is connected with the preparation of the rider and horses for riding in a group, because a lack of discipline may ruin the pleasure of recreation for other participants. Group riding sometimes takes the form of competition in which the skills of horses and the horsemanship of riders are compared, especially in the sphere of breaking in a horse.

We can distinguish the following forms of horseback tourism:
a. travels, touring on horseback trail rides;
b. distance runs;
c. sports horse trail rides.

Travels and touring on horseback can be divided into individual and group ones. A horse trail ride is an organised group ride on horseback in the country supervised by an experienced leader and following a set of rules defined in advance and which include the principles of competition. Typical trail rides under FEI rules were not held in Poland until 1990 (Czabanska, 1980). A sports horse trail ride is an equestrian discipline which aims at proving the speed and endurance of horses. Competitions can be held in one day or over a number of days. They consist of one or a number of stages. The stages are divided into sections each of which ends at a check point, i.e. a stopover, during each a veterinary check-up takes place (Kydd, 1981; Przepisy jezdzieckie, 1991). Distance runs are a form of competition in riding. They are classified according to their character and way of organisation. A set route must be covered in a time limit by means of various horse steps (Gless, 1982; Grabowski, 1984).

### ORGANISATION OF TOURING AND HORSE TRAIL RIDES

Organisers of touring and horse trail rides have to meet high standards. These include ensuring the safety of both people and horses, providing equipment, checking the participants' kits, planning the route and checking it, determining speed limits which depend on the type of countryside and ground, checking the preparation of horses and if they are able to cover the route, considering the likelihood of the occurrence of ailments or even illnesses in horses and preparations to look after the horses should the need arise. Each trail and tour must be accompanied by a car carrying equipment. The presence of a veterinary doctor is desirable.

The success and attractiveness of tourism on horseback is determined by:

- the choice of the horse;
- the fitness preparation of the horse;
- choice of saddle and accessories and the preparation of equipment;
- organisation of service, and selection and checking of the route;
- preparation of the route;
- organisation of the tour;
- professional care for the horses in case of injury or illness.

### PREPARATION OF THE HORSE

Preparations for setting out must commence with the selection of the horse in terms of its character. For trail rides as well as for passages the best horses are those which are well balanced, willing to work and with the right step. Watering the horse is one of the basic problems during a rides. A horse should be prepared to drink and eat not only in its own box, but in various places and at various times of the day. The best horses are aged 7-8, well balanced and with a lot of experience.

### ORGANISATION OF TOURING ON HORSEBACK

It is the duty of the organiser to provide the group with a competent leader. A group with more than six horses must have two instructors, one of whom leads the way and the other follows behind.

The route must be commenced in the morning. If the planned distance is 50 km, the tour takes 6-7 hours. Combined with two stopovers of one or two hours the tour extends to 9 -10 hours.

Early feeding of the horses must take place at least one hour before setting out and in case of trail rides two hours before the start. The horse should be warmed up half an hour before setting out. Some riders warm up over the first two kilometres which are covered in a walk. Before saddling the horse the saddle and accessories must be checked, especially those parts of the saddle which remain in direct contact with the horse's back and the hooves must be cleaned thoroughly. After saddling the horse the troop is formed following a pre-determined order. After covering approximately two kilometres the girth must be tightened so that it is not too loose. This is done without dismounting from the horse.

The troop travels at the speed of approximately 8 km/h. This results from a well balanced mix of walk and trot. The speed of the walk is 6 km/h, whereas that of the trot is 11-12 km/h. In travelling on horseback there is no need to gallop which requires increased effort, because the time of the tour is unlimited. During the travel the leader must avoid all beaten tracks and uneven surfaces, and cover all stretches of hard surface at a walk.

The place for rest should be chosen in such a way that it ensures a stopover between consecutive two hour marches. When approaching the place of rest the riders should dismount from the horses and lead them, not forgetting to loosen the girdle. First the horses must rest. They can be fed and watered one hour before and after effort. This determines the length of the break. On hot summer days it is advisable to take a longer break, ideally during the midday heat.

In order for touring to be successful it must be well thought through. Figure 22.3 shows the route from Sopot to Ostrzyce. It consists of three sections and two breaks. The length of the route and places for rest have been marked in kilometres on the left, whereas on the right the names of the places along the route are shown. Figure 22.4 shows a possible frame for the preparation of programmes for recreation and tourism on horseback (Wyznikiewicz-Nawracala, 1995). Figure 22.5 shows the scheme which is used for the preparation of a one-day, three-stage passage on horseback from Sopot to Ostrzyce (from the Gdansk Seaside to the Kaszuby 'Switzerland' area).

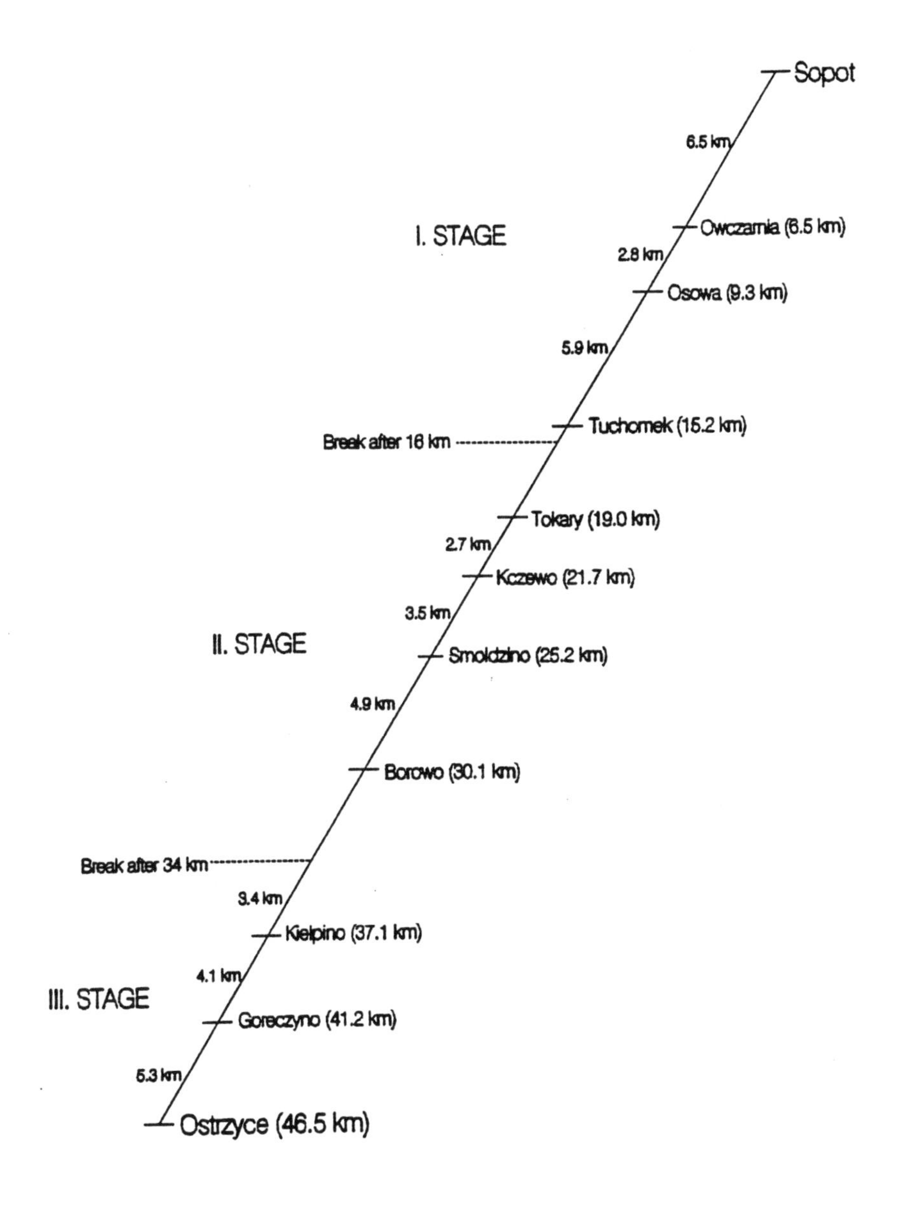


**Figure 22.3: The route from Sopot to Ostrzyce**

| Accommodation places | Campsites | | Horse Hostels | Organization of meals | Programme | | |
|---|---|---|---|---|---|---|---|
| | | | | | Riding | Recreational | Touristic |
| Hotel<br>H | I | toilets, shower, kitchen | Forestry and stables | Canteen<br>C | Riding lessons<br>L | Trails:<br>on bicycles | |
| School hostel<br>Sh | II | umbrella, roof, water | Forest carpark with an umbrella roof | Restaurant<br>R | Cross-country riding | by car | |
| School classes<br>Sc | III | "wild" | Private farm | Bar<br>B | Touring on horseback<br>T | canoes | |
| Private accommodation<br>P | | | Adapted centres | Self-catering<br>S | Trail raid | | |
| | | | | | | lake | Landmarks<br>L |
| | | | | | | tennis court | Monuments of nature<br>M |
| | | | | | | sports grounds | Regional open air Museums<br>RM |
| | | | | | | mini sports stadium | Historic Monuments<br>HM |
| | | | | | | hippodrome | Regional Industry<br>RI |
| | | | | | | | Wildlife Reserves<br>WR |

**Figure 22.4: The pattern for the preparation of programmes for recreation and tourism on horseback**

| ROAD | Characteristics of the destination | | | | | | | |
|---|---|---|---|---|---|---|---|---|
| | Ac-com-mo-dation | Horse Hos-teis | Meals | Programme | | | Dis-tance (km) | Stages (min) |
| | | | | Riding | Recrea-tional | Touristic | | |
| Sopot | H | | C | T | | L: Trójmiasto (Gdansk. Sopot Gdynia) Baltic See<br>M: old tree Reserve on Zajęcze Wzgórze | 0.0 | I: 2 h 10 min |
| Owczarnia | | | | | | M: Springs of Ev's Valley | 6.2 | |
| Osowa | | | | | | | 9.3 | |
| Jez. Wysockie | | | | | | | 10.3 | |
| Jez. Tuchomskie | | | S | | | WR: wildlife Reserves | 16.0 | 1 break 1 h |
| Tokary | | | | | | | 19.0 | |
| Kczewo | | | | | | | 22.7 | |
| Młynek | | | | | | RJ: old mill | 24.3 | II: 2 h 15 min |
| Smołdzino | | | | | | | 25.2 | |
| Sitno | | | | | | M: nature Reserve | 28.0 | |
| Borowo | | | | | | | 30.0 | |
| Mezowo | | | S | | | M: old larch Trees | 33.7 | 2 break 2 h |
| Kielpino | | | | | | | 37.0 | |
| os. Bernardyno | | | | | | | 38.7 | |
| Goręczyno | | | | | | L: church 16th - 17th c. | 41.0 | III: 1 h 50 min |
| Ostryce | H | | | | | | 46.5 | |
| | | | | L | | M: Wiezyca Peak | | |
| The followed route | | | | | | Σ | 46.5 km | 9 h |

**Figure 22.5: The scheme of realization of a one-day, three-stage touring on horseback from Sopot to Ostrzyce (from the Gdansk Seaside to the Kaszuby "Switzerland")**

## REFERENCES

Altkorn, J. (1994). *Marketing w turystyce*. Warszawa: PWN.

Buttle, F. (1986). *Hotel and Food Service Marketing*. London: Holt, Rinehart and Winston.

Cooper, C. (1993). 'An Introduction to Tourism.' In: C. Cooper, J. Fletcher, D. Gilbert and S. Wanhill. *Tourism Principles and Practice*. London: Pitman.

Cowell, D.W. (1990). *The Marketing of Services*. Oxford: Heinemann.

Czabanska, E. (1980). 'Przemarsze i podróze konne, rajdy turystyczne i dlugo-dystansowe'. In: *Kon Polski,* No 3, pp.22-23.

Dietvorst A. (1994). 'Dutch research on leisure, recreation and tourism'. In: *Progress in Tourism, Recreation and Hospitality Management*, volume 5. London: John Wiley & Sons, pp.116-131.

Gilbert D.C. (1993). 'Marketing management'. In: C. Cooper, J. Fletcher, D. Gilbert and S. Wanhill, *Tourism Principles and Practice*. London: Pitman Publishing, pp.230-240.

Gilbert D.C. (1994). 'The European Community and leisure lifestyles'. In: *Progress in Tourism, Recreation and Hospitality Management*, volume 5. London: John Wiley & Sons, pp.116-131.

Gless, K.H. (1982). *600 Rad dla milosników koni*. Warszawa: PWRiL.

Grabowski, J. (1983). 'Terenowe próby koni - rajdy'. In: *Kon Polski* No 1, pp.36-39.

Gronroos, C. (1978). 'A Service Orientated Approach to Marketing of Services'. In: *European Journal of Marketing*, volume 12, No 8, p.589.

Holloway, J.C. and R.V. Plant, (1988). *Marketing for Tourism*. London: Pitman.

Klisinski, J. (1994). *Marketing w sporcie*. Warszawa: RCMSKFiS.

Kotler, P. (1982). *Principles of Marketing*. Englewood Cliffs: Prentice-Hall.

Kydd, R. (1981). *Distanzreiten erklart*. Gifhorn, Zeunert's Verlag.

Przepisy jezdzieckie, (1991). *Rajdy dlugodystansowe*. Warszawa: Polski Zwiazek Jezdziecki.

Stanton, W.J. (1981). *Fundamentals of Marketing*. New York: Mc Graw Hill.

Wyznikiewicz-Nawracala, A. (1995). *Turystyczne i rekreacyjne formy jezdziectwa w agroturystyce*. Gdansk: Zeszyty Naukowe AWF.

# Chapter 23

# Tourism and the crime rate in Poland

**Wieslaw Alejziak**

The analysis of the present situation and the forecasts for the future, as regards the development of tourism in Poland, point towards perceptible growth tendencies in the tourist industry. An especially strong growth dynamic exists in the case of tourists arriving in Poland from abroad. This growth can be seen both in the volume of tourist traffic and in the revenues flowing from tourist services.

At the same time, however, we cannot fail to notice the disquieting increase in the crime rate and other manifestations of social pathology, and indeed a general worsening of the state of public safety. In the opinion of many experts, the rising crime rate and the ineffectiveness of the Polish public safety authorities (state and local police, public prosecutors, courts, etc.) are perceived as one of the factors that could bring a halt to the growth tendencies recently observed in the Polish tourism market.

These facts, along with the large and constant significance of tourism in the social and economic life of Poland, prompt us to pose the question:

Is there a direct (or indirect) link between the development of tourism and the increasing incidence of crime and other social pathologies? Are there characteristic dependencies between these phenomena? If so, is it possible to verify these dependencies scientifically, and to determine the properties that govern them?

To date we do not know whether tourism in some particular way generates (produces) an increase in crime and other social pathologies. It can only be presumed that an increasing crime rate would naturally result from the inflow of tourists and the increasing number of people in a given area. But does the crime rate increase proportionally to the number of tourists who arrive, or are there other dependencies (e.g., does the crime rate increase faster)? Does the impact of tourist traffic change not only the rate of increase, but also the nature of the crimes committed?

Unfortunately, we cannot give any answers to these apparently simple questions. These issues have not so far been raised, either by specialists in criminal law, criminology, or victimology, or by scientists interested in research on various aspects of tourism. While the theoretical base resulting from research on both phenomena (i.e. on tourism and on crime) is already sufficient to allow certain conclusions to be drawn and generalities to be stated as regards each of these separately, nevertheless there has to date been no research that brings together the issues raised by the two phenomena in conjunction with each other. The problem of social pathologies, especially the rising crime rate in cities heavily visited by tourists, has not yet been subjected to serious analysis and study. What is more, despite the obvious increase in both the scale and the significance of these phenomena in recent times, there are no signals that any such studies are planned. The results from research on current research priorities in tourism, conducted in 1984 by H. Leo Theuns, indicate that the issue of the links between tourism and crime (and other social pathologies) is not perceived as an essential area of scientific interest for tourism research.This issue was not mentioned in any of the eight divisions mentioned by Theuns comprising some 46 research topics (Theuns, 1986).

At the same time, tourism itself, in all its complexity, and with the great benefits it can bring, has in essence an ambivalent character. It turns out that tourism can just as well bring grievous problems as benefits: it can destroy the environment, disintegrate the social structure, demoralise the youth, and so forth. In essence, the destructive capacities of tourism are virtually as great as the benefits it can bring. One of the manifestations of the potential destructiveness of tourism may well be an increase in crime and other social pathologies.

Tourism, which for centuries has been connected with 'adventure', by its very nature creates many opportunities for crimes to be committed. These involves both tourists and the local population. In addition, it seems that the concentration of tourist traffic 'attracts' many criminals, especially those involved in various kinds of thefts (pickpockets, car thieves, hotel burglars, etc.) It seems that the inflow of tourists, in addition to the - in a certain sense - natural increase in the number of common crimes (theft, burglary, robbery, and the like), has a particularly strong impact on the growth of certain kinds of crimes and infractions (highway accidents, smuggling, currency violations), as well as social pathologies (alcohol abuse, prostitution, vandalism, vagrancy, etc.).

## Is Poland a safe country for tourists, especially foreigners?

In reports on the Polish tourist market, which often provide the basis for the decisions and strategies adopted by foreign tour operators, Poland is listed as a 'higher risk' country, as regards both the safety of the tourists themselves, and the operations of the tour organisers. For this reason, many foreign travel bureaus decline to organise excursions to Poland, or, if they have already decided to do so, they typically give their customers information warning them of the threats they may encounter in Poland. The most common mentioned threats include theft, especially the theft of automobiles and expensive tourist equipment; various kinds of con games and frauds; and more recently phenomena emerging from nationalism and certain youth subcultures which, because of the philosophy (ideology) they espouse, are hostile to tourists. This situation significantly limits the possibility of promoting Poland on the international tourist market.

On the other hand, many problems have recently been caused by the mass influx of foreigners from certain former socialist countries. Regarding tourism as an additional source of income, they come to Poland in large numbers and sell the goods they bring with them at markets and bazaars. While illegal trade is not in itself a particularly dangerous phenomenon, it is often accompanied by much more serious crimes.

Another problem is created by political refugees, potential applicants for asylum, and nomads following their wandering lifestyle. They often regard Poland as only one stage (predominantly the first stage) in their search for their own 'place under the sun'. As a result of the temporary nature of their stay and the likelihood that they will soon leave the country, along with the costs entailed by their travels, their general lack of financial resources, and their ignorance of Polish law, they often come into conflict with Polish law, or become a source of certain social pathologies, such as vagrancy and begging.

The phenomenon of crime committed by foreigners visiting Poland is something new, as a problem of considerable social significance. The political and social transformations, especially the democratisation of passport regulations in the former socialist countries, and the liberalisation of Polish visa requirements, has caused a mass influx of foreign tourists to Poland. Citizens of former socialist countries account for a considerable portion of this dynamic. Unfortunately, they also create the most problems with law and public order.

## DO TOURISTS COMMIT CRIMES?

Tourists who leave their homes and head for tourist destinations may equally be either perpetrators or victims of crime. In the case of crimes committed by tourists, a distinction should be made between situations where crimes are committed without premeditation (committed more or less as a result of an opportunity that arouse during the tourist excursion), and situations where the entire trip has been undertaken with the intention to commit acts forbidden by law, and tourism fulfils only the role of camouflage, concealing the actual motives and intentions of the criminal.

It should be emphasised that among all the various classifications and typologies of the motives underlying tourism, there are none which would presuppose tourism undertaken for criminal purposes. We presume that the intention to commit crimes precludes the classification of a trip as 'tourism'. A person who leaves his place of residence in order to commit a crime is not a tourist, but rather a potential (or actual) criminal who happens to be travelling. In practice, however, it is only rather difficult to distinguish genuine motives for engaging in tourism from motives which are only declarations that a given departure or arrival is 'touristic' in character. It often happens that the real motives for the trip are concealed under the veil of the alleged needs, motivations, and purposes of a 'tourist'.

An analysis of police reports indicates, however, that 'genuine' tourists also violate the law. These violations include not only accidental violations (e.g. traffic violations) and common crimes (theft, robbery), but also crimes that are particularly closely connected with tourism, such as customs and currency violations, art smuggling, illegal commerce, hotel thefts, etc.

Can the worsening state of public safety bring to a halt the growth tendencies of the Polish tourism market? Answering this question requires detailed and methodologically correct research. In the final section of this article, I have taken the liberty of briefly presenting a preliminary research concept for studying the links and dependencies between tourism and crime in Kraków.

## TOURISM, CRIME AND SOCIAL PATHOLOGIES IN KRAKÓW: A RESEARCH CONCEPT

In view of the thematic diversity of this subject, the research will be interdisciplinary in character, involving issues in criminal law and penal (criminological) sciences, sociology, and tourism. The particular disciplines to be covered include criminology, victimology, sociology of tourism, sociology of criminal law, and certain specialised disciplines in tourism (psychology of tourism, economics of tourism, organisation and management, statistics, tourism policy). Given the lack of similar research and the insufficient scientific literature, as mentioned above, I presume that the research will be characterised by considerable elasticity, as regards both its scope and its methodology.

## PRIMARY RESEARCH GOAL

The basic goal of this research is to conduct a scientific survey of the issue of crime and certain social pathologies in tourist destinations, and to indicate the ways and means by which the unfavourable effects resulting from the influx of tourists can be counteracted.

The cognitive goals include the following:

- to test whether dependencies exist between the nature, extent, structure, and dynamic of tourist traffic on the one hand, and these same parameters and measures of the incidence of crime and certain other social pathologies on the other;

- to attempt to develop a universal (and methodologically correct) research method that would allow similar research to be conducted in other tourist destinations and regions;

- to develop some sort of 'balance sheet' of the gains and losses resulting from an influx of tourists. As yet we do not know whether it is more often the case that crimes are committed by residents of Kraków against tourists, or that tourists commit crimes against the local residents.

The practical goal of the research is indicated by the fact that the issue of public safety in tourist destinations must be taken into account when forming and implementing tourism policy. This involves both the state's tourism policies (on the macro scale), and regional and local policies and strategies. If we have a diagnostic account of the links between tourism and crime, if we understand the dependencies between the volume and form of tourism on the one hand, and the nature and mechanism of the crimes committed on the other, it will be easier to take effective countermeasures. Thus it is also part of the present author's intentions for the research to be concluded with a report, including concrete proposals for possible changes in legal regulations, the organisation of public life, and the functioning and operating methods of the municipal services, so as to take the specific character of Kraków as a tourist destination into account to a greater extent than has been the case to date. The report will also provide practical advice for the tourist industry. It would seem that Kraków's experiences could serve as a model for other tourist destinations.

The subjects of the research will include all those persons who have fallen victim to crime, or who have committed crimes or other acts regarded as social pathologies within the city limits of Kraków, insofar as these had some connection (direct or indirect) with tourism.

The temporal scope of the research will cover the period from 1989 to 1994. In particular cases, this period may be extended. The spatial scope of the research will include the land located within the city limits of Kraków.

The objects of the research will be a range of sub-issues (fields of research). Behaviours and actions included under the concepts of 'crime', 'infraction', and 'social pathology' (e.g. prostitution, drug addiction, vagrancy and begging, sports-related pseudo-tourism, attitudes towards tourism and tourists in the ideologies of youth sub-cultures, etc.) will be subjected to analysis.

In relation to each of the crimes mentioned, the statistical analysis will deal with crimes committed by tourists separately from crimes committed against tourists. The research will also cover certain crimes and improper practices in the operations of tourist institutions.

The institutions of public safety will also be included in the analyses, including especially the state police and the municipal security service. These analyses will deal with the organisational structures, functioning, and operating methods of these services, with respect to the prevention or limitation of the negative phenomena produced by the mass influx of tourists to Kraków.

## RESEARCH HYPOTHESES AND QUESTIONS

The primary research hypothesis is that there exist scientifically verifiable links and dependencies between tourism on the one hand, and crime and other social pathologies on the other. Several sub-hypotheses have also been established:

The influx of tourists causes an increased crime rate and the growth of certain social pathologies, and the increase in the crime rate is not directly proportional to the increase in the volume of tourist traffic.

Under the impact of tourist traffic, changes take place not only in the volume of crime and social pathologies in a tourist destination, but also in their structure, dynamics, nature, and geographical distribution.

The organisational structure, functioning, and operating methods of the public services do not sufficiently take into account Kraków's tourist function, both on the level of planning and in practical operations.

The research questions include the following:
- Do 'genuine' tourists commit crimes?
- Who most often falls victim to crime, and who most often commits crimes: the tourists, or the residents of the tourist destination?
- Can tourism be used (is it in fact used) as a tool for the criminal activities of organised crime (the Mafia)?

## RESEARCH METHODS AND TECHNIQUES

The thematic diversity of the research requires that a broad and specially selected research apparatus be applied. The process of realising each of the separate fields of research (cf. the 'objects of research' above) will consist of the following steps:
- specifying and determining the problem;
- gathering information about the phenomena and processes being

researched, and about the ways and means used to counteract them;
- analysis of the system being researched (by breaking it down into sub-systems, or even elements);
- diagnosis (through the synthesis of the information gathered);
- (model) solutions.

The interdisciplinary and multi-facted nature of both phenomena under consideration (i.e. tourism and crime) brings about the necessity for the research itself to be interdisciplinary. It will thus be necessary to apply statistical and sociological methods, and methods derived from organisation and management, and so forth.

The basic method for gathering research materials and collecting information about the extent, structure, and dynamics of crime and other social pathologies in Kraków will be a comprehensive analysis of statistical reports from law enforcement agencies and court authorities. The following elements of criminal statistics will be subjected to analysis:

Police and prosecutor's statistics. In view of the fact that these records include all criminal acts, regardless of the outcome of later criminal proceedings, they give the most complete picture of the crime rate. The analysis of data contained in the materials and reports of the Regional Police Headquarters in Kraków will provide the basis for specifying the volume, dynamics, and structure of crime in general, and for breaking down crimes into those committed by tourists visiting Kraków and those committed against such tourists.

In these records, the statistical unit is a person convicted by a binding verdict. The so-called 'criminal pages' of persons accused and convicted will be subjected to analysis. In view of the rules governing the way these records are kept, and especially on the wide span of time that elapses between the crime and the verdict, the scope of time covered by the research may be extended in the case of court statistics.

Penal statistics. Here the statistical unit is the person under confinement. The primary document is the 'W-3' report, which contains an annual report on persons under temporary arrest, convicted, and punished.

As in the case of crime, statistical analysis will be of fundamental importance in the issues pertaining to tourism. The statistical data will provide a basis for an analysis of the volume, structure, dynamics, seasonality, and other characteristics and measures of tourist traffic.

The statistical methods will be supplemented by empirical material collected by using other research methods, including in particular sociological methods, such as interviews, questionnaires, various forms of observation, etc. These methods will be applied as needed, and will be of use in investigating particular research problems (e.g., questionnaires in relation to prostitution, interviews as regards hotel safety and security, participatory observation in the case of sports-related 'pseudo-tourism', and so forth). In research on the organisation and functioning of the public services, it will be necessary to apply methods from organisation and management, document analysis, etc.

The research is explanatory in nature, and will thus be aimed towards discovering the links that exist between the phenomena of interest, and in particular towards testing the correlations between an influx of tourists and an increasing crime rate in tourist destinations. In the statistical analysis of the research materials, we will use several kinds of statistical techniques and tools. In a situation where we are dealing with a preponderance of quantitative (measurable) figures, descriptive statistical methods will be used, specifying the phenomena and populations tested with a system of varying parameters (averages, standard deviations, etc.).

Nevertheless, the basic variables in criminology most often have a 'non-gradual' character (i.e. the given characteristic either occurs, or not), which will require that other procedural methods be applied. In performing analyses involving correlations and evaluations of the strength of the links between the growth of tourism and an increasing crime rate, the methods applied with include Pearson's linear correlation factor, Spearman and Kendall rank correlation factors, and measures of dependency used in non-parametrical statistics (e.g. chi distribution). In some cases it will be necessary to used approximating methods, including extrapolation, for example, to make predictions regarding the phenomena under research.

After the empirical materials have been gathered and statistically analysed, they will be subjected to further analysis, intended to make connections between the cause-and-effect links discovered and the results of the research on the system of social intervention and crime prevention. At this stage, we will use a method of diagnostic analysis especially adapted to our research. Its basic characteristic is the critical analysis of the status quo as regards what is needed to solve the problems. This analysis will consist of a detailed analysis of the existing solutions, the discovery of the improprieties and errors in these solutions, suggestions as to the best way to avoid them, and proposals for changes. In the final analysis, this should lead to the optimisation of the solutions and a proposal for an ideal model (or perhaps alternative models).

## BASIC TERMINOLOGY AND THE CRITERIA USED TO CLASSIFY THE PHENOMENA UNDER RESEARCH

By the term 'tourism' the author understands 'the entirety of the phenomena of traffic over an expanse of space, connected with voluntarily and temporarily changing the place of residence, and the rhythm and surroundings of life, and with coming into personal contact with the environment visited (natural, cultural, or social)' (Przeclawski, 1993).

We will be interested only in the so-called 'arrival tourism', which may be defined as "the whole of the relationships and phenomena connected with the stay in a given area of persons arriving there, provided that such arrival does not result from the intention to resettle or take up permanent employment". We ascribe a similar meaning to the expression "tourist traffic in a given area". (In our research this refers to tourists coming to Kraków.)

The term 'social pathology' means "...phenomena of the social behaviour of individuals and specified social groups that is contrary to the values of the given culture".

The fundamental issue, both in the criminal law system and in criminology, is the term 'crime'. If we accept as a binding definition the contents of the law presently in force, we may assume that the term 'crime' should be understood to mean an act which poses a social danger, is specified as such in a particular piece of legislation, and is illegal, culpable, and punishable by virtue of a particular statute. The term 'crime rate', despite the fact that in Poland it is not an element of legal language (i.e. it is not a statutory term), is one of the most commonly used terms in criminology. In our work, the term 'crime rate' will mean "the total number of acts which are forbidden and punishable by law, and are committed in a given territorial unit within a given period of time".

In criminological literature, a distinction is made between the actual, reported, confirmed, and adjudicated crime rates. In our research, we will interest ourselves in the last three categories, depending upon our needs, and upon the source materials and statistics available.

The inexactness of the terminology and the criteria used for classification purposes makes it impossible to precisely limit the terms 'tourist' and 'traveller' (i.e. a person who arrives for reasons other than tourism, or for reasons of which tourism is only one). As far as the main goal of the research is concerned, the precise distinction between 'tourist' and 'non-tourist' is not all that important. We presume that both kinds of persons, to a significant extent, behave similarly, and use the same services and accommodations (transportation, lodgings, food, etc.).

While in the case of materials from public prosecutors and courts the identification of tourists as such will not present too many problems (since the files contain complete information on the identities of the perpetrator and the victim, and often their statements and pleadings), in the case of police materials such identification can be rather difficult (especially if the perpetrator was not apprehended). Nevertheless, in the desire to obtain complete information on the scale and structure of crime, daily police reports have also been subjected to analysis, despite the fact that they often contain only information about the event, and the name and address of the victim and the perpetrator (if known). In a situation where it is difficult to say, on the basis of the information available, whether or not a given crime had some connection with tourism, it has been assumed that following are reliable indicators of such connection:

a. the fact that the victim or the perpetrator has declared that his/her stay in Kraków is touristic in nature;

b. the place where the crime took place (hotel, hotel parking lot, museum, tourist service point, tourist attraction - e.g. Wawel - or tourist route - e.g. the Royal Way);

c. the type of objects stolen (video camera, camera, tourist guidebooks and maps, car with foreign license plates, etc.);

d. national origin (in the case of foreign tourists).

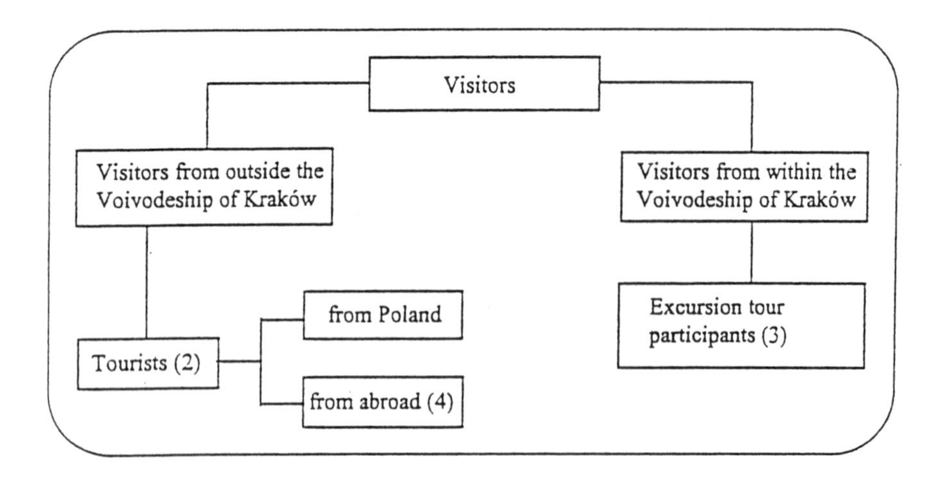


where:

1. all persons not having a place of residence within the city limits of Kraków who are temporarily present in Kraków (with the exception of persons in active military service or serving time in a penitentiary);
2. visitors in regard to whom we have information available to indicate that during their stay in Kraków they pursued the fulfilment of tourist goals;
3. visitors from the voivodeship of Kraków (outside the city itself) in regard to whom we have the same information as in (2);
4. all foreigners visiting Kraków (all counted as tourists, regardless of the purpose of their visit).

**Figure 23.1: Visitor classification scheme**

The terminology used in the research is that of the World Tourism Organisation for the classification of international tourist traffic, with some basic changes, however, in the criteria used for classification purposes. (In WTO statistics, the prime criterion is spending at least one night in a lodging facility within the country visited.) The classification scheme used is presented in Figure 23.1

In 1993, preliminary (pilot) research was conducted, which confirmed the hypothesis that there exist verifiable links and dependencies between the volume and structure of tourist traffic and the volume and structure of crime and certain social pathologies occurring within the area of concentrated tourist traffic.

## REFERENCES

Theuns L.H. (1986). 'Priorytety w badaniach turystycznych. Przeglad opinii ekspertów ze szczególnym uwzglednieniem krajów rozwijajacych sie (Priorities in Tourism Research: A Review of the Opinions of Experts, with Particular Attention to Developing Countries)'. *Problemy Turystyki* I.1.

Przeclawski K. (1973). *Turystyka i wychowanie (Tourism and Education).* Warsaw: Nasza Ksiegarnia, p.12.

# Chapter 24

# Developing tourism education in Central and Eastern Europe

**Greg Richards**

The contributions to this volume make a wide range of recommendations about the future development of tourism and tourism education in Central and Eastern Europe. As the development priorities for tourism as a whole have already been discussed in Chapter 1, it seems appropriate to conclude with a brief consideration of the priorities for developing tourism education in the region.

## CURRICULUM DEVELOPMENT

The most pressing need in CEE is the adaption of tourism curriculum to the changing needs of the market and the tourism industry. This is not simply a question of adding new elements to existing curricula. Tourism education in CEE has developed from very different roots than in most EU countries. In the West, tourism has developed very much from a management background, and is firmly linked to the productive aspects of tourism activity (Richards, 1995). In CEE the predominance of social tourism in the domestic market led to a view of tourism as a social phenomenon, rather than a commercial `industry'. Whereas tourism courses in the West can trace their origins to hotel schools or management departments, in CEE developments have stemmed from geography and physical education.

Changes in the tourism curriculum will also require an expanded debate about the balance between academic and vocational education. This is an argument which has long raged in the west, and which even now shows little sign of being resolved. The rush to acquire marketing and management skills by many in CEE also has the potential danger of narrowing the range of subjects offered in the curriculum. As Chris Holloway has pointed out in Chapter 12 of this volume, there is a need to preserve `liberal' behavioural science elements in the tourism curriculum. The neglect of behaviour sciences in Western countries has arguably already produced too narrow a vocational focus in many curricula.

There might be a case to be argued for the development of a common core curriculum for CEE countries (or groups of countries within the region). In contrast with the European Union, where the argument about a common core curriculum revolves around a distinct identity for `tourism' courses, the argument in the case of CEE might be based on a need to guarantee the inclusion of less applied aspects in the curriculum.This approach has already been adopted in the ATLAS Action Plan (Richards, 1995), and also featured in the proposed Action Plan for CEE (see below).

## ACADEMIC STANDARDS

The vacuum left by the dismantling of former state education systems and the opening of western influences has produced uncertainty about the equivalence of qualifications in international terms. Many institutions in CEE are therefore seeking assistance from Western partners in finding an appropriate level at which to pitch their educational programmes. A number of programmes have already been developed with support from the west, as demonstrated in the national analyses for Hungary (Chapter 5) and Slovenia (Chapter 10). These courses are usually designed according to Western academic standards, often with external validation or accreditation. There is, however, a danger that unquestioning acceptance of Western standards could lead to a dilution of the strong elements in the current curriculum.

## ACADEMIC EXCHANGE

The decline of former systems of educational exchange between CEE countries has created a need to build new systems. At present, it seems that the orientation of such schemes will predominantly be an East-West one. Many CEE countries are already prepared for participation in SOCRATES ahead of membership of the European Union. This will raise considerable questions about the ability of CEE partners to engage in reciprocal exchange schemes with EU institutions. The knowledge of CEE languages among students from the EU is likely to remain low, and this will increase the need to provide courses in English and other EU languages. Such pragmatic solutions will, however, reduce the potential of academic exchanges to increase cultural integration between CEE and the EU member states. There is also the danger that a predominance of East-West exchanges will reinforce the idea that Western ideas and models are inevitably superior to Eastern ones.

It is therefore important that the development of East-West exchange is also accompanied by a re-establishment of intra-regional, or East-East exchanges.

## EDUCATIONAL RESOURCES

A common problem in all areas of CEE is the lack of financial and other resources to develop and implement new curricula and to underpin academic exchange. In some cases, resources are being found from the private sector, particularly in the area of vocational education, and EU programmes help to provide support through the TEMPUS and PHARE programmes. In most cases, however, the resources available are insufficient to address the vast scale of the problems encountered. New means therefore need to be found to help support developments in CEE, both through material aid and through the exchange of expertise and know-how.

## SUPPORTING FUTURE DEVELOPMENTS

An important function of the Kazimierz conference was to create an ongoing dialogue between educators in the EU, and their Central and Eastern European counterparts. In addition to the contacts built up through the conference itself, a number of proposals were put forward during the conference for further action which could be taken by ATLAS and other organisations working in this area. It was considered particularly important to involve institutions from CEE in the ATLAS Network, and to initiate projects which would be of particular benefit to CEE members. To this end, a special Action Plan for Central and Eastern Europe was drawn up and presented to conference delegates.

ATLAS will work closely with other interested bodies to ensure that the Action Plan is implemented in the coming years.

## APPLYING THE ATLAS ACTION PLAN IN CENTRAL AND EASTERN EUROPE

One important outcome of the Polish conference was a draft action plan for Central and Eastern Europe, which will build on the activities already underway under the ATLAS Action Plan agreed at the Tilburg conference in 1994 (Richards, 1995). The main points of the draft action plan for Central and Eastern Europe (CEE) are:

### 1. Extend the ATLAS network and information exchange systems to CEE

ATLAS will extend its membership in CEE, enabling it to offer the same support and advice services to members there as currently operate in the EU. Particular emphasis will be placed on measures which help to exchange experience between western and eastern members of ATLAS. The ATLAS network in CEE will be strengthened by appointing national coordinators in CEE, and by encouraging representatives of universities in CEE to join the ATLAS Executive.

**2. Organising further ATLAS events in CEE and involving CEE members in SOCRATES projects**

In order to stimulate further communication and network development in CEE, ATLAS will facilitate the organisation of events which will bring ATLAS members together in CEE. Members from CEE will also be encouraged to join existing and future ATLAS projects to be undertaken in the framework of SOCRATES, particularly as CEE join the SOCRATES programme.

**3. Support the development of tourism curriculum in CEE**

ATLAS will support curriculum development by strengthening the European dimension of courses, providing advice on curriculum design and working towards the recognition of courses.

**4. Stimulate student and staff exchange both between east and west, and between CEE countries themselves**

ATLAS will help members to establish the contacts necessary to create and extend exchange schemes between the EU and CEE. Attention will also be paid to reviving academic contacts and exchanges between the individual CEE countries.

**5. Provide support for the development of links between education and industry**

ATLAS will provide advice on building links between educational establishments and industry.

**6. Support the provision of market information and analysis in CEE, for example through transnational research**

ATLAS will investigate the potential contribution that its members can make to developing tourism market information in CEE, for example through a multi-country study of consumer attitudes to tourism in CEE.

Since the Action Plan was drawn up in September 1995, some progress has already been made in implementing aspects of the Action Plan. In particular, the extension of the ATLAS network in Central and Eastern Europe has proceeded rapidly. Before the conference was staged, ATLAS had three members in CEE. By April 1996, this had grown to 14 members, spread across 6 countries. A number of CEE members have also participated in the development of SOCRATES projects on curriculum development, including the development of a European Core Curriculum.

Since the conference was held in Poland, there have also been signs that the economic problems facing a number of CEE states have begun to ease. Polish GDP grew by 7% in 1995, unemployment fell and price increases were running at around 25% a year, compared with 500% in 1990. In the Czech Republic inflation has fallen below 10%, and GDP grew by 5% in 1995. These trends offer hope for the future development of tourism and tourism education in the region, but there is still a lot of work remaining to be done.

## REFERENCE

Richards G. (1995). *Tourism and Leisure Education in Europe: Trends and Prospects.* Tilburg: Tilburg University Press.